CONFLICT and TRIUMPH

Also by Jewell Nicholson Cunningham

Look At Your Hand, 1984

Fifty Years of

CONFLICT and TRIUMPH

IN THE MINISTRY WITH THE MAN CALLED "MR. MISSIONS"

JEWELL NICHOLSON CUNNINGHAM

Edited by Florence Biros

Additional copies can be obtained from:
    Jewell Nicholson Cunningham,
    P.O. Box 4489, Tyler, TX 75712-4489

or from:
    Son-Rise Publications & Distribution Co.,
    R3 Box 202 New Wilmington, PA 16642, (412) 946-8334

Typesetting by Thoburn Press, Tyler, Texas

Printed in the United States of America

ISBN 0-936369-12-4

Dedicated To

My Three Children

Their Encouragement Has Made
The Tiring Job Possible

TABLE OF CONTENTS

Foreword *by Loren Cunningham* xi
Introduction *by Florence Biros* xiii
  1. More Than Heredity 1
  2. Subject to Change 6
  3. Tom's Story 16
  4. Backwoods Preachers 24
  5. West Fork, Arkansas 30
  6. Moving On 36
  7. Wilderness 41
  8. California or Bust 48
  9. San Joaquin Valley 53
10. Dora 58
11. Independence? 67
12. Burnt-Out 71
13. Promise of God 76
14. Firebaugh 82
15. Monterey 93
16. Ventura 101
17. Pioneering Again 106
18. My Isaac 114
19. El Centro 122
20. Out of the Desert 129
21. West Los Angeles 138
22. Mr. Missions Is Called 147
23. Long Beach Call 154
24. Open Doors 167
25. Samoa 174

26. Roma, Roma! 183
27. A Question of Worthiness 195
28. Apartment Complex 202
29. South Pacific Island 206
30. Fulfilled Years 215
Appendix 1 — The Greatest Missionary Offering 224
Appendix 2 — Missions Giving on the Missions Field ...226

ACKNOWLEDGMENTS

I want to thank Florence Biros, for her patient, skillful editing of this manuscript. Thanks also, to my husband Tom, who is known around the world as "Mr. Missions," and who has put up with me for 55 years. This book is in his honor. Special thanks to Janice, the writer in my family, for her help. Thanks also to the many typists whose work helped make this book a reality.

We extend a special acknowledgment, too, to all the friends who asked for this book as a sequel to my former book, *Look At Your Hand*. Friends have asked, "Tell us about Tom's work." All right, herein you find such a record. I'm surely the one to tell it!

Many have retyped and edited this work, but I still claim that it is primarily in my own words. Thanks to all.

Jewell Cunningham

FOREWORD

by Loren Cunningham

My sisters, Phyllis and Janice, and I had the privilege of growing up in a family that truly knew and loved the Lord and were committed to Him and His word. We learned to hear His voice, to love Him and to love His ministry. Because of our parents' attitudes, we never considered it a sacrifice but only the highest calling of all to work for the Lord. When we lived in a tent, the back of a church and later an attic, we still knew we were privileged to be in His ministry.

From the vantage point of growing up in this family, I can say that Mom and Dad are real in their walk with God. I'm glad they've written this book in order to share the ways of God they've learned over many decades.

They have something to say to this generation, especially to the pioneers within the Body of Christ and the world of missions. The same biblical principles and the same Holy Spirit works today as in the past.

INTRODUCTION
by Florence Biros

"IS THAT REALLY YOU, GOD?"—reading Loren Cunningham's life story had touched my very soul. The trials and tribulations, conflicts and triumphs of *Youth With A Mission*'s international leader were masterfully shared throughout its pages by Janice Rogers' pen.

Janice, I learned, was Loren's sister. She, too, was wrapped up in her family's style of existence, full-time ministry for Jesus—both she and her husband worked through "YWAM." The only other sibling, Phyllis Griswold, the eldest of the Cunningham children, had also dedicated her life to service for Christ. Her forte is teaching, along with a special talent in music which both her sister and brother share with her. All three Cunningham children had gone through physical ordeals and years of constant dedication to the cause of Christ.

What kind of parents could have produced a trio of such dedicated offspring? That question had crossed my mind when suddenly over the phone a stranger's voice announced to me, "This is Jewell Nicholson Cunningham." I knew from reading Loren's story that this voice belonged to Loren, Phyllis and Janice's mother!

"Could you help me edit my new book?" she queried and I agreed. Even over the telephone her spunk and determination was evident. And so, several weeks later I found myself winging my way across America from Pennsylvania to a YWAM base at Tyler, Texas.

On my first day there, when Janice came to share lunch with us at her mother's home, I asked the obvious question: "Didn't you want to help get your mother's book in shape?"

"I'd have liked to, but I have too many things going on right now! I simply don't have time. She wanted it done right away."

Later that afternoon as Jewell and I sat in her modest home known as "Uncle Tom's Cabin" she related the origin of some of the trinkets and memorabilia that lined the walls. We'd just begun to peruse her manuscript when the phone rang. "Hello, son!" she exclaimed and embarked on a conversation. Loren had just flown into New York from Europe and was waiting for a plane to take him to Virginia Beach to film a teaching series for the Christian Broadcasting Network.

When the phone rang again, Phyllis was on the other end of the line. Jewell explained to me, "Phyllis and her husband are selling their California home to go to Hawaii to help Loren."

Later that evening Tom Cunningham also called his wife from California where he was busy raising funds for missions. After more than fifty years of marriage a spark of joy still came to Jewell Cunningham's dark eyes as she talked with her husband, the man known as "Mr. Missions" to Assembly of God members along the west coast and called "T.C." by those who know him well. Thousands have come to love and respect this devoted man of God with such remarkable wit and endurance. In his late seventies, he still gives his all for his Jesus and the great commission. When Jewell hung up from talking to him she turned and said to me, "Tom's agreed to go to Belgium in the fall."

During that week at Tyler I shared in the intimacy of their home and the graciousness of my hostess. Through that experience I came to realize the diligence and devotion each family member had for their precious Savior.

As I worked so closely with Jewell I came to know about the conflicts she shares in the following pages and watched her triumphant spirit which comes through her love for Jesus. Mrs. Cunningham was every bit the Jewell I'd expected and more. Her grit fanned a spark of determination as she told me, "Now, I'm a-telling you, girl, this is my story and I want it in my words." And so, as close as it is possible, the following pages share her thoughts and ideals, in actions and words.

Each day at four o'clock she falls to her knees in prayer for the world, the nation, YWAM, all God's servants, her husband, her children and every other conceivable need she can think of during this time specifically set aside for talking to the Lord.

She prayed earnestly for this book and so it is with great honor and joy that I have a part in sharing the conflicts and triumphs of a couple whose ministry has spanned the globe for far more than half of a century. They have carried the divine commission to spread the Gospel, traveling from one continent to another, from Maine to Miami, from California to the east coast of America. More than anything else, it is my prayer that this sharing of T.C. and Jewell Cunningham's life will do exactly what her favorite phrase says: "PRAISE WONDERFUL CHRIST!"

With the world out there we looked
at it's possibilities from youthful
eyes. Fall 1936

Our first child, Phyllis Dorene
A doll at six weeks

Pastor Tom at Covina in 1944
got his second daughter,
our third blessing

For this son I prayed, and like Hannah
said, "I'll give him back to you Lord."

1

MORE THAN HEREDITY

How my heart ached as I stared down at my beloved Papa on his death bed. He'd been so forlorn, thinking he had nothing to leave his five children.

How I wanted to console him! "Papa, Papa," I spoke haltingly, "you're leaving us the greatest heritage anyone ever could — the heritage of the Pentecostal way of serving and worshiping God. I have often claimed that I wouldn't trade places with the President's daughter!"

At such a trying time those words were difficult to voice to my dying father, a dynamic man of God, but I felt I had to say them. Our chosen way of life hadn't been easy, but in his last fleeting moments I wanted my Papa, R. C. Nicholson, to know his family thought all the conflicts and triumphs of his life had been worthwhile.

Yes, we surely did have conflicts! Born in Indian territory just six months before Oklahoma achieved statehood, I was to find out poverty had become a way of life for the Nicholsons. Papa was only a sharecropper and I was the third little mouth he had to feed. There were five offspring — four daughters: Marylydia, Pebble, myself and Frances. Brother Coy, second from the end, was the only male offspring and found himself outnumbered from the start.

"I just growed like Topsy," the character from "UNCLE TOM'S CABIN." Being the third little girl, I shadowed the two older ones, but they seldom included me. At one time our house was nothing more than a six foot hole dug into the earth with a clapboard top and a roof over it, called half dug-outs in the Territory days—I'd crawl up the steps to watch them through a knot-hole.

Once Marylydia and Pebble spied me and stuffed a corncob in the hole. "Yah, yah!" they sang mockingly. "You can't see out any more!"

Our life was made up of many physical conflicts. Long before I began school at age eight, I went to work in the fields helping with the crops—hoeing in the scorching summer sun and picking cotton in the fall.

During our few leisure hours I entertained myself, until Coy became old enough to play with. Since I'd taught him how to tie his shoes and kept him out of danger so often, my little brother had become my pal for life. In turn he'd always come to my rescue if someone began picking on me at school. "You leave my sister alone!" he'd holler. If shove came to push, he was even willing to fight for me.

But when Papa found Jesus, our lifestyle changed dramatically. For five years the entire family traveled dusty Indian trails in a covered wagon as he preached and pioneered churches all over the new state of Oklahoma.

My beloved Papa's teaching and his Godly example made the Lord become as real to me as He was to my father. One Sunday morning when I went out to pray and get alone with God, I knelt beneath a big tree in the tall timber across from our house. There God filled me with the Holy Ghost.

My body began shaking so that I couldn't get the yard gate open to get back to the house. When my family heard me talking in tongues, they came running out into the yard. Papa declared, "I'm so glad for you, Jude! Each of us needs to find the Lord's fullness!" (He always used my nickname when he was particularly pleased.) That spectacular event took place two months before my tenth birthday.

That "fullness" Papa spoke of has kept me full of joy to this day. Even in my valley experiences, I have always felt a deep-seated peace within. In times of sorrow, deeper than the tears that seemed to well up of their own accord, there was still an undying hope and joy. From the time of my being filled with the Holy Ghost until now I have grown in grace, seen visions and heard the voice of God in our daily times of worship, as did other members of our family.

Preaching is my calling. When I was twelve I had known that He was calling me, but had only preached once. I tried so hard to resist that call on my life until one September morning of the year I was seventeen. My resistance invited God's hand of chastisement. While at my private place of prayer I said, "Lord, make me willing to obey Your call, even if You have to take me to death's door."

I can still see myself making my way back down the path from the pasture following that request. My head felt feverish even as I entered the camphouse where we'd been staying. My mother felt my brow. "Jewell, you need some rest!" she declared and put me to bed on a cot. I was coming down with malaria and for days Marylydia and Pebble took turns placing cold wet cloths on my forehead, trying to bring my fever down. I became unconscious and stayed in the state of delirium for two whole weeks.

The entire family prayed night and day for me. Often Papa lay on the floor by my cot all night, talking to His Lord about the problem into the wee hours of the morning. When I was conscious I could hear him speaking in tongues or pleading in English, "Please, dear Lord, heal my daughter!"

Doctor Hines, a friend of the family, came and took my temperature one morning. One hundred and four degrees! That day I happened to be in a semi-conscious state and could somehow grasp the gravity of my condition. "There is nothing medically I can do for the worst stages of malaria," the good doctor declared. "All we can do is pray." Miracle drugs had not been invented then.

I lingered on. My only nourishment was a tablespoon full of buttermilk or water occasionally as my parents would raise my head up and pour liquid down my throat. When I opened my eyes it seemed like dear Coy was always looking down at me with those big brown eyes of his just brimming with tears. Frances, then age 10, went out into the brush to pray for me, and in her earnestness she, too, was filled with the Holy Spirit.

"I want everybody here to say good-by," I told my parents one day. "I'm going to go to be with Jesus. Don't pray for me to be healed any more."

Instead of doing my bidding, they began to pray up a storm. But then, suddenly, their voices drifted off. I could no longer move. I felt as though I were being lifted up and out of my body. From a space above I heard the Lord speak to me as He had at the age of twelve while I was praying at the creek bank when he told me to go and preach His Word. Again He spoke, "Now will you go? Or will you come to be with me now?"

I knew He was giving me another chance, saying: "Now, will you go and preach — or will you come and be with Me?" I understood fully what He was asking. In my heart I said, "Yes, I'll go preach," for I was too weakened to have either breath or voice to argue. I knew His will for me was to go preach rather than go with Him then — yet I also knew He never goes against our free will.

Immediately upon making my mental decision, I felt a surge of blood race through my veins. First my feet tingled and then the tingling spread up my legs and body. When I lifted my arms, they moved! I opened my eyes and raised myself up. To my family I announced, "I am healed and I'm going to preach!"

"Victory!" I shouted, rising from the cot and lifting my hands in the air. I got out on the floor with the others and began rejoicing in the Spirit. Papa said, "Now, Jewell, lie back down and rest!" Poor Papa, always advising and rightly so! I rested, but the next day I got up again and began to eat meals. The following Sunday I preached in the church which Papa had started in Duncan, Oklahoma, twenty miles away. Still too weak to stand on my own, I had to hold on to the pulpit.

The story of my recovery and obedience to God's call would not be complete if I failed to tell that I chilled every day for the next three months. I still took turns preaching with Marylydia and Papa in spite of the chills during my "bootcamp" or "wilderness" experience. I'd chill each day, then feel well enough to preach again when it came my turn. By this time we were on the road again.

That sickness ended my battle with myself and my will. Through the prayers of my loved ones I was raised from my deathbed to begin preaching. I knew I'd been chastised. Not all illness can be termed as chastisement, but I'd asked for it and mine had been in answer to my prayer. The Bible says, "Whom He loveth, He chastiseth."

My high school days were interrupted by my call to preach. In later years I had the privilege of going back to minister in the school I'd been attending. My old professor was one of the first to shake my hand and say, "Jewell, I wish you Godspeed."

That first year of ministry I battled self every time I got up to preach. I have often thanked God for Papa's discernment during that time. My father had an uncanny ability to know just what to say when I was discouraged and he never let me beg off when he knew it was a trick of the devil to bring me low and keep me from fulfilling God's call. During the times I was tempted not to minister but did so in spite of my feelings, God's anointing rested upon me far greater than the norm.

2

SUBJECT TO CHANGE

Life is change! For fourteen and a half years the seven members of the Nicholson family had traveled together as the Nicholson Family. But then, without any warning, our lives changed. How well I remember Mama walking into our bedroom to speak to us girls. We asked, "What's wrong with your face? Something happened to it during the night." The way it was drawn on one side made one fact perfectly clear. We girls knew our beloved Mama had suffered a stroke.

Three weeks later she seemed to be so much better that she asked Papa, "Let's go and pray for Mr. Gross." Her concern was for a rich cattleman whom her unsaved brother-in-law had asked her to pray for. Mr. Gross lived 20 miles away, so Papa and Coy took her in the family vehicle.

Since my mother never took anyone's salvation lightly she got down on her knees in Mr. Gross' home to seek the Lord's guidance in that situation. While kneeling, she felt a nudging of the Holy Spirit to lay hands on the man. Without lifting her body from its kneeling position she moved on her knees across the room and began to pray. Momentarily she stopped to put her hands to her own head and cried out, "Oh! Oh! My head hurts so bad!" She had suffered another stroke.

When word got back home we rushed to be at her side, interceding for her all night. As we all stood around her bed and watched Mama struggle for breath, even our own Uncle Bud Darnell, a wicked sinner our Mama'd had on her prayer list these many years, was touched. He tried to help her breathe by lifting her arms.

I could not help but think about the time only a few years before when at the age of eighteen I'd gone off to evangelize for the
first time. It was as if God spoke to my heart then and said, "You'll
not have her very long." Even with that memory I sang, "Jesus,
Jesus, Jesus—sweetest name I know," interspersed with my tears
and words of intercession.

"O, God, if it be thy will," Sister Wisely, a prayer warrior
along with Mama was saying. "Even now, O Lord, wilt thou
spare her?"

Marylydia asked me, "Jewell, why do you sing?" Such a question!

I suggested to my sister, "Let's all sing so she can hear us as she
enters the Gates." I knew by then that it was God's will for her to go.

When she died in Mr. Gross's bed on August 4, 1928, at four
in the morning, I wasn't surprised. Heartbroken, yes—but not
surprised.

I stood beside her casket and said good bye to her earthly re-
mains. As the singers sang of the Resurrection, the thoughts came
to me—"Do not see her (never more)—But only see her gone
before." Certainly no other fourteen-year-old ever felt more grief
than Frances did at that moment. All five of us stood together, trying to comfort one another and the precious balm of the Holy
Spirit reached down and lifted our downcast spirits, assuring us of
where our Mama was. Heaven had become her home. The Lord
replaced my spirit of heaviness with one of joy.

Her death inspired Papa to make a verse:

> "Once was seven
> Now 'tis six.
> The band is broken;
> It can't be fixed.
> I'll keep all that's left*
> And just hide behind the cleft!"

---

*"I'll keep all that's left"—This prophecy was fulfilled—3 out of 6 are left.
And, one, youngest to die was 69—the other 3 of us are in our later years now.

Two years later, in need of a mate, our Papa married Bernice, the widow of Brother Roberts. Our father had officiated at the funeral of Bernice's husband just two years before we lost Mama. At that time, in a surge of independence, Coy and I often went off preaching together. Once we had to hitchhike for 300 miles. Each time the "Lord was faithful to provide" a ride every time we had need of one. God gave us several calls to help out with our guitar and mandolin as a brother and sister team.

We went to San Juan, New Mexico, to help Papa hold a revival. One Sunday night, while preaching a revival in a small New Mexican town, it was my turn to preach — I developed a sick headache just before the services were to begin and felt too washed out to even think of going up to the church from Papa and Bernice's bedroom in the church basement. SOMEONE ELSE CAN HAVE THE HONORS, I thought. I'LL STAY IN THE BASEMENT UNTIL CHURCH IS OVER, THEN I'LL GO TO MY OWN ROOM ACROSS THE STREET. BUT I CERTAINLY DON'T FEEL LIKE GOING OVER THERE ALONE.

Soon after I went to bed the music upstairs gained momentum. As the loud music began, the throbbing in my head increased. Stomping and clapping followed — sounds I loved when I felt able to participate. But that night I just craved peace — and QUIET.

After a quick survey of my surroundings and a fast mental calculation of how long the meeting could last, I decided the walls of that "high-class dugout" were devastating to my morale. Thoughts raced through my mind. THIS IS HOW IT WILL BE WHEN YOU DIE. YOU'LL BE SIX FEET UNDER AND THEY'LL BE ON TOP OF THE GROUND SINGING AND SHOUTING. I needed to get out of there! My nerves were getting bad, my head was pounding. I was shaking inside.

Suddenly I remembered I didn't have any of my clothes with me. So I pulled on one of Bernice's dresses and put on a pair of her shoes. . . . I swam in them! With my hair stringing down my back and her shoes flopping up and down on my feet I blew out the lamp and climbed the ladder to push open the trapdoor which opened right at the altar above. Pausing for a moment, I thought to myself, "You're the Sunday night speaker and look at you!" I decided I would descend the ladder to find the matches and relight the lamp, but realizing that would be impossible to do in the darkness that enveloped me, I knocked on the trapdoor. Through the floor I heard one of the men who was sitting in the favorite "men's corner" at the rear of the altar say, "Some one wants out of the basement."

I made certain my second knock was louder. They opened the door and I scrambled out. As I ran across the room and out the side door, some one from the back screamed, "What was that?" Never in my life was I more thankful for fresh air and freedom!

On another trip, Papa, Bernice, Coy and I traveled back to Duncan, Oklahoma to hold a revival at the First Assembly of God. The church still had some charter members on its roll who had been at Papa's first Pentecostal meeting there. This was the same church where Mama's funeral had taken place.

Our meetings had gone on for a few days when Tom Cunningham came in from Oklahoma City where he had resigned his job as foreman for a large construction company because he felt compelled to find his own preaching ministry. (Five years earlier he'd come to our hometown of Duncan to play guitar at one of his father's revivals. Only sixteen years old at the time, I thought he was so good looking that I said to the boy I was with, "If that fellow was a little older, he'd beat your time.")

As I walked down the aisle of the well-filled Duncan church on a Saturday night, I noticed a man on the piano stool with his back to the crowd, tuning his guitar. One of the ladies stopped me and asked, "Do you know that man sitting up there?"

"No," I answered. "Should I?"

"Yes, that's Tom Cunningham. He used to be around here."

I did recall Tom because he could play the guitar so well. The lady could have added, "He used to go with my daughter."

I went to the platform. Passing by Tom I said, "How are you, stranger?"

"I'm well," he answered. "How are you?"

"I'm well enough."

A look of concern flashed through his gray eyes. "Aren't you well?" He seemed sincerely interested in my well-being.

"I'm okay," I told him. Then he agreed to help my brother and me sing a song before my sermon. A kind of motherly love surfaced in me when I noticed boils on the back of his neck.

The lady who'd stopped me was his hostess. After the service she introduced him to the girls and I watched him pick out a beauty and walk her out of the church. I took my Bible and walked the three blocks to my room — alone.

A broken engagement and a broken heart were still plaguing me because of a certain blonde young man in South Texas. I had broken off with him because of being uncertain as to God's will in our relationship. A verse I sang often stated my feelings well:

"Jesus said, 'If you'll go, I'll go with you
Preach the Gospel, I'll preach with you.'
Lord, if I go, tell me what to say,
For they won't believe in me."

That was the formula for my ministry — always put God first. In traveling from place to place I'd had proposals of marriage, some of interest and others not so much appreciated. After my last serious consideration of a proposal, I wrote in my diary, "The Lord is the Lord of my life and anyone not all-out for God, I'm not interested in." I'd been fortunate thus far, with Papa's prayers and keen perception, to avoid a pitfall in wedlock.

Dear Tom looked so clean-cut and irresistibly handsome as he played his guitar that Saturday night. I was hard-pressed to concentrate on my sermon as I walked to the pulpit. A few casual remarks were almost the extent of our communications for some months to come.

That night I had a hard time falling asleep. Looking out the window at the stars, I thought they seemed to be talking to me. While I was deep in thought I heard a voice — the same voice I'd heard at age twelve when He called me to preach His Gospel. But that night He was saying, "Tonight you've found your husband."

I answered, "No, Lord. Don't let me be deceived. You know I've earnestly sought You for my life. I love You more than husband, family or any earthly thing." Then the time also came back to mind when after my heartbreak I'd prayed at a lonesome altar, "Lord, I'll go alone if it's according to Your will. Amen." Then I fell asleep.

Tom showed no more concern for me. Being torn up over a broken engagement of his own and moving, leaving a good paying job in response to God's call, could he be blamed for walking that girl home from the services? How difficult it was for me, but I kept silent about my secret message from the Lord as I helped my father and brother preach during the meeting another two weeks.

The following Saturday Coy and I took the youth group from the church to hold a street meeting at the small town of Rush Springs. On the way I handed Tom my Bible and said, "Here, Tom, you say you're called to preach. Why not give it a try?"

He didn't refuse. Instead he asked, "Jewell, do you mean it?"

"Yes," I declared emphatically. Listening to him on that street corner, I knew he was meant to be a preacher.

Another time we accidently met on the sidewalk for a moment. I gave him a word of encouragement from the Lord about "picking up your cross." We didn't meet again until three months later, in June, 500 miles away. We'd gone our separate ways — he with his father to hold revivals and I with Papa and Coy to do the same in the Ozarks of Arkansas. Coy and I held street meetings while we waited for Papa's scheduled time for us to return to his hometown to help him hold services at the church which we as a family had helped to start.

Coy and I went to Berryville to hold a park meeting. While carrying our instruments to the park we met Brother Medley, one of Papa's converts, and agreed to help him start a church there.

In my daily prayers I always included Tom. I had a burden to pray for him. "God, make him what You'd have him to be." I was falling in love with someone so far away — no letters, no contact. When Tom came to visit Coy one day before leaving Duncan, Papa's commentary was brief but complimentary. "NOW,

THERE IS A MAN!" I had confidence in Papa's judgment, even though he'd driven some of my suitors away by force. That word of Papa's helped me confirm my feelings and affirm the voice I'd heard from the Lord.

I believe I got my intensity from Papa, for he really got action when he moved by his feelings. In watching for possible pitfalls for his three preacher girls, he didn't regard our feelings any more than the feelings of anyone he felt was unworthy of us. We would live to see the day when we would have reason to thank him. So, when Papa saw beyond Tom's boyish looks and expressed with such certainty that Tom would be A MAN, I was so pleased, remembering my secret message from God.

Why shouldn't parents help with the choice of companions for their youth? We choose the dentist, doctor and school; we give them other Godly advice. Why leave out the one that means so much to their entire lives? It would save tears later if parents would act responsibly.

Out back of the Flinn sisters' house stood a storage room which I used as a hideaway prayer closet. There I prayed, "Lord, it's been three months and I don't know where Tom is, but please, Father, keep Your hand on Tom."

Coy and I took Brother Medley's daughter to Fayetteville, Arkansas, to attend an all-day meeting which included one of those very famous down-to-earth meals. My heart flipped when I glanced up and saw Tom Cunningham, one of the first to greet us. He seemed to like banana pudding. Since he sat near me I made certain one dish of it remained at our end of the table.

After dinner Tom and I went for a stroll and took some pictures. I laughed heartily at his jokes, enjoying the fact that I was the sole target for his attention. Through our discussion I learned he was helping his father in a meeting not far from us.

After I returned home, a note came from Tom asking, "Will you be my cook?" Was he thinking I'd feed him a lot of banana pudding? Before I could answer his note, Tom came to visit on a Monday morning and found me scrubbing on a washboard. He didn't get down on his knees nor tell me that he loved me, but as he stood by watching me scrub he said to me, "I want to make a suggestion. Do you want to know how to get those clothes clean without rubbing?"

"Yes," I replied, to which he answered smugly, "Well, send them to the laundry."

I laughed. In his next breath he said, "I want to make another suggestion."

Thinking it was going to be another one-liner such as he was famous for, I declared, "Hop to it."

"Let's get married."

Caught off guard, I asked, "Are you serious?" Previously I hadn't looked up at him as he stood by the washtub, but now as I glanced up and saw his expression, I knew he meant it.

"It'll be a lifetime. Give me thirty days to think about it, Tom." Since I KNEW what I wanted, I decided to see how sincere he was by making him wait for an answer. He walked away to return to his father's meeting but was back the next night asking if I didn't have an answer.

"Tom," I reminded him, "it hasn't been thirty days yet. I'll give you a dollar not to bring it up again."

With a hurt look he declared, "I'll take it and show you I won't." With that, he left without saying what I was fishing for. I wanted him to say he loved me.

Brothers can be of some help once in a while, so I suggested to Coy, "Let's all go to the Cunningham meeting tonight. It's MY turn to throw the ball."

After the meeting Tom finally came over to speak to me. When I asked what his plans were, he replied, "I think I'll go back to Oklahoma City to my job."

"No, Tom, don't do that!" I begged. "You're called to preach." Coy invited him to spend the night with us, so I had another chance to talk to him. Cars are good for private talk, but the divan is much better. There we sat after all the others had retired to their rooms — two would-be lovers huddled alone, the lights not turned too low.

Again he asked, "Jewell, will you marry me?" As always the same question was locked in my mind. He still hadn't told me he loved me. I found out later that he's not one to ever make much ado over his feelings.

"Tom, you'll find your answer in the book of Ruth, chapter 1, verses 16-18."

He read, "Entreat me not to leave thee, or to return from following after thee: for whither thou goest I will go; and where thou lodgest I will lodge; thy people shall be my people, and thy God my God: where thou diest, will I die."

Closing the book he asked me, "Do you mean it?"

I answered, "Oh, yes, I mean it." That proposal would have probably have come sooner if I'd done like Ruth and uncovered his feet and lain down at them, but all we'd done was hold hands until then. Putting his big arms around me, he said, "Then love me."

Another scripture had to have been written for me in that special moment. "The swallow has found her nest and a place to lay her young." As I looked back, I'd put God first, not my motherly instinct. A dear man was going to be my husband.

The following Sunday Tom and I, together with Coy and his fiancée (Brother Medley's daughter Retha whom he'd known for only three weeks), were married in a double wedding ceremony carried out in Oriental style. Retha and I walked with our maids up one aisle; Tom and Coy with their best men came up the other one. I had taken out of the trunk the wedding dress I had made for my marriage to the blonde and Tom wore the suit he'd bought for his marriage to the brunette. He'd said, "If you're wearing yours that you got for another, I'll do the same." Reverend Rousey, an Assembly of God pastor of direct Jewish heritage, first asked Tom the question, "Will you, Tom, take this woman to be your lawful wedded wife?" then proceeded to ask each of us to give our consent.

Since Tom hadn't really established his ministry, we had to borrow money for the license to get married. The preacher had to wait for the first dollar we received to pay him. After buying gas and the license, Tom had one nickel left, so he bought me some gum. He spent his last five cents on me, saying, "Here's your wedding present!"

Melissa, one of the Flinn sisters, saw to it that our wedding supper was prepared. Physically incapacitated, she directed the fixings from her bed. June nineteenth was the day the slaves got their freedom. It worked in reverse for me, though it's different to be a love slave.

A honeymoon? What's that? We had one week before we were to help his dad finish his revival and begin our first one. That honeymoon week, Tom swam in the creek while I waded. We explored caves and attended a singing convention. That special time of getting truly acquainted passed so swiftly. Not having had any romantic "going steady" time, we found we had some adjustments to make in order to learn how to give and take. Just getting his guitar and my mandolin tuned and getting our voices to blend was no small job. Coy and I had well-blended voices, but he and Retha were also learning to sing and play their instruments together. Tom's guitar picking was the best as he picked the tunes and kept time with chords while I accompanied him on my mandolin.

Since Tom was just beginning to preach, he tried to get me to do more preaching and let him lead the music. I realized that his lack of confidence could cause a conflict in our marriage, so I told him, "No, every other night is your time." Through "sharing alike and faring alike" we have triumphantly shared the pulpit for over fifty years of ministry.

3

TOM'S STORY

Private times of conversation were nearly non-existent until after Tom and I were married. When we finally found time to share things from our past that we had never known about each other before, I realized that my own childhood was not the only one full of conflict and poverty.

Born into the home of J. H. and Lucy Cunningham on November 25, 1910, Tom supposedly tipped the scales at a whopping 18 pounds! Even then he made a BIG impression! His arrival was number four in the family, following Arnette, Gertrude and Sandra. Finally, James Henry, Jr., nicknamed "Toad," rounded out the family of five.

Since Tom's mother died when he was only five years old, he only had five distinct memories of her. One evening he shared his remembrances from when he was a small child. "Once mother sent me to market to buy what we call 'head cheese'—the cheapest part of the hog you could buy. That day the butcher gave me four slices for ten cents. Normally, he'd have given us only three! Jumping across the gutter, I ran all the way home, yelling at the top of my voice, 'Mama, he gave me FOUR slices!' She hugged me and grinned, saying, 'Shush, Tommy!'—trying to get me quiet.

"On another occasion a little friend came to our place. In those days in the South a pitcher of ribboncane syrup was as much a fixture on the table as the salt shaker. My little boyfriend poured out the syrup and then licked the top of the pitcher clean. 'My goodness, that's not very polite!' Mama scolded, then took a rag to wash off the pitcher before she would let me pour any syrup on my own bread.

16

"Months before this, I can remember her giving me a snack of cornbread with syrup poured over it. Was that good! I couldn't have been more than 4½, but I can almost taste it now.

"On another occasion, Mama came in from shopping and brought us some cookies from the bakery — such a treat!

"Another thing I remember was the time dad's youngest brother, Uncle Wade, took me for a haircut. Because I twisted around a little too much, the barber caught my ear with the shears. The barber exclaimed, 'I'm so sorry. It was an accident.' But I'm not sure to this day whether it was an accident or revenge. I raised so much Cain that my uncle left the shop. When he came back he quieted me by giving me some balm for my wounded feelings — a little bag of candy. Sandra, who was just three years older, wanted the candy and Toad, 2½ years younger than me, demanded some too. The only safe place I could think of where I could eat all the candy I wanted was up under my bed. Crawling back as far as I could, I tried to ignore my mother's pleas to come out. At first she sweet-talked me, but I refused, cramming that candy down as fast as I could. Finally she laid down the law. 'Tom, you HAVE to come out!' She took the candy from me to divide what was left with the others.

"My last memory of my mother certainly made an indelible impression on my childish mind. My mother, brother and I were confined in a sanitarium in San Antonio, Texas, during a small-pox epidemic. During our three-week stay, my father never went to bed. Occasionally he left us to bathe and change clothes, but other than that, he just caught catnaps as he sat in our room. Mama and my brother had severe cases; mine was not as bad.

"Complications arose because my mother was six months pregnant at the time, but she seemed to be getting better. My father had brought her clothes to the sanitarium and she was planning to go home. Suddenly she drifted into a coma. How well I remember the hustle and bustle of the nurses and doctors. As small as I was, I recognized the concern on their faces, but couldn't understand what was really happening when they started to work over her in earnest. Pop was standing right there, clinging to her

hand. Tension filled the room. Before she lapsed into uncon-
sciousness she told my father, 'I want to pray for you and the children.' These were my mother's last words.

"Today's medical skills could have saved her life by taking the
baby by Caesarean section. Instead, she died shortly after the
fetus died. When her last breath was drawn, the doctor slipped
the sheet over her face and turned away, shaking his head. He'd
done all that he could. My father began to weep and the nurse
who had cared for her and grown to love her during those three
weeks buried her face in her apron. Sobs shook her frame. At age
five, I couldn't take it all in. Wide-eyed, I stood watching—little
realizing the treasure of which fate had robbed me. Months turned
into years and years turned into eternity. I was forced to drink
from the cup of disappointment to the bitter dregs. One of the
memories of my childhood was how I envied other boys my age
when I would see them being lovingly cared for by their mothers.
Time after time, I would slip away and hide to weep until it
seemed as though my childish heart would break. My mother was
thirty three when she died on May 14, 1916.

"Because Mother's death was smallpox-related and that was
such a dreaded disease then, my father was told, 'You can't have a
public funeral for her.' The undertaker brought the casket to the
sanitarium ward and we knelt around it there on the floor.

"The three of us were put in an ambulance for the drive home.
My three sisters, who were being cared for by my father's mother,
ran out to meet us when the ambulance pulled up. Since Mama
was thought to be getting well, they expected to see her emerge
from the ambulance. 'Where's Mama?' they asked. Such a sad
way to learn of our mother's death and burial!

"The county health authorities moved us out of our house,
totally sealed all the doors and windows, then used a heavy
fumigation agent of some kind to kill the germs. They stacked up
all our bedding—mattresses, quilts and pillows. Then they
poured kerosene on them and lit it. Poof! The bedding started to
burn. I remember watching it. Nothing was offered to us to replace any of these essentials. Losing them was our hard luck.

Smallpox was considered conquered at that time, but we lived close to the Mexican border in an area with a heavy Mexican population. There were still major outbreaks of the disease in countries such as that. It was because the authorities feared the threat of its spreading that we could not have a public funeral. The only service was during the brief time we stood around the casket in the sanitarium when Papa read scripture and prayed."

Tom never stopped telling me his background that night. My heart ached for my new husband as he talked, but I realized he needed to get all his past hurts and childhood conflicts off his chest. He sighed as he continued, "Our long hospitalization, the death of our mother and all related expenses took their financial toll. In later years I heard my father say, 'It took the loss of my companion as God's dealing with me to move into a full-time ministry.'

"After he bought train tickets for his children and gave my grandmother a bit of money to help care for us, Papa had only five dollars left to his name. He got in his car and drove to Ballenger, Texas, for his first revival meeting which was really the launching of his full-time ministry. Then later Papa remarried.

"For a time, we children lived with them. But later his second family included four children, broke up and he put us in the homes of friends so we could go to school while he went evangelizing. Arnette, the oldest, had left home at age 18 to live with friends. Gertrude lived with our maternal grandmother.

"Toad [My brother's name was James Henry, but papa nicknamed him 'Toad'] and I were left with friends of my dad's during the time he took our youngest sister, Sandra, to his sister's where she lived until her graduation from high school and her marriage shortly after. Later that week he returned and packed our clothing into separate cardboard boxes, loaded us into the Model T Ford, and took us on a three-hour journey to Mr. and Mrs. Grover Eddings' home where I was to stay. Mr. Eddings was a fairly successful farmer who lived in a spacious farm home. Neighbors gathered there on Saturdays as was customary in those days. Quite a few people met there — neighbors visiting neighbors, including the elderly couple who were to take my brother into their home quite a distance away.

"Papa hugged my brother and me and told us good bye. Then
he got in his car and drove off. Wanting to escape curious eyes,
Toad and I went to the barn to play. After a time a call came for
him. As he turned to go, there was no farewell, just a sad look exchanged between us. An elderly gentleman lifted the chubby six-
year-old up into the seat of the old-fashioned buggy, climbed up
beside him, tapped his horse and started down the long country
lane to the main road about a quarter of a mile away. I watched
them from the hayloft until they turned and disappeared behind
the trees lining the road. I wept in my loneliness. The sun seemed
to have set in the mid-afternoon. Would I ever see my father,
sisters and brother again? When the crowd dispersed at twilight
Mrs. Eddings came looking for me. She was a kindly young
woman. In the 100 yard walk between the barn and the house, she
told me, 'Tom, I thought a good deal of your mother and we had
been good friends.' With this assurance and the kindness shown
me, I began to settle into the routine of living with this wonderful
farming couple. Theirs was only one of the several foster homes in
which I was destined to live before I was old enough to set out on
my own.

"While Toad and I had still been living with Dad and our stepmother, she had a garden and especially liked raising green beans.
We boys didn't like green beans, at least not well enough to have
them every day, so I thought of a plan. I got some shears and clipped
the roots close to the ground. After the plants died, my stepmother said, 'Well, this is the last of the beans. The cut worms
must have eaten them.' These mischievous habits of my childhood
were pretty well cured by the time I was grown and on my own.
The several different foster homes and hard work for my keep provided the fire which partially consumed that dross.

"Papa always chose our foster homes for us. He never deserted
us nor were we ever wards of the court. In that day, if children
had clothes, food and a warm place to sleep, they were considered
to be all right. People didn't think about a social upheaval having
any bearing on children's lives, however we know now that emo-
tional problems come from such treatment. Today we consider it

brutal for a man to talk to a nine-year-old child as one did to me: 'We only took you for the work you could do.' But we must consider the customs when people had to work fourteen hours a day. Public jobs, even if they were covered by a labor contract, required a ten-hour workday. That's the way it was."

Tom grinned as he reminisced further, "One funny thing I remember happening when we stayed at Grandma's concerned a little stool that Dad sent to Toad and me. Once when Gertrude wanted to sit on it to put on her stockings and shoes, I made quite a fuss. I wasn't going to allow it, but Grandma ordered, 'Tom, you let your sister sit there.' I found a big safety pin and straightened it out, then got behind her and sent that pin through the cane bottom of the stool to quite a depth. Gertrude jumped straight up eighteen or twenty inches! I was caught red-handed — the pin stuck in the chair! She never used my little stool again! After Grandma got through with me, I wasn't able to sit on it for some time either.

"As far as my family roots, my paternal grandfather was well-educated. His dad was a big plantation owner in Chattanooga, Tennessee who had sent him to school in Europe for a while. When the slaves were freed by the Emancipation Proclamation, my great grandfather had 75 slaves who were set free. Like all Southerners, he'd put everything he owned into Confederate money. After the Civil War he had no funds of any worth, no slaves to work the large plantation and so they had to move. My granddad took his sons and moved from Tennessee to Texas.

"About 1907, one time when Papa had been praying about whether or not he should preach, he began speaking in tongues. He was certain he was going crazy. His Baptist pastor told him, 'If you get to praying too much like that, you'll lose your mind.' Pop began to say, 'Oh, God, don't let me lose my mind!' Shortly after that a woman came from Houston where they'd had a much-publicized camp meeting in 1906. She began to tell Pop of her experiences in the Holy Spirit. That let him know that he wasn't losing his sanity. About eight years after Mom died, he found and joined the Assemblies of God.

"Papa's ministry before Mother's death had been an off-and-on thing. He started in a Baptist church and I can only remember Dad as a minister. Mama had taught Arnett and Gertrude to sing in the services when they were small children.

"After Mama died, the family broke up and Papa entered full-time ministry. The only time he took secular work was to help support his vocation. Those jobs included helping with an old sawmill. Then he ran a big logging engine in East Texas and Louisiana and later was an engineer on the T&NO (Texas and New Orleans) Railroad where he studied and learned the scriptures so well that he earned the title 'The Walking Bible.' Pop was a fellow who could literally do anything well.

"Jude," Tom said, using the nickname Papa had given me, "I prayed through the first time at an old Holiness altar in a little sawmill town in East Texas at the age of eight. Like many kids, I didn't make too deep a commitment. I had a lot of experiences coming and going. I actually came back to the Lord at age 15 and started traveling with my dad in revival meetings.

"The call came early on my heart to follow in my dad's footsteps, but I fought it. I learned to play the guitar and helped Pop with the music in his meetings, but left at age 19 and worked for 2½ years in Oklahoma City. Because I'd landed a good job in the construction business, God had to speak to me in louder tones to get my attention. He let me almost lose my life once. I was working on the Biltmore Hotel which was then under construction in Oklahoma City. We were nailing together the forms for pouring concrete around the steel framework of the 24th floor of the 26-story building, as was the method of construction in those days (1931-32). Due to a freakish accident I was left dangling over the outside of the 24th floor, clinging for life to a small load of lumber that had been hoisted up by a crane. It was only a matter of seconds until I was pulled back to safety, but what a life-changing experience. I almost squeezed the 2 x 4s into toothpicks! When my feet were back on the six inch girder of the framework of the building, I dropped down to the floor below that had already been formed. I walked to the interior of the building and sat down on some lumber. It was then that my nerves gave way and I began shaking like a leaf. Inside me a voice whispered the words found in Romans 11:29: 'For the gifts and the calling of God are irrevocable.' I didn't need anyone to interpret that for me. I stayed on the job a few more months until the building was completed, then told my superintendent I was leaving and where I was going. He thought I was a fool and said as much, but when I left the construction business to follow God's call, I felt compelled to leave. In spite of the superintendent's protests I left his good-paying job behind."

Tom finished the conversation there. I'd done most of the listening and ached as I heard some of his early ordeals. But I had great hopes for a better future for him.

Tom, with bag packed leaves from front of Faith Tabernacle, West Los Angeles for first trip abroad where he caught the vision for world evangelism. 1950

Where Tom made his consecration
while working on this hotel when
it was under construction

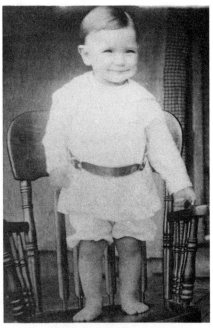

Tom stands alone. Here
he's practicing for future
years of making a good impression

The family beside the church
Somerton, Arizona, Late 1938.

Tom, his brother and sisters, 1965.
The first family reunion in 46 years.

4

BACKWOODS PREACHERS

Girl preachers? There weren't very many a few decades ago, but before Tom and I ever met, Marylydia and I had the distinct privilege of being accepted as "Petticoat Preachers in the Pulpit." She and I had been holding revivals for the Assemblies of God for eight years by the time Tom Cunningham decided he wanted me for his bride. Jokingly he had commented, "She went to the back woods with me to get started." Tom and I held our first meeting together in a schoolhouse called Debuque. This meeting place was located out in the back country fifteen miles from Harrison, the county seat of Boone County, Arkansas. We'd only been married two weeks.

Looking back now, we realize that if you want a great revival it's best not to get newlyweds! Truthfully, our minds weren't always on the goal of saving souls. The Lord blessed anyway, for many prayers were going up from the believers there who knew how to pray.

The Kenyon family who lived down in a canyon welcomed us to their lovely-but-small farm home. Our quarters consisted of a bedroom with a small table and the use of their kitchen stove to prepare our meals so that we could learn to be on our own.

We were always being given foodstuff for offerings. The little Kenyon boy watched as sack after sack was carried in to us. Wide-eyed, he'd declared, "When I get grown, I'm gonna be a preacher and the people will bring in the grub, bring in the grub!"

One morning while Tom was eating a hearty breakfast and I was sitting beside him, to get his attention, I plopped my head on his lap. "Tommy," I teased, but he didn't react the way I'd hoped. His mischievousness was something I was about to learn about. Deliberately he let a spoonful of mussy food fall into my face and I came up fighting mad! He learned then that I was willing to fight. (We've sparred many rounds throughout our marriage, but have never come to blows!)

During serious times we prayed together, but still I yearned to keep up my regular habit of daily getting alone somewhere with God—a most difficult feat, I thought, while living with a "trailer." Having been used to being on my own, I was suddenly at a loss as how to handle a man trailing me around all over the place. When I'd go to my private place to pray and be alone with God as I'd done all my life, I'd no more than start off my prayers when I'd hear footsteps and Tom would be behind me. Deciding there had to be some adjustments made I said to him, "Tommy, I love for you to pray with me, but sometimes I need to be alone with God." He understood my need to have devotions alone in my private prayer closet as the Bible tells us to do. As the song says,

> "Get alone somewhere with God.
> Where shall I go to pray?
> Go to the rag-strewn attic,
> Kneel before him in prayer.

He'll hear and answer you there." Since then Tom and I each have had our own times alone in prayer throughout the years, but we have also had a family altar time every day.

Throughout our three weeks of ministry at Debuque, at twilight Tom and I would walk side by side the two miles over the small mountain to the schoolhouse where we held our meetings each evening. Such joy to have someone share my zeal for the work God gave me! It gave me an inner pleasure to have him beside me carrying my good shoes while I carried the Bibles and the songbook. Between us we also carried his guitar and my mandolin.

Although starting time was set for 8 o'clock, we sometimes got there late. The folks would be sitting and waiting. We never felt we had to hurry-scurry. People had patience back then. Since no stopping time had ever been set, we were free to minister as long as the Spirit kept directing the programs. That was commonplace then, and all the Christians respected the trend to let the Holy Spirit have time to operate and be felt in the songs, testimonies and sermons. Early dismissal never seemed to matter, for above all, no one wanted to hurry those seeking God at the altar.

One night an elderly lady came up front and asked, "Can I help someone here at the altar?"

"Sure," I answered. "If you want to."

Then I overheard her say to a young woman who was seeking at the altar in prayer, "Little lady, have you asked your husband if you should join this church?"

"No!" I interrupted. "She doesn't have to ask her husband or anyone. Her relationship with the Lord is strictly her own choice!" It was then that I realized we needed to know something more about those who ministered at our meetings.

Souls were being saved at the old plank altar and the revival became even better after we fasted and prayed for a couple of days. That fasting resulted in a special blessing for me—and besides, the meeting picked up in the spirit.

Mr. Kenyon and Tom had killed and dressed a goat which had been brought for the evangelists and they'd put the goat meat in the spring to keep it cool until it could be cooked. I called for two days of fasting and the goat meat spoiled. Admittedly I didn't want to cook that meat for Tommy, but I had a hard time convincing him I hadn't called for a fast for that reason.

Rowdies threw rotten eggs at us. Folks tried to make excuses for the behavior of those delinquent boys and protect them from prosecution. In those days disturbing public worship could mean a stint in the local jail. (Today it seems the slogan "The law is for the lawless" is forgotten in the U.S.A.) Tom and I didn't prosecute the offenders. We ducked the rotten eggs as best we could, but when the schoolhouse began to stink like a sulfur factory, we decided we had to move. We moved about a mile down the road under some large trees, but to our dismay, so did the egg-throwers! One night a well-aimed egg nearly hit Tom on the head as we sang our special song. When it smashed and splattered on the tree behind us, he just kept playing his guitar as though nothing had happened.

Still the meetings continued and folks kept coming. One night my heart was warmed as a light approached. Two older folks found their way there by carrying a lantern. I had not been sure they would follow when we moved our meetings a mile further for them to walk. Others — walking or riding in horse-drawn vehicles — came too. A few even arrived in cars, which were scarce back then.

In the peak of the depression we seldom got any money in the offering, but folks gave us enough food to keep us well-fed. If we'd have pooled all our financial resources, we couldn't have even bought a new mantle for the gasoline lamp. When one burned out, we had to take a couple of chickens the fifteen miles into town and sell them for a quarter a piece to buy new mantles.

Once Brother Roberts, the man in charge of leading a meeting, took it upon himself to try to raise money in an offering for us. "How many will give the Cunninghams the first dollar you get?" Four hands went up in the air, (But they must have never earned another dollar, for to this day none of those four people have ever given us the promised four dollars!)

After about three weeks the large regular crowd of farmers gathered for the closing Sunday services. Meeting back in the schoolhouse again, we started first with singing. Then it came time to take the offering and Brother Roberts tried his pitch again: "How many of you will give a gift of food for these young folks to take home?" (That in itself was a joke — we had no home.) Hands shot up all over that one-room schoolhouse.

The next day Tom and I drove my father's truck along the country roads gathering up our gifts. That pickup was such a sight! Its cab top had been completely torn off in a wreck. As we traveled along the crooked main road, it was heartwarming to see men waiting along the roadside with their offerings. One man hollered up from such a steep incline that Tom and I pondered how we could get down to get his gift of tomatoes. Finally we yelled out, "Thanks anyway, but we can't reach you!"

At the end we surveyed our collection — a dozen jars of canned fruit, lots of potatoes and onions, nine hens and a billy goat. I stayed in the back of the truck as Tom drove to town to sell our loot. My job was to keep the goat off the chickens on the way. Passers-by probably thought we were honest-to-goodness hill-billies.

The hens, potatoes and the goat (who literally "got my goat" before we were through with him) brought a total of four dollars. We got our promised four dollars at last! Since the Flinn sisters had always been so hospitable to both of us, we gave them the vegetables and fruit as a payment of sorts for all their kindnesses.

A few years after our "honeymoon revival" Papa went back to Debuque and built the Liberty Assembly of God Church there.

The church where we'd been married five weeks previously became the target for our next revival efforts. For the three weeks we stayed there, Tom and I preached twice each day and thrice on Sundays to the two extra groups that Pastor Rousey was shep-herding, besides at Rev. Rousey's church. I began to feel the strain of trying to preach too often as well as trying to get ac-climated to married life. Exhaustion set in and my health became a concern, so I tried to find more moments alone. To calm my nerves I'd walk around the upstairs porch that graced two sides of the house.

Our home life and living quarters were fantastic. Tom and I stayed in an upper room of a lovely house and ate downstairs with our host family. Their two daughters refused to let me do any washing or ironing. What a change from spending hours rubbing Coy's and my clothes over a washtub that Monday six weeks be-fore when Tom proposed to me.

After having the morning prayer meeting at the church each day, Tom and I would walk across town to the park. There we'd sing a few songs, give a short message and invite people, "Come on over to the meeting tonight." As part of our routine we held a jail service on Saturdays. Our first convert there was a bicycle thief named Odey. "Oh, Jesus, forgive me!" he wailed as we prayed with him through the bars. The entire church rejoiced over the next convert, for she was the town's most notorious lady, though the converted youth may have been our best fruit.

Years after holding that set of revivals I met one of our older acquaintances from there who told me, "I met a lawyer who told me he was converted after hearing 'that girl' preach." Those words assured me that it doesn't take a person highly educated or expert in theology to reach the souls of men; it simply takes the anointing of the Holy Spirit. Some folks in Yellville accepted our message; others didn't—like the infidel who stood on the street corner yelling "That's a lie!" while Tom preached.

We went from Rev. Rousey's church to hold open air meetings with Papa in Belfont. Those meetings weren't well attended. How we'd hoped for a big attendance for our revival as we had relatives and old friends in the area, but since they didn't agree with our teachings, they stayed away. One old Dutchman never missed a chance to stand up and testify. It wasn't difficult to discern that a rift had come between him and his wife.

Since the meetings weren't accomplishing what we'd hoped for, we closed them and Papa went elsewhere. On the last night we came with our suitcases packed because we planned to drive on right after the service. When Tom and I were getting into the car, the old Dutch brother came with his bags in hand saying, "Phere shall I ride?"

"You don't understand. We're leaving now."

Shaking his head, he agreed, "I go mit ye."

When we refused him as kindly as possible, he turned away sorrowfully declaring, "I don't know phat I shall do then." Since that time many have wanted to "go mit us."

5

WEST FORK, ARKANSAS

Sometimes it seemed as though our lives were never going to triumph over the physical and financial conflicts. Tom and I sought out places to conduct evangelistic meetings and preach on the streets — just for gas money. Since meetings were not opening up for us, Tom got a job in the cotton fields, but wouldn't let me help him. One day I wrote in my diary, "I've been away from Tom for four hours now — the longest time in these four months of marriage." This became a lifetime pattern. We were like two ships sailing. Waves would wash us apart, then we'd be back touching again. Up and down on the sea of life. Glorious, grievous, groovy and sometimes really gritty — just to stay afloat.

Tom's cotton picking wages were low, yet they amounted to enough to take us further west, out into the Panhandle of Texas where we held meetings in schoolhouses with Frances and Cecil. Such joy! Even on Monday nights folks showed up in force. When we moved our meetings to the Rocky Fort schoolhouse, the farming people there showed the same appreciation. Such a pleasure to minister to the country folks! They were most receptive.

Everything was not in our favor. Our car had a flat tire one evening and it kept us from getting to the meeting on time. Yet when we came in the crowd was waiting. Cakes and goodies and chickens and other grocery staples were given us. Even though all of their kindnesses knit our hearts with theirs, we finally felt that it was time for us to say goodbye and find our way back east. We felt led to go.

Papa had still wanted to hold the family together, even after we'd all married and occasionally would suggest reunion revivals together. When we were all together Marylydia had shared a vision about the Nicholson evangelistic family which confirmed this was not God's perfect will. Tom and I had occasion to recall her vision. "I saw a load of telephone poles all tied together," she had said, "and God said that we are to be separated to carry the message." None of us took it to mean that we weren't already doing that, but that the Lord was saying, "Scatter and be more effective." We scattered.

In the two previous years Dad and all five of his children had taken on mates, and so, after fourteen years of being called "The Nicholson Evangelistic Family," we began to go through the painful throes of separation. At that time our family held the record of having the most ordained preachers in one immediate family. Ten, including the five in-laws, Papa and his four children — all but Pebble the prayer warrior and exhorter.

Six of us met at Aunt Liza's home for a night's lodging. The next day we held a prayer meeting on the creek bank to discern how God wanted to lead us. Coy and Retha claimed, "We feel led to go to the far west coast." Cecil and Frances, Tom and I felt God's spirit leading the four of us to Arkansas. The word that we received from the Lord was, "Go south ten miles out of the city of Fayetteville." God knew we didn't, anyone of us, know about a little town called West Fork.

The Vaughans went on ahead of us, but by the time we got our car going, we found them coming back. We hollered to them, "Why the change in direction?"

"They didn't want a meeting. No welcome."

"Well, let's go out here a piece away from the road and ask God again," I suggested. Was the Lord kidding, or did we not hear plainly? After our prayer in the little scrub brush, we four felt it was just the devil trying to turn us back. So we turned our cars east again. How easy it is to run into conflict. How could we have doubted when God had so clearly stated, "Ten miles south of Fayetteville"? Here we found a small town of West Fork.

At West Fork we located a house across the street from the Assembly of God church. Since it looked unoccupied, we peered through the window. Upon inquiring, we located the owner. "Yes, I'll be glad to rent you the home. I haven't been back to get the furniture since Mama left," he told us. "You can rent it for five dollars a month." Tom had one dollar to hold it so we moved our few possessions in and that old house became our home.

Spacious! It was so large that we closed up two of the back rooms. Each couple had their own bedroom with a good bed and dresser. The place also had plenty of chairs and rockers and a stove to burn wood in. The kitchen was well-equipped with everything needed to cook our meals. The big range was one like I'd always wanted, with a warmer on the back upper part by the stove pipe. I knew a little about making the fires and cooking. The men stayed busy collecting wood and milking the cow they'd borrowed from a farmer, carrying out the garbage and bringing in water. "Hey, Tom, milk the cow yet?" Cecil and Tom would jest and fuss about who did what job, but it was all in fun.

The first night in our new home, we got our instruments out and started singing and playing. The sound spread out into what had been a quiet little neighborhood. Soon a crowd of our neighbors stopped by to ask us, "Who are you folks and where'd you come from?" We learned that some of them belonged to that church across the street. "Come on in! Let's get acquainted!" we invited.

The next day the pastor of the church heard that some strangers had moved into town. When he came to visit he was surprised to find out who it was. The day before he'd not welcomed the Vaughans, so we assured him, "Pastor, we didn't come to cause any trouble. We feel that God led us here!"

He asked, "Then will one of you bring the message on Sunday?" Everyone voted for me because I was the senior preacher. God so anointed my sermon that Brother W's words still stick in my memory. "My God, what a sermon!" Such freedom we had at the service that night! Such singing and preaching! Everyone felt the anointing. We were asked to continue with nightly meetings.

We had come in obedience to the Lord, and it seemed we were receiving His spiritual unction from on high. Glory to God! He'd not only prepared a house for us, but He was giving us revival!

Although revival thrived, since it was nearing Christmas, Brother W decided to close the meetings, for he wanted to see his daughter perform at the school program in town. Such a ticklish score to settle, but Tom went to discuss it with him. The pastor was somewhat discouraging in his remarks. "Brother, you can't reach these people. They've heard some of the best."

Undaunted, my Tom replied, "God can even use a child who is anointed. It doesn't take any special type of preaching for God to move. . . . Just obedience to the Holy Spirit." But Tom's efforts were of no use. The meeting closed. It just so happened that a case of flu broke out and canceled the Christmas program so we approached the pastor again.

"Can we hold prayer meetings since folks are feeling that revival should continue?" He agreed and prayer meetings were moved from house to house. Folks were hungry for the Word and God was filling their hearts.

On Christmas Eve Cecil and Tom went into Fayetteville and preached on the street to the Christmas shoppers until a deputy came by and ordered, "You'll have to move on — you're blocking the sidewalk." They moved, but then concluded their meeting.

Our husbands wanted to bring us Christmas gifts, but they didn't get much of an offering. Tom bought me a green mixing bowl for fifteen cents. It still helps decorate my house; it's just right for a hanging basket.

Christmas Day we wanted to have an all-day meeting. It's always been our custom to celebrate the Lord's birthday in this way. "No," Brother W protested, "the church is in no condition."

"What kind of excuse is that?" I asked my family. "I'm beginning to think that it's the pastor who is out of condition."

The next time he came to visit, I found the nerve to tell him before he left, "Brother, I believe I have a word from the Lord for you." He respected my hard preaching so he listened. I knew I was stepping on soft, untreadable ground by saying what I really felt. "Brother, you seem to be through here. You carry a burden for another place. I heard you say that — so why don't you go there?" Just like a thrown brick-bat, my words didn't fit the princi-

ples of etiquette, yet he humbly answered, "You're right." With
that he walked away.

Tom and I went from there twenty miles north to Springdale
for revival in the Assembly of God Church newly built by Pastor
and Edith Murrell while Cecil and Frances had begun a series of
meetings in a country schoolhouse in the West Fork vicinity. Tom
and I also saw great results. The first night Tom preached, the
lights went out. That didn't stymie my husband. He finished his
message in the dark and souls groped their way to the altar to pray
for salvation.

A couple of grown boys came seeking God for the infilling of
the Holy Spirit. They fasted and then the next day went out of
town to pray. At a waterfall near where they were holding their little prayer meeting, one of them felt God tell him, "Get under the
falls and you'll be filled." "Obedience is better than sacrifice," for
when he obeyed, he received the promised blessing of the infilling
of the Holy Spirit! The other boy tried the same thing, but came
out with nothing more than a sopping wet body. That obviously
was not God's way for him. There was no magic in the waterfall!

When we returned to West Fork, we heard the news that the
pastor had gone, leaving on the pulpit a simple curt note with two
scriptures and an explanation of his reason for leaving. We
assumed that he'd gone on to find his ministry where he'd been
called.

Wouldn't it be great if God could always get men to move
when He says "move"? Most pastors seem to think the field will be
unfruitful if they don't stay. God does give a few lifetime jobs in
one place, but the whole world is a mission field. We were to learn
later that many times it is much easier to leave than to stay put.

The deacons came and confronted Tom. "Would you consider
filling the pastor's unexpired term?" Tom hesitated, then replied,
"We'll have to pray about that. Jewell and I are evangelists." We
prayed and felt God would have us take the pastorate for the un-
filled time. But the weather was cold, and I'm sure that factor partially encouraged us to stay. The church also voted, and Brother
Charles Pepper, the Presbyter of the section, came to install Tom

in his first attempt at pastoring. I served as his assistant, the first time of many to follow.

With the pastorate came a better, yet unfurnished house several blocks away from the church. Since we no longer had a car, we walked to visit the saints, who nearly all lived within walking distance of the church. We even trudged into the country several miles to visit the Roses. Their welcome mat was always out for us to spend the night.

The town had no paved streets and was a kind of Eden with its well-kept lawns, fruit trees and flowers in season. I made my favorite jellies and jams from the fruit. We received so little money—the tithes never amounted to much on Sunday. Once we received a pound of butter with a dollar bill tucked inside. So precious—it even came gift wrapped!

There were visits to the sick and Tom preached his first funeral. He'd only attended one public funeral, and his mother's had not been public, so he asked me what he should do. I said, "Preach Jesus to the live ones. That's what I did at the only funeral I ever preached." He chose an appropriate text: "It is appointed unto man once to die and after that comes the judgment." We learned that the man had not ever professed to being saved.

Several distinguished visitors came to preach at that church including both of our fathers and Brother Burris, the Arkansas District Superintendent. What do you feed such a distinguished preacher? When Brother Burris came we dug down deep into our little "kitty," got out our nickels and pennies and bought steak. I cooked vegetables and made cornbread. Brother Burris said grace and then asked, "Mind if I just make myself at home?"

"Sure. Dig in and help yourself," Tom answered. With that, he shoved everything else aside except his glass. Then pouring his milk, he crumbled the cornbread into it. . . . And we'd sacrificed to buy him steak!

6

MOVING ON

"Come and seek God till you get what you've come after," Tom said nightly. Tarrying services were really paying off for the "Chronic seekers." Everyone was promised, "Get to praying and believing and God will fill. God has promised and you are hungry!" Then folks began to receive the Holy Spirit. We girls stayed home to pray and intercede but each night we'd ask, "Who got it tonight?" Some outstanding men such as Donald Walker, Woodrow Smith and Robbie Harris received and were made preachers. Within two weeks, twenty had received the promised Holy Spirit.

In dire need of finances to pay the regular bills, Tom began a project to raise money. He rented a piece of untilled land some distance from town and planted corn which he would sell to pay church bills. Single-handed he weeded and tended it. The crop was beautiful because God was on our side and sent the sun and rain to make it grow.

Summer meant time for outdoor meetings, so we pitched a tent and asked Sister Edith Murrell, our lady preacher friend, to come. It was her turn to become our guest evangelist. My Tom discovered a new gift then — that of being a peacemaker. Everyone had to walk to and fro from the tent which was stretched out on an open lot close to the riverside. As we walked, two men got to discussing who was going to be the song leader. The argument got so heated that Tom got right in between them and began his passionate life-time activity, that of making peace between two Christian brothers.

Another night a lady came carrying two buckets full of huckleberries. Handing me one she said, "And here's one for the evangelist. It took me all day to pick them." Few gifts have been that impressive.

Baptism followed the tent revival. Tom baptized the converts in the West Fork of White River, the beautiful stream which gave the little town its name, while singers and onlookers watched. One woman, so afraid of drowning, clung to Tom and tried to climb him like a tree! Frances and I stood on the other side with wraps of a sort, ready to greet the wet ones.

"God helps those who help themselves." We needed fire wood. Tom went to the country to help Brother Rose cut some wood and haul it into our yard. After cutting wood all day he came home and found me standing at the ironing board. Pushing me aside gently, he finished ironing his shirts himself. Not that I couldn't iron them to suit, but I was expecting our first child. He was determined that I wouldn't overdo again for I'd already spent two weeks in bed to keep from losing the baby. He had brought me flowers then and he still does occasionally. Flowers speak louder than words.

Tom preached on "The Old Paths" and had both our fathers bring a message. My father declared, "How a person lives is how to measure his Christian faith." The coming of the Lord was on everyone's mind. Staying ready for Him was the principle thought carried by the two elderly preachers. "The Spirit was there in a mighty way, Jude," Tom told me, as I was not attending the services.

Our prayer chain kept the church in good condition, though some began to skip regular services even on Sunday nights to work the new challenge of jigsaw puzzles just like people today watch TV and attend ball games instead of church. Their missing services concerned us. "Forsake not the assembling of yourselves together . . ."

July's heat and humidity caused us to swelter. With no fans of any kind all we could do was raise a window to catch any small bit of breeze. Counting the days until the baby's arrival, I'd hem diapers and Tom helped with my punched rug whenever he wasn't busy with church work. I wanted to make our place as pretty as I could for Tom, so I made rugs to throw here and there. One Sunday we held a foot washing service. Essential or not, God can use this humbling service to crack some hard hearts. And He did.

Nearing the time for annual elections, we were also anticipating our first family increase. Tom was praying about the first and very much concerned about the second. Both of us were getting itchy feet to get back into evangelistic work. Still, we didn't want to go before God's time and before the arrival of our new addition.

I went into labor on one hot night during the July heat wave. Old Dr. Houston, a local general practitioner, was called. He'd bragged to me, "I've delivered thousands of babies in my lifetime."

After waiting with me for a while he declared, "Jewell, you just aren't quite ready. I'm going to take a nap in the living room." He was called again at midnight; once more at 4 A.M. Frances came to be my nurse. Doc Houston said to me, "I'll have to put you to sleep and take the baby." No hospitals were close by and I felt I had no need of one. The baby's birth was between me and God and nature.

Doctor Houston went back to his office for forceps. While he was gone Frances received a word from the Lord for me. "Jewell," she said, "the Lord tells me you are going to have a beautiful girl who will play the piano from one end of the keyboard to the other."

I held fast to her message as I drifted off into oblivion from the chloroform. Later I learned I had been under four hours or more and had been given too much anesthetic. The lady who'd administered it had never done that before. When I finally awoke, I asked, "Please, can I see my baby?"

Tom clasped my hand in his and said, "Jude, Doc told me to send for your folks to come. He thought there wasn't a chance for you and the baby to make it." The baby had been all but left for dead, but Frances persistently pleaded with the doctor. Over and over she said, "Try to bring the baby around. I've had a message from God!"

Doc said, "All right" and asked for some water. I guess he thought the baby'd be a spastic when he saw her condition.

"Poor baby," I said when I first saw her. Such a pitiful sight! Too weak from the labor, I could no longer stay awake and drifted off to sleep.

By the time I awoke, all the other members of the family had arrived. Many had traveled a long distance. They were a praying crowd and what we needed most was prayer.

Later they helped me by cooking the meals and caring for the baby and me. Too weak to do much mothering, I was especially grateful that Frances had been there—not only to nurse me, but also to persist with the old doctor when I didn't even know what was going on. After four weeks of being bedfast I was up and going again.

Tom wrote in his diary, "July 25th, 1933, a baby girl came to live with us—born at 10:45 in the morning." The new daddy was kept busy washing and caring for the new baby's colic night after night. Although he still had his pastoral duties, the first Sunday after her birth he relaxed by swimming in the river after the morning sermon. We were both glad we could say, "Finally the three of us are by ourselves." We felt the triumph after the conflict.

At church we dedicated our little girl to the Lord, calling her Phyllis Dorene. Over the years she has proven my sister Frances had a real revelation from God. Phyllis not only plays the piano from one end of the keyboard to the other, but her trained voice has blessed countless numbers. Being involved in missions and teaching school, she has offered hospitality even to strangers. The devil was cheated. God's word was triumphant.

It was nearing the time when the congregation at West Fork, Arkansas planned to vote on a man to be their pastor. Our names were expected to be on the ballot so we were praying for guidance and hoping the church would choose someone else. We both yearned to get back into evangelistic work, yet Tom seemed to have put out a fleece before the Lord. He said he felt we couldn't freely leave if we were re-elected.

On election night we waited for the votes to be counted. The clerk finally announced, "The vote is for the Cunninghams."

A family of four had come in late so Tom saw their arrival as an opportunity to turn his fleece over. We were not rejoicing at the election results, so he said, "To be fair to the latecomers, we feel the vote should be taken again." We neither knew or cared if this was according to parliamentary procedure. The vote was taken for the second time. We lost! The die was cast and we resigned ourselves to the situation. Tom and I realized that our term there had been a form of triumph, for we know now that every evangelist should pastor at some point to better understand a congregation and its daily problems, especially the pastor's problems.

Our day of farewell came and we had to say goodbye to the church that had given us so much. Tears flowed freely as we got into our Chevy that Tom had practically rebuilt. Once again we started off with no knowledge of where we were headed.

7

WILDERNESS

Wilderness! When you're a preacher in a wilderness, what do you do? Without a church or a home of any kind we decided to drive over to Harrison where the dear Flinn sisters lived. They'd put us up while we were on our honeymoon, so jubilantly we returned to them with the fruit of our marriage—our baby daughter. The two sisters fell in love with Phyllis and willingly offered to babysit for us as we accepted calls to preach around. In return for their many kindnesses, Tom patched their roof.

A call came from Coy and Retha in California. "Come on out," they coaxed, "there's plenty of fields here that need harvested for the Lord. God has given us good meetings."

We'd come in contact with a girl named Ruby Paul who was engaged to a soldier stationed in Imperial Valley, California. She wanted to see him so badly that she declared, "I'll be glad to pay for the gas if you'll take me there." Both Tom and I felt her offer was our way to get us where the Lord wanted us, so after our last ministry, a fellowship meeting at St. Joe, Arkansas, we prepared to leave.

With Ruby Paul, her few belongings and our baby in her basket crammed into the back seat of our old '29 Chevy, we headed west. Tom drove most of the way, but occasionally I'd take the wheel. At Little Field in West Texas we stopped overnight to visit kin at my cousin's home. My father and stepmother were visiting there and were so pleased to see us and the family offshoot. But stopping proved to be a mistake. We should have taken to heart Jesus' words, "Salute no man by the way."

41

Papa declared, "We want to go with you to California," so Tom and I left our car in Little Field and all five grownups plus the baby piled into my father's smaller car.

"Thump, thump!" Suddenly the car swerved and we began thumping along the highway. Tom got out and confirmed we had a flat. Upon surveying the rest of the tires, he exclaimed, "These tires are all bad!" Throughout our trip my poor husband sweltered in the heat as he fixed one flat after another. How we both wished we'd have continued in our own car! It not only had good rubber, but we'd been doing fine on our own.

Upon reaching the outskirts of the beautiful city of Roswell, New Mexico, we knew we didn't dare look for a first-class place to sleep. None of us had any extra money. In an outlandish little tourist camp apartment, we rented a room with two regular-sized beds. My stepmother and Ruby shared one while Papa, Tom and I shared the other. Tom was scrunched in the middle. The baby slept in her basket on a chair by my side of the bed. In the dark of the night Tom awakened us screaming, "Give me air! At least there's plenty of that!"

With all due respect to Papa, I declared "I think we have a Jonah on our boat." Tom suggested to my father, "Maybe you and Bernice would like to go back to your meetings in Texas. This doesn't seem to be working out very well." They agreed, so we backtracked after repaying Ruby Paul so she could buy a bus ticket to El Centro. We went back to my cousin Joe's place where Tom shocked grain and did other farm work. Joe bought our trailer and canned fruit I was taking to, of all places, California! He gave us twenty-five dollars for the whole lot!

After Tom and I seriously sought the Lord in prayer we both felt it was right for us to go on to California. But a letter we received sounded like a "Macedonian call." The Winningers, our sinner friends from Oklahoma, had gone to east Texas to the oil boom, and they'd written us to come start a church. Not considering the seasons nor anything else, we took our twenty-five dollars and headed east. Since it was already late fall, we realized Texas was a closer target than California. We had to travel night and day to get there in a few days, even with both of us driving. How could we do otherwise? Our funds were sparse, but we felt sure we'd find riches, a home and a meeting place once we'd reached our destination.

On a stopover in Dallas we bought something new for each of us to wear, fixing ourselves up for an appropriate entrance. Lessons sometimes come hard. Outward attire is important, but not so much as the inner man. It wasn't long before we realized too, that California would have been a better place to spend the winter. God does lead and help us with the planning of our lives if we will only listen. How often we set the stage and build the system, but leave Him out!

We found in East Texas an oil boom — an area of oil 50 miles long by 10 miles wide. Derricks like tall fingers pointed up to heaven. God wanted a church in Arp where others had tried unsuccessfully to start one. Was God challenging Tom and me with the difficult task?

After wandering around we finally found our oil drilling friends at London, Texas. The Winningers put us up for the night, but couldn't find us any place to preach. We visited Tyler after a Brother Lewis talked to us about having a meeting there, but he didn't want us to hold it right away. Can you imagine living in a car with a baby for two solid weeks, sleeping in the seats? That was what we were forced to do. Our only income came from the few coins people pitched on the sidewalk when either Tom or I preached on the streets in one of the small towns nearby. At least with those few coins we were able to buy milk and bread, and gas for the car. We were "having to preach to live." A couple of towns had deputies who did not welcome us and were interfering by having us move our meeting — Henderson and Tyler.

Our constant roaming and seeking brought us to the District Fellowship Meeting at the Gladewater Assembly. I thought we'd surely find our call there, for before they'd even had a church building, their folks had sent a letter with train fare for my sister and me to come and hold their first revival. Since we'd already had a commitment, we'd sent the money back. Alpha Fortenberry Henson came in our stead, and from her revival that church was born. Surely some of the Gladewater folks would still remember me!

Those meetings were well attended. That first day I had no lunch or supper. With the last two cents Tom had in his pocket, he bought a handful of peanuts from a vending machine, my entire meal, but at least our nursing baby was well-filled and didn't cry. The next day a man approached us and said, "Here are two dollars. God told me yesterday to give you folks a dollar, but I failed. Now He's having me double it." I could have told that brother if he'd been obedient, he would have been a dollar richer and I would have had more to eat than peanuts!

Tom and I went in search of Longview Assembly, but were misdirected and wound up at a Free Pentecostal revival where we joined in prayer with a lady who was praying inside. By doing so, we ended up meeting a brother in Christ after the service who invited us to stay at the "prophet's chamber" in his big house. Oh, the joy of sleeping on a bed for a night, after being cooped inside the car for so long!

We moved on to Kilgore where we met an evangelist named Weeks who let us stay in his home for two days while we preached on that city's streets. Brother Weeks also gave us spiritual advice, "The little town of Arp is without a church." Like the Apostle Paul, we were looking for a place where Christ had not been preached. At that point it seemed that all other doors were closed except the door of home missions. Since we had no other call, we felt we were to start a church in Arp. It looked like God had us cornered.

"Where can we find Arp?" Tom asked. Brother Weeks' directions took us down muddy roads crowded with wagons and stalled jitneys, through piney woods, past oil derricks, past houses and hovels, workers and cars loaded down with household goods on top. People there needed the Gospel! A burden for them began burning inside both of us. Arp was the place! Tom and I stopped and prayed, then asked a man, "Are there any Pentecostal folks in that little town?" We asked others until someone directed us to a Brother Allen. We found him on his farm which hadn't been cultivated in four years. He'd been living off his oil royalties. After talking with him, we sensed he wasn't very interested in our call. "Too many have tried and failed here," he said and walked away.

Not so easily turned aside Tom and I went to see a Sister Massey, the town's school teacher whom Brother Allen had told us about. "Could we hold prayer meetings here in your home?" we asked her, but she said she couldn't let us because her husband wasn't saved.

We decided to return to Brother Allen's and try again. He came out and stood in the cold wind with snow falling all around him. "We want to come to your house tonight for a prayer meeting," we informed him.

"Then go invite the two other families," (Sister Massey and a family with several children) he answered us reluctantly. After driving into the snow-covered piney woods to change clothes and eat our bread and drink our milk in the car, we drove into town to invite the other folks to Brother Allen's place.

There was no real faith responses that night after I gave the message, "The House Was Built Because the People Had a Mind to Work," but God certainly anointed the singing as we all praised Him together. What bewildered us was the unconcern.

We'd been getting many calls to preach in churches like Henderson and Tyler; calls came for revivals in other towns. A call to take the Athens church had even come from their pastor who was leaving, but we'd both felt we were to stay in Arp. That even meant dropping an offer we'd had from St. Joe, Arkansas, where we'd been unanimously elected. Our call to Arp had been so specific. Why had no one cared to take us in? Motels were nonexistent there.

We got a tent from Rev. D. D. Lewis which Tom had to put up himself, until a stranger passing by offered to help. By the time we finally had found a spot for the tent the wind was blowing strong and cold. Warming the tent we feared would be a problem. We even thought about using oil drum stoves with gas piped into them. The committee (Tom and Jewell) decided to abandon the tent idea because of the number of difficulties. We went back looking again for another meeting place. To our advantage, Sister Massey had decided to put us up at night, although she couldn't take care of us during the day. So we preached on the streets to get money enough to buy bread and milk.

One day we came across an odd-looking building—an old abandoned blacksmith shop—just as dirty and black as soot could make it. Big enough for our purposes, it also had plenty of parking spaces around it.

After hunting up the owner, we learned we could rent the building for $5.00 a month. Tom had enough to pay the first week's rent, so we set to work surveying the needs to get the building in shape. Not only did the roof have to be patched, but the entire place was filthy. We raked and carried out trash, then rented boards to build a platform and benches. We rented the lumber on credit—promising to pay later. Using most of the dimes tossed to us at our daily street meetings, we bought building paper to cover the black walls. Tom was up on the roof mending the last hole to make it weatherproof when Mr. Allen came by. Looking up at Tom, he asked: "How're you going to light it? Looks like you do mean business about getting a church started."

"I sure do," Tom answered. "I aim to have gas lamps, I guess."

"No," said Mr. Allen. "You take this ten dollars and have the electricity hooked up." We thought, "They'd better come, or we'll turn the whole town over to whatever happens to people who don't know they're having a visitation from God!"

The meeting place was finally ready. We put the baby in her basket on the rough home made altar and the three of us dedicated the building. But where were we to stay? The little 7' by 9' lean-to in the back of the building was better than sleeping in the car, so we wallpapered it with newspaper. It became home. We had a stove to heat and cook with. At the other end of the room was a ¾ size bed and a sort of shelf table Tom had built on the side of the heater. Across from that we stood my wardrobe trunk on end and opened it up, making a combination wardrobe and dresser with a mirror on top. Phyllis' basket was on a box by the side of our small bed. Cozy!

Sister Massey loaned us her piano and played for our meetings. Revival was on! Weeks passed, and the church began to get established. Two murderers, one who had not yet had his trial (Brother Allen had paid his bond to be free until his trial), prayed through at that rough wooden altar. By February of 1934 several souls had found salvation in that embryo of a church. One woman suffering from pneumonia got up out of her bed and came to services. She was both saved and healed! Tom found an old abandoned Methodist church in the country, which he bought for a mere $25.00. Later on the blacksmith building was torn down and the Methodist Church was dismantled and rebuilt on the lot.

Brother Joe Wilkerson from Duncan came by and started a revival for us. God used Joe at Arp. One backslider was saved, and we felt we were to turn the church over to Joe. He accepted and stayed long enough to see the little church moved to the location of the blacksmith shop and the believers set in order with the Assemblies of God.

Were we to start again for California? Did God intend for us to minister out West? We felt we should go, as we started out with no thought of gas and food money to get there.

In 1969 Tom and I returned from the General Council in Dallas in our Cadillac to visit Arp. They met in a nice large church on a better corner instead of our little country church. The youthful pastor gave us a warm welcome, asking us to stay for the service. But we declined. After 35 years, we found Mr. Allen still on his farm and bid him a belated, "Thanks and God bless you" for helping us get that church started.

In 1983 Tom preached the celebration of fifty years of the Assembly of God church in Arp in the big brick church which was the third one after the little Methodist church that was put in place of the old blacksmith shop turned church, which we left there to worship in.

8

CALIFORNIA OR BUST

On our second start to California we stopped at Lufkin, Texas, to hold a revival. Measles broke out and brought our revival to a standstill—disappointing to us, but evidently the last discouraging blow to Pastor Petty, for on our last night he resigned during the service. The congregation suffered from a double shock—suddenly they found themselves without revival or pastor. Blame the measles and the devil!

Tom and I continued on our way, stopping off at Cache, Oklahoma, where we sought out Marylydia for her blessing concerning our trip west. She gave us a lot of negatives, then added, "But, Jewell, it's too far!" What would she have said if she'd have known we had only one dollar to our names? We had the letter from Coy and Retha inviting us the second time, but now they had a church where we were to hold a revival—no money, though, accompanied the invitation.

"Surely God must have something special for us out west for the devil has tried so many times to discourage us and hinder us from going there," I told Tom. My husband agreed and had faith enough to continue that long journey with just one dollar to start with and a wife and small child in an old car ready for the dump. We had no promise of tomorrow's food or gas, only faith to believe God was in the venture and He would provide!

The first day's journey got us to Atlas, Oklahoma where Brother Burns welcomed us and offered us a night's stay in his home. After prayer the next morning, Tom found the good brother had pressed a roll of three one-dollar bills in his hand. No one had told anyone that we were broke.

48

Further on during our journey toward West Texas we stopped over at Hollis, Oklahoma to preach on the streets. Listeners tossed a few coins our way after the service and a sinner man by the name of Johnson, also a stranger, gave us a much-needed inner tube.

Upon entering Childress, Texas, we wandered up familiar streets to the Sheets' home where Alvin and Haley had always put out a welcome mat. Brother Sheets considered Papa his "spiritual father" for Papa was instrumental in leading him to the Lord. Haley's comment as we left the next day pleased me no end. "Jewell," she whispered, "you sure got yourself a pretty man."

"Thanks," I responded, "I was looking for one."

At Las Cruces, New Mexico, we stopped over to see my folks who were holding revival services there with Pastor Smith. Tom and I expected to pay our regards to them, then be on our way. But for the second time Papa also had acquired the bug to explore the west. Coy and Retha had invited my father to come to their church in Exeter, California, too. When Papa's meeting was over he planned to move on west. Cecil and Frances had been at Las Cruces helping Papa in the meetings. That closed, that being the last Sunday night — so the next day we all started out west. They with their baby Lavelle would follow in their car. And so the three Nicholson cars, loaded with people and baggage, headed toward California.

As we continued on through the desert occasionally we'd see a jack rabbit or an Indian riding a spotted pony. Once in a great while we'd pass another vehicle with people who were also brave enough to encounter the desert heat.

Arizona scenery caused us to marvel as we viewed it for the first time, but after long, hot and uninteresting days of travel we were grateful to arrive in Tucson where we found a night's lodging in a rented building used as the Assembly of God Church, spreading our pallets on the floor.

Reaching Pheonix by Saturday, we attended church, where the folk were in revival. At the close of the meeting a Sister Murphy asked us, "Wouldn't you all like to lay out your bedding on the church floor so you can sleep tonight? We haven't any place other than that where we can house all of you." Thankfully, we took her up on her invitation, spreading our pallets again, and in the morning she had all of us to the parsonage for breakfast. That was our first encounter with Sister Murphy, but knew immediately she had a spirit full of love. It doesn't take long to judge one's spirit. Jesus said love's the main ingredient by which we can know a disciple.

We went on to Glendale where we attended their Assembly's Sunday morning service. The elderly Rev. Skull was in charge then as a relief pastor. One lady pointed to Papa and exclaimed, "That's the man! That's the man I saw in a vision! He was to come to us for a revival!" Perhaps the rest of us should have gone on to California and left Papa there, for they wanted a revival to begin immediately. It should have been suggested to Papa.

A big dance hall at a nearby park was offered to us by the custodians so we could hold a meeting. But to our dismay, we learned we'd been voted out, when we returned to the church that evening. "When everyone voted, they agreed there were just too many of you," we were informed, so we drove the scenic road to the town of Wickenberg nestled in the foothills.

Papa must have been stepping hard on the gas pedal of his car, for when we drove up and parked, we found Bernice and my father already seated with the pastor and his wife in their backyard.

When the preacher and Papa came to the fence and looked across at us in our parked car my father announced, "My children, the Cunninghams."

"Come on in," the pastor greeted us as his wife scurried to get some more chairs from the kitchen. When our third car drove up, I couldn't help but notice a change in the pastor's facial expression. From his first joy at having Papa and my stepmother arrive, his mood went to consternation, then to dismay. The Vaughans were introduced by my father and they were also brought seats. Then the pastor looked us over. We heard no more questions of concern like, "How was the trip?" or "How has God been blessing?" Instead he declared, We will take up an offering to get something for all of us for supper."

As broke as we were, how could that be? While the rest searched for fitting words, I spoke up. "If you don't care, brother, we'll go out to the church and pray. We don't need supper. We're getting used to fasting."

While our family prayed — and we were getting a bit loud — footsteps came from behind us. The pastor's voice boomed, "Let the house come to order!"

Papa then arose from his kneeling position. Looking here and there he asked, "Where is my hat? Where did I put it?" He never was one to fight back. (I needed more of his good qualities.) He and I joined the other family members who were already outside. Tom had disgust written all over his face, for on top of everything else, we had a flat tire.

From out of the crowd which had been gathering, a familiar voice called out, "Jewell, Jewell!" It was Sister Freeman. A friend from my girlhood meetings, she insisted we remain for the services, but we got no further encouragement from the pastor. That flat tire kept us from moving on. Trapped! When the meeting began the preacher suggested, "Tonight let's have a good service. Let two or more people pray." After his short sermon he called on Papa to pronounce the benediction.

Dear Sister Freeman invited all of us to her house to sleep. She made beds all over the place; some of her own children slept on quilts spread on top of the dining room table. Sister Freeman expressed concern for her church. "The women have been meeting to pray for freedom in the church," she told us. Later we were told God heard the ladies' prayers and moved that pastor. Praying, spirit-filled daughters can cause action! Tom had not a nickel for gas, though we could fast. Mr. Freeman loaned us $5.00, which bought enough gas to get us to our destination, and Tom sent the $5.00 back. It was the only time we had to borrow on our trip.

On through the desert we traveled. Since there was no such thing as air conditioning, we rolled down all the windows to catch even the tiniest bit of air. Somehow we made it through. The other two cars had gone over the pass to the San Joaquin Valley through the mountainous roads, but Tom and I drove directly into the outskirts of San Bernardino and on into Los Angeles County to the "City of Angels." Before World War II, when it was far less congested, the city was a most beautiful sight to behold. We spotted an open air meeting place as we cruised along; another spectacular attraction to us was a special prayer place called the Cave of Adullum. We didn't tarry then; we knew brother Coy was waiting. But we had an inspiration that however wicked now, it was a "City of Angels" back then.

Following the old Grapevine Road across the Sierras to the 200 mile-long fruitful San Joaquin Valley, on our way to the small town of Exeter, we watched wild flowers blooming in profusion, green cotton fields already producing bolls, vineyards as well as orchards and orange groves ripe with fruit. Back in the San Fernando Valley we'd already stopped to pick an orange, one straight from the tree, the juiciest we'd ever tasted. As more and more orange groves became evident we saw the first of the transients from the dust bowl who were camped along the roadside hoping to get work helping pick the oranges and cotton (for cotton was the one crop still picked by hand).

Passing by tractors and men working in the fields, fat grazing cows and dairies for plenty of milk, we felt as though we'd entered Canaan. God had brought us through to Exeter, California! There Brother Coy came running out to greet us "Welcome." Yes, we felt it was God's timing. God WAS going to give us the spiritual lift we needed and make us a blessing.

9

SAN JOAQUIN VALLEY

During the Easter season God sent revival. Folks were being filled; the Holy Spirit was at work. News of God's stirring spread and people came to our Exeter revival from other cities. Deacon Miller, who had known Coy and Retha when they'd ministered for him in Maricopa, came nearly a hundred miles for the meeting.

Tom got a job in the peach orchards to help with our personal needs and was fired — the first and only time in his life. While gathering peaches with all his might and mane (as he did everything) the boss said, "Here's your money. You're too hard on my trees." That was a triumph as well as a defeat. The Lord did not send us to California to harvest that kind of fruit.

All ten of the family members went to other churches in the valley — to Dinuba and to Woodlake. *

The Dinuba church hosted the revival for our family of ten and brought food to the five-room house where they put us up. The Holy Ghost kept filling souls nightly as we took turns preaching.

After those meetings, Papa took care of Coy's church and we three couples went to Los Angeles to the Christ's Ambassadors convention at Bethel Temple, the oldest and only Assembly of God church in the city. An elder statesman in our movement, Rev. Louis Turnbull and his wife Josephine were the pastors.

---

* The Green sisters were the founders and pastors of the tabernacle at Woodlake which is no longer in existence. Later, as District Home Missions Director, Tom helped Brother Simpson get a new church built. Often seed sprouts even if it looks as though it has died in the ground.

Oh, the joy and excitement of those three days of services. The youth were the convention leaders, but the elderly ministers were welcome to preach. A free wave of the Holy Spirit just swept through the sanctuary as hundreds of youth from across the state raised their hands and sang to the glory of God. It didn't matter whether a youth or one of their pastors spoke, the messages were anointed. Heaven must have been stormed with that convention's worship and praise.

While we were in L.A. we visited Angeles Temple. Baby Phyllis began to whimper during the service and I was politely asked to take her out.

Were churches not meant for little ones? In our modern times it seems Jesus would have been mistaken if he invited the little ones to come unto Him—provided He was even present in the church service. The sooner we let the little ones come and observe, the better. Some denominations do it right. They take time during the regular service for the pastor to "feed the lambs" instead of sending them out to a puppet show. We need to triumph over this conflict—the battle over having children again in the pews.

Our offspring are more intelligent than adults give them credit for. The years for the main impressions on their minds are these early years. "Train up a child . . . ," the Bible says. How old is a child?

More than once I have been asked to leave with my little ones. But one time when the great orator Raymond T. Richey was preaching, he called to me from the pulpit, "Don't mind the baby, I can preach over it. He will be a preacher. Cry aloud and spare not." It seemed like a prophecy spoken for our young son, Loren.

Our babies heard their parents preach. When one of us was not available to hold our infants, they would be in their baskets. When no one else could keep them quiet, they'd be brought to the platform where they could hear and see me preach. There they quietly absorbed the truths of God.

Children are a blessing, not a burden—not to be abused or neglected; certainly NOT ABORTED. Dr. Norman Vincent

Peale was asked, "Shall I bring a child into this awful age?" To this he replied, "Yes, bring them in. They will be candidates for heaven, so get them here." God doesn't give anything to hinder us in His work, we set the stage for how our children affect our ministry. My grandchildren will make a long trip to hear "Mama" preach or eat my homemade buns.

As Westerners, few of us understood how the "Reds" had been taking over the governments in the Eastern hemisphere. Tom and I had hardly heard the term "Reds" when we visited Los Angeles on "May Day" in 1934. We were not aware of the Communistic thrust worldwide at that time so were amazed as they marched through that city's streets. Later we learned that they stormed the Los Angeles city plaza, tore the American flag from its flagpole and raised the red flag in its place. Other socialists did the same in cities like Paris and London.

"What do you suppose is happening, Jude?" Tom asked as we watched the hoards of people and the frantic Los Angeles police. We bought a newspaper and found out what the crowds were all about. From that day forth the Communists have harassed our democracy — threatening our freedoms.

We three Nicholson's and our spouses searched throughout the city for an old preacher friend of Papa's. We checked every lead and even searched the yellow pages to see if he was listed as a painter, his avocation. There we found his location.

George had been a young zealot for God. As a pioneer evangelist, he preached with such fervor and intensity that people flocked to the altar. How well I remembered the nights when we prayed together around a campfire during our covered wagon days. Brother George would share with us what God gave him in the spirit. During World War I God brought him back from training camp with a discharge and a memo from his superior, "This man is not a soldier and never will be."

Our search finally paid off. When we pulled into a very ostentatious-looking house, George answered our knock. "Don't think you'll remember us. We're the Nicholson young folk. This is Coy . . ."

"Coy?" he asked, recognizing the name, for few people have ever been named Coy.

"And here's Retha, Coy's wife," I said, continuing my introductions. "And here's Frances and her husband Cecil Vaughan." After I introduced Tom I told him, "We just wanted to share with you what Papa's been doing."

George invited us in to meet the lady of the big house and we learned that God's young enthusiast had backslidden. He would get her mansion when she was gone. For three days we stayed with them, praying and fasting, for we felt this was why we had found him—to get him back right with God. George would kneel and pray with us. Oh, he sounded sincere, but God's discernment showed us he was not. Phonies wouldn't be so plentiful if we exercised the gift of discernment more freely in the church.

George would dismiss himself, go to his room, lock the door and not come out again until morning—leaving us praying for him. About 4:00 one Thursday morning, Tom and I got up and started praying anew. While we were praying, we heard George praying aloud in his locked room. "That sounds natural, doesn't it?" I asked and called to the others. We were overjoyed at hearing him pray in earnest. "Oh, God, forgive me! I, who have prayed all night at the altar for souls, need to be saved. I, who have preached to others, need forgiveness. Forgive me and I'll preach again." How genuine his words sounded.

Without waiting to speak further to him, Tom and I began packing our things to head east. Frances and Cecil decided to stay and get George's feet re-established on the right path.

George did come out before we left.

There is not one soul this side of the grave which cannot be saved. His mercy reaches to the lowest hell—even to the brink of the grave. However, someone who is in touch with the Lord has to intercede for the Holy Spirit to return, I perceive, remembering that event, and the scripture of the sixth chapter of Hebrews, verses 4, 5, and 6.

How I wish this story had a better ending, but I don't know any. Saul didn't have a good ending to his story, yet he'd been chosen of the Lord above his fellow men. He stood the tallest physically as well as otherwise, but he had only one altar. Abraham, on the other hand built an altar everywhere he sojourned and the Bible calls him by a title worth more than if he'd had a Doctorate in Divinity or a Ph.D. God called him FAITHFUL.

At that 4:00 A.M. prayer time, Tom and I felt led of the Lord to go to New Mexico where we'd been invited by Brother Billy Bates to start a church at Dora near Portales. We left hoping Cecil and Frances could get George rededicated. We had to be on our way to New Mexico.

10

DORA

"No one should be wandering through the desert on a day like this!" Tom declared as we spied a lone hitch-hiker on the road near Albuquerque. With that, he brought the car to a stop. "Get in," Tom offered, "and sit up here beside me." We had all our belongings crammed inside to go to Dora, New Mexico, to start a church for Billie Bates. We'd made a bed in the back seat where Phyllis and I were riding. Tom and I had been taking turns driving, resting and holding Phyllis.

The young fellow got in and after eating some dry bread we offered him, he confessed to us, "I haven't eaten for days." He appeared ill from the first, and seemed to get even sicker as we drove along. Tom stopped every few miles just to let him get out and roll on the ground crying with pain. We determined he was having an appendicitis attack.

He let us know immediately after entering the car, "I don't want to be a Christian!" but we just ignored that and prayed for him all that night.

Worried about our passenger's problem, Tom stopped by a house along the way. The owner evidently feared strangers for he would not come out of his home. Through a closed door he told us, "There's no doctor here, but there's one in the next town." Reluctantly he gave us directions to the doctor's house.

Upon our arrival there the young man got out and fell writhing with pain on the physician's front sidewalk. That doctor had such little concern for human misery he wouldn't even come outside after we had to admit none of us could pay for his services. Whatever happened to the Hippocratic oath?

We felt we had no other choice than to go forty miles out of our way to take our ailing passenger to a hospital in Albuquerque. Arriving at daybreak, the first hospital we found was Catholic. The head sister's greeting was one we'll never forget: "We will do what we can to help him and find his family. You have been good Samaritans thus far, but we'll take over now."

After leaving the hospital we pulled over to the curb to nap. At six that morning we were roused from our sleep by a policeman rapping on the car window. He thought we'd been there all night, which was against the city ordinances. When Tom explained to him, "Officer, we came here on an emergency trip to the hospital," he was very kind to us and helped us on our way.

Years before when I'd been holding a revival in the nearby city of Mt. Air, I'd come to this same hospital with friends who were admitting a young girl with a malady similar to our suffering hitch-hiker. Why had they taken her to the hospital? Because she was one of the rowdies disturbing the services where I was trying to preach that Sunday afternoon. I learned that night she had taken seriously ill and I was asked to go with the friend taking her the hundred miles to Albuquerque — the only hospital. She later became a minister herself. That young lady had come to repentance and acceptance of Christ as they drove her in. It took all night for us to make that trip and so did this trip with the young man. When we visited him the next morning, we saw that Christ had also won in his life.

Traveling on to Clovis, we came to Brother A. C. Bates' house. Since it was Saturday, he asked us to stay over and preach the following day. After the luxury of a warm bath, a night's rest on a good mattress and washing our clothes, we ventured on down the road ten miles to Portales to the place where Billie Bates had asked us to come to establish a church in a small place called Dora.

Times were so bad that we wondered why we'd left Los Angeles to come to such a dismal spot. From "Canaan" (California), Grandma Bates had been no encouragement. She was too honest. She'd told us, "You children will starve out there. Everyone depends on relief or the Red Cross." Our determined answer had been, "But God led us."

At Dora we sought out a place to hold a revival and asked the trustees about using the Pep schoolhouse situated about three miles from town. Our revival was to begin on Friday, June 8th, 1934. Tom and I anticipated that everyone from the surrounding area would be there early to get a seat. After all, it wasn't every day that they had a chance to hear noted evangelists from California!

Some young girls helped us clean out the building and dust the seats. Our tiny Phyllis had never been so filthy as when she crawled over that floor in her church clothes while we worked.

The audience for the opening night of our "Great Revival" included only our host family and the three of us. What a let-down! Saturday night attendance was the same. On Sunday we attended their Union Sunday School. People came in late. The Sunday School Superintendent did not profess to be a Christian! Members told us he'd been seen playing cards the night before — preparing his Sunday School lesson??

The youth group had no interest in getting together for anything but a good time — fun at the expense of others. Our work was cut out for us! Often Tom and I asked one another, "Why did we leave California where so many doors were opening, to come to this?"

Sunday night I preached from Matthew 1:23: "And they shall call His name Jesus." Jesus became our subject for the next few weeks. People had no way of knowing what denomination we were from. We spoke of nothing but Jesus, not of denominational differences.

A little green one-room house became our home. I papered the walls with newspaper because we got it for nothing. I loved sitting in the shade with Phyllis on my lap, waiting for the nightly services at the school house. As Grandma Bates had warned us, we experienced hard times financially even though the meetings were beginning to gain interest.

Souls were coming to Christ! Word spread and folks began coming in increased numbers. Some came in cars, others in wagons. The breakthrough hadn't yet come, but God showed us this was a seed-planting time.

Since we lived just a mile from the schoolhouse we walked there in the evenings and caught a ride back with someone after the services. Someone loaned us a cow for Tom to milk and food was brought to us.

Monday night we scanned the crowd and found the schoolhouse was nearly as full as it had been Sunday night. Tom came on strong with a very warm text: "Hell." He pictured Hades as a place to stay away from. I was pleased to hear him preach on fire and brimstone. It looked like it would take a lot of heat to melt those folks' cold hearts! (Not hellfire heat, but the Holy Spirit's warmth.)

When Lurlene, Brother Billie's daughter led testimonies, very few spoke a word of praise for the Lord. The few Christians who were there were from various denominations. The spiritual drought seemed to penetrate our souls too. We were doing all we could to keep on preaching with fervor, but our hearts were heavy with discouragement. Our call had been to "build a church" and that's what we intended to do.

Why do new calls to ministry come when you don't need the enticement of extra decoys? A letter arrived from a church in Parnell, Oklahoma, asking us to be their pastors. Without hesitation we answered: "Thanks for your confidence in us, but we have decided to stay here until a church is established."

We enthusiastically sang such songs as "Dry Bones," "My, Didn't It Rain," "Jesus, Hold My Hand" and "Old Time Religion." We needed that! Tom and I have always found songs of praise and worship to be as uplifting to one's spirit as attending the Cherry Festival in California, as exhilarating as viewing the Grand Canyon.

The town of Dora seemed as dead as the Petrified Forest we'd visited once. It was worn and rugged, reminding us of the Indian antique village with its art and the old wooden wagon from 1846 which bragged with its sign, "I was driven to Arizona before many of you were born." To me, the old schoolhouse by that wagon compared to the Pep Schoolhouse in Dora.

Would the folks in Dora ever make Christ welcome? "God will help us get something moving," we felt. "Some bones are already beginning to shake. The old wagon isn't just a monument any longer. It's rolling! The Gospel wagon's moving. Souls are being saved."

One night a young man in the congregation stood under great conviction but refused to come forward at the invitation. A few days later we heard he was close to dying, so dear Tom took his Bible and walked several miles to see him. Upon his arrival at the lad's home, Tom found the family gathered around his bed. The young fellow's face bore the look of near-death.

Still conscious, though, he recognized Tom coming through the door. Without giving my husband a chance to say a word, the sick boy stated definitely, "Preacher, you may as well go home with that Bible if you've come to preach to me."

Tom began, "Oh, I just want to . . . ," but the lad interrupted, "I don't want your religion. I'll take my chances." Heartsick, Tom turned and trudged all the way back home. Within a few days the young fellow died—taking his chances. (Proverbs 29:21 and Romans 9:19 explain the dying man's right to make his choice.)

The revival picked up momentum, so we began all-day Sunday meetings. Oh, what food! Fried chicken, pies, cakes. One couple, Uncle Frank and Aunt Mandy, not only filled their stomachs, but made several trips carrying food to their horse-drawn vehicle. They claimed they couldn't afford to run a car, but we'd heard that those people were the richest in the country. Big ranchers, but such misers!

At one prayer meeting Uncle Frank was leading a prayer for much-needed rain. We'd been hoping for a gullywasher around Dora, but our hopes fell when he turned to his wife and asked, "What is that county down in South Texas where our farm is?" After she told him the name, he continued with his prayer, "Yes, Lord, that's where we pray for rain."

One day Sister Hicks was praying with Aunt Mandy while a violent storm raged outside. Sister Hicks was listening attentively to Aunt Mandy's prayers. She told me later, "There we were being blown away and she was praying that God would bless Frank that day."

"It's all right for her to have her husband in mind," I commented. But Sister Hicks continued, "She wasn't praying for Frank's safety, but was asking God to bless him and help him make some money!" After sharing such incidents I was not surprised at what Frank said to me when I approached him again after making my rounds for funds for the new church building: "What do you want? I gave a dollar already!"

Every place has an Uncle Frank and Aunt Mandy. Currently when I hear someone fretting about prophecies, about recession and inflation that will drive us into depression—". . . What are we going to do?"—I am reminded of the Aunt Mandys and Uncle Franks I knew during the Great Depression. So afraid they might starve, they no doubt brought on a quicker death for themselves by their worried state of mind.

"Hold on to your life and you will lose it . . . Take no thought for your life, what you shall eat or your body, what you shall put on . . . Look at the lilies and consider the sparrows how the Heavenly Father cares for these, His lesser creation. Will He not more so do it for you (His higher creation)? Oh, ye of little faith!"

Are riches wrong? No, it is the trusting in them which is condemned. Solomon said in Ecclesiastes 5:19: "Every man to whom God has given riches, rejoice in his labor, as it is a gift of God."

When we moved our meeting to the northwest of Dora, new people began to attend and most of those from the south side continued to come. After that we also held open-air meetings right in Dora. Then the rains we'd been praying for came! It rained and rained.

One twelve year old boy was the only soul who found salvation in the open air meetings. After two or three weeks we closed on a discouraging note. The meeting had been rained out and only one soul had been saved.

Back at the Pep schoolhouse we continued to hold regular services until we could proceed with the building program. Years later that lone little boy became our pride and joy. He not only became a successful pastor, but built a Christian school in connection with his church enlargement program. The brethren elected Leonard Hicks as Presbyter, then Executive Presbyter of the Southern California District Council. He proved to be a choice convert. Triumph came in spite of the rain!

June 19, 1934, was our second wedding anniversary. As Tom and I were celebrating with all-day prayer and fasting, a severe wind and sand storm interrupted our afternoon prayers together at the schoolhouse.

The next Saturday we returned to Portales for the regular park meetings, aware that the people who came to hear the service seldom had any money to give. But that day, after sitting on the grass under the big oak trees for the preaching, they not only responded with handshakes but with a good collection. After someone passed the hat, Tom counted the offering. "Three dollars and ten cents!" he cried.

The next Saturday we came and started the meeting as usual. A cocky deputy, accompanied by a fellow officer came, grabbed Tom by the arm and marched him to the sheriff's office, leaving the other officer outside the door.

I said to the people in the crowd, "We'll be back next Saturday." I then started to the sheriff's office with several people following me. One fellow said to the crowd, "Let the lady through." Then he said to the deputy, "Things like this will get folks in your eyes like onions."

Going in I asked Tom what was happening. He said, "It may be 'the can' for me." The arresting deputy had gone to the District Attorney to file a complaint. Shortly he returned and was almost apologetic as he released Tom.

In a few days we learned what caused his change of heart. The D.A. had said, "You mean you arrested a preacher while he was preaching? No, I won't accept a complaint against him. But if he comes and files a complaint against you for disturbing public worship I'll accept it." Those were heart changing words for the deputy.

The sheriff offered us the courthouse auditorium and that is where we carried on our Saturday meetings for a few weeks. But it was too hot in the auditorium and there were no fans, so we quit in Portales and went to the streets at Elida, west a few miles, until the Reds followed and bothered us there too.

Tom bought wheels and axles and began to build our trailer house so we'd have a place to live near the plot where we were going to build the church. "Where was the money going to come from?" we mused.

I'd been patching and re-patching Tom's five shirts. If I turned the collars, four would still be good enough to wear. When he tore his only pair of pants I found him mending them himself. Tom was always good at doing what was needed.

The next Sunday the Baptists were to take their turn to preach in the schoolhouse, but the preacher said, "Tom, you and Jewell need to preach today." After the service we had a big feast on the grounds. The afternoon ball game took only a segment of our church crowd. At the Baptist preacher's request Tom preached in the morning and again at 7:30. A good start on our trailer came in the offering—fourteen dollars in cash and promises!

On Monday night when Tom and I walked up to the front at the schoolhouse, we found the place was packed out! When we tried to stop the preaching, some of the people encouraged us by crying, "More! More! We need more!" Folks wouldn't let us close the revival. Monday is always labeled a blue day, but God anointed us that Monday! The revival continued in the evenings while Tom worked days on the trailer. The number of believers grew. No wonder Brother Billie had been so concerned about his community's needs. All it take is one person with a vision such as Nehemiah, who said, "There was no man with me and no beasts save the one I rode on" as he viewed the ruined city and got the burden to rebuild Jerusalem's walls. (Nehemiah 2:12)

Brother Billie had the burden and did something about it. We'd come at his invitation, and with God's help we were seeing the groundwork completed for a church at Dora.

Preaching in itself did not seem to be enough, so Tom announced one evening, "We're going to hold tarrying services and have intercessory prayer every day next week." Conflict can only turn into triumph when we persevere!

11

INDEPENDENCE?

Adobe bricks were made by first digging up a piece of good clay dirt. The hole in the ground was filled with water, then with straw which has been hauled from a straw stack. It was Tom's job to get into the hole and wade around to mix the mud. Then we'd carry it by the bucketfull and pour it into forms which lay on the ground that looked like ladders. While one set of bricks was drying, more mud would be poured into a second form. When completely dry, these bricks would endure. Bricks were stacked one on top of the other much as manufactured bricks are laid with more mud as the mortar.

We bought two by fours for rafters, other board and shingles. We tried not to leave the people in debt, and didn't.

At times I had nothing to make a fire with, so I'd walk around the building and pick up shingles that had dropped to use as fuel so Phyllis and I could keep warm in our trailer. Before the shingles were available, little Phyllis, holding tightly to her bucket, trudged along behind me on the other side of the barbed wire fence as we picked up "cow chips" for the fire.

Such a welcome change came when we bought a small new King heater which got red hot when fired up with enough fuel. Placing a sheet of metal on top made the top level enough to be used as a good cook stove. One skillet had to cook everything. After cooking each item, I removed it for the next. We had steak, potatoes and my fried corn meal ho-cakes. Milk came from the borrowed cow we had staked outside. Occasionally the school bus would stop out front and a child would come running in with a package containing butter or some other delicacy.

Meat was plentiful because Tom had cut some of the slaughtered meat and hung it in the rafters of the unfinished church. He jokingly told visitors, "You'll have to excuse the meat." No refrigeration was necessary then for we had freezing weather. Snow covered the ground. Each day God supplied our needs.

Before we had the cow, I often felt like Old Mother Hubbard who found her cupboard bare. One morning when Tom noticed that we had oatmeal, but no sugar or cream to pour on top, he excused himself to let Phyllis and me eat alone. Can't say that dry oatmeal is my favorite either, but it sure beats an empty stomach!

That day Tom fasted and prayed. A work force had promised to come and help, but we had nothing to feed them. Before noon a stranger came to me and said, "I've been authorized to give you an order for a bill of groceries at the store." When I noticed the authorization came from the county welfare department, I was thoroughly surprised and said, "We didn't ask for welfare!"

"I know you didn't," she answered softly, "but I've been authorized to give it to you." That was the first and last time we ever received welfare of any kind, but we accepted it then as an answer to Tom's prayer. After the woman had gone, I motioned to Tom to come inside. "Here," I said, "take this signed order and get to the store quick."

That day we praised God for the noon dinner which He had provided for several men. No one else knew how nor from whence it came. As far as we were concerned—it came as a gift from the Lord!

The well-constructed one-room building held our crowd, but we lost many of them when we had the Superintendent A. C. Bates dedicate it as Assembly of God. Sister Holley, daughter of Billie Bates and wife of Pastor Holley, told us that during the years the building was in use, before the new superintendent ordered it to be sold, seven young women and men had answered the call and became preachers. Billie Bates' two or three children made gospel workers and one of these was Sister Holley. God had rewarded Brother Billie's efforts.

We all were thinking that it would be good when we would finally get our church built to hold services there instead of going around to first one schoolhouse, then another as we were doing. We rejoiced in the fact that God was helping us accomplish the task for which we had traveled from Los Angeles several months past.

It was nearing springtime. The winter had been rough. The weather was so cold that we never could get the church building warmed up, even with the oil cans for heaters.

We would get on the telephone party line and ring the six rings to get everyone all over the country to listen in. We'd announce, "Bring pies to the Saturday Auction and we'll auction them off for a church building fund." They would bring pies of all kinds. Tom would go and auction them off. Some of the cream pies which everyone especially liked would be auctioned off piece by piece. Some of the crowd said, "Preacher, you missed your calling. You should have been an auctioneer."

Now we were getting the elite — the ranchers, homemakers, farmers, and folks who will make a church. Mr. Capps was there, a rancher and owner of a spread, but wouldn't come forward to get saved. He in his large cowboy hat and boots wanted to leave, but we detained him at the door and talked with him until he accepted Christ and went forward to testify to it. The Bible says to "Go out and compel them to come in."

One day, when Tom was up on top of the church putting on the last shingles, I got a letter from the mailman. I called out, "Tom, it's from California!" Down he jumped and we opened it with excitement. It was from a man named Miller in Maricopa. Where was that, and who was he? Then we remembered that it was the place where Coy and Retha had preached a revival, and Mr. Miller had come to our revival in Exeter. This was the beginning of something good — I could feel it in my bones! The deacon was writing us to say that they were without a pastor, and on Coy's recommendation, they were asking us to consider it. Tom immediately began to pray, and hurry up with the shingling! We often sang a special song called "Goodbye, Hallelujah, I'm gone!" The rest of the time there (a few weeks more) was spent finishing the church. Actually it was not really finished: the windows were not completely set, and we still only had a cement floor. But we did have seats, benches with backs, a platform and a borrowed organ. Tom had also built a make-shift puplit. I'm sure he didn't intend to go very far without a fancier one.

While at Dora, Tom had a bit of diversion. With his ambition and good bass voice, he started to attend a singing school. The man there told him that he had a million-dollar voice, but that he'd have to give up preaching to train it right. "If you stick with me as your manager," he said, "you'll never have to work again." He was making a little less than that preaching, but preaching is what he chose to do.

On the night of our dedication, our church was full for the first time. It was getting harder and harder to think about telling them that we'd be leaving soon. Brother Musick began the first revival for us in the newly dedicated church. It closed March 20th because of the dust storms.

March 24th was our last service together in our adobe church. Tom's text was "Why speak ye not a word in bringing the king back?" We had to tell them we were leaving, and we did it at the morning service. The folks cried. That night we never got to the sermon, because about the middle of the service a dust storm hit and the building just wasn't dust-proof. The gas lights were soon like matches in a dark room. We hurriedly told the good people goodbye. They were those whom we had learned to love by working alongside, praying with, and preaching to, for ten months. They had made their way into our hearts, but now it seemed we were being beaten out of a chance for a last service together and a decent goodbye. We felt our way to the door and blinked at each one, trying to see who we were shaking hands with for the last time until "over there."

I told Loren to go outside and
practice his trumpet, so he and
his dog used this outside cabin.

My granddaughter, Sheri
at the piano.

Loren and Phyllis
sing a duet.

Our three children often
sang together at home.

A. C. Bates and family. He held a tent revival for us in Maricopa, 1935

At six months, Loren flashes that well known smile that helped him get attention and gather young people from many countries to "Help Turn The World Around."

Loren being used of God at *Youth With A Mission*'s Twenty-fifth Anniversary.

12

BURNT-OUT

Tom looked very sad as I left him standing on a street corner in Clovis, New Mexico, where Brother Billy, Phyllis and I had taken him to catch a train to California, to see about the call he had. He was expected to be there on March 31, 1935. He didn't realize that they had already agreed for him to be pastor. He had said, "No, you'll vote on me — and it'll be a peaceful meeting." Deacon Latham held a vote. Then he found Tom out in the parsonage rooms and said, "Brother Cunningham, it's yours — not one vote dissenting." Maricopa was not only a burnt-out oil field, but it was burnt-out spiritually. Our Daddy, though happy for the call, sure hated to leave us two behind in the dust storms. Water would have to be hauled. It would be bad, this he knew.

Back home at Dora, I soon realized how lonesome it was going to be in our trailer house by the side of the road without my husband for two whole weeks. Dust always blowing, and now everything was left up to me. I had to re-learn how to milk — an art I'd never really quite mastered. The next morning I put the divanbed up, tried to milk the cow, cooked breakfast for Phyllis and myself, then wrote a letter to get it in the mailbox by nine so Tom would have mail waiting for him when he arrived in Maricopa, California. The second night was bad, sand blowing so I couldn't see but a few feet away.

One afternoon a rap came at the door. A group of ladies from the church came bearing gifts and yelling, "Surprise! We've come to give you a maternity shower!" They couldn't have known their presence was even more delightful than the presents. Since those

71

days we've been honored by so many showers, birthdays, anniversaries, with going-away gifts and coming-home gifts. Church altars have even been filled with gifts for us. We've found our table loaded with groceries. None of these times have been more deeply appreciated than that baby shower given for me by the ladies at Dora. All of that kind of love made it more difficult for us to leave them.

Days dragged on for Phyllis and me, alone in the trailer and miles from the nearest neighbor, with Tom so many hundreds of miles away. Often we prayed, but every time I knelt down, my little girl was already on her knees. "Dod bess Daddy." Such sincere praying for a one-and-a-half year old!

But the awful dust storms! Wonderful California climate was like a calling card to us. Sunday found me spending most of the morning just scraping the dust from the trailer. Grit—true grit— had filtered into the church. I cleaned it by myself, then preached to the few who came later that night. It was spring, but still a north wind was blowing, yet Monday was wash day and I had to hang out the clothes. And how my hands ached! The dust was beginning to get on everyone's nerves. Some farmers sold out, others died from pneumonia caused by dust in their lungs. These times made it easier to think about leaving there.

On April 11 a card came saying Tom was on his way home! Was I glad! That two weeks was the longest we'd ever been apart. When he came in I hardly recognized him. A growth of beard and an unkempt appearance was so unlike him. After greeting me with open arms, he said, "I wanted to save money so we could get back to California, so I caught the cheapest ride I could find. I paid a trucker five dollars just to ride in his cab. Such a rough ride!"

That same day I packed my clothes while Tom went to get the car tags. He was still planning to drive our old Dodge he had rebuilt out of parts and pull the trailer, while sending our little girl and me ahead on the train. Phyllis and I left the depot at Clovis on April 15, 1935.

It took two nights and a day to get to California. Speeding through the deserts of New Mexico and Arizona, the baby and I found ourselves enjoying our trip with the other passengers, yet often I thought of how lonesome her daddy must be.

Coy met us at the Bakersfield depot; he was pastoring at the little town of Oildale close by. Saturday he took us to Maricopa to see our new place to live — an apartment built on the rear of the church.

As I walked through my new quarters, joy bubbled inside. One bedroom, a living room and a kitchen with a real cookstove that burned GAS. No more picking up cow chips and shingles for the stove! The entire place was comfortably furnished. It even had a screened-in porch with an extra bed. We could have company in style!

Deacon Hazelet bought a brand-new crib. Phyllis was so tickled, thinking it would always be hers. But it was for the new baby.

My job was to fill the pulpit until Tom arrived in three weeks. Back at Dora, Tom was having trouble trying to get our old Dodge to get up and go. When I wrote him that Phyllis had been sick and was exposed to the measles, he left everything behind to come to us — all that furniture and the beef tamales I had made and canned, the lye soap I had made, my coveted copper bottomed boiler and tub, all my pillows and covers and other things I had made — he left and someone else enjoyed them, I hoped — we never did get anything, or news from it.

Together we had failed God. Tom felt like giving the trailer house and all the contents to missionary Kinzie Savage, but we didn't. Someone took it, at our loss.

I began our ministry at Maricopa on Easter Sunday, April 21, 1935. At 3:30 A.M. I was up and preparing for the sunrise service. No one ever told me, "Sister Cunningham, you need to rest up." God sustained me during the three services that day, even though I was expecting our second child in three months and had just endured a long and sleepless train ride.

Nature is a wonder of which God is such an intricate part. I have seen mothers-to-be working in the cotton fields pulling cotton sacks right up until the night before their babies were born. I believe all who trust their fate into God's hands are taken care of; but for those who wholly trust themselves into man's hands or abort that which nature has started, all is not well.

Tom finally arrived, and I was grateful to have our little family settled into our new home. Our task was to try to help Maricopa's church become self-supporting. At that time it was still dependent on its mother church, Taft First Assembly of God pastored by Leon Hall. As we tarried and prayed, we knew there would have to be growth by unity. God began to melt hearts and bless.

My husband tried out his carpentry skill by adding a porch to the small parsonage attached to the back of the church. From there we could enjoy the mountain range which separated the valley from the sea. Our folks often took trips to the ocean. Once we went along, so we got to view the Pacific for the first time and returned with an abalone shell.

The valley was uncomfortable and hot in the daytime, but at night the sea breeze wafted through the mountain range to cool us off. I really liked the house — the first real house we'd had since the little three-room rented one in West Fork. I could hardly wait to put out my quilt and embroidery pieces. I made myself several dresses to wear. Hopefully I'd get back down to my right size again.

We began calling on folks, asking them to come to the church on the corner. Tom started Bible studies after holding a short, fiery and fruitful revival. He announced confession meetings to accompany our prayer sessions — a good way to see feuds settled.

An orchestra was in the offing, and I think we'd have welcomed anyone who wanted to join — even someone who had nothing more than a dishpan to beat. Tom tried to learn to play his new trombone, but liked the guitar too much to leave it lay. I still had my sax and looked forward to getting back wind enough to play it. My Dad used to joke, "God can use any tune except a spittoon!"

How I'd love to go back in time and do all those things over again. The Lord said, "Those who leave all — houses, land, loved ones — for the sake of the Gospel, shall receive a hundredfold in this life, plus eternal blessings." It's all more than worth it!

Someone appropriately wrote a verse which said it all: "Only one life will soon be passed, only that which is done for Christ will last." At Maricopa our spirits were lifted as we watched those who had been burnt-out spiritually become alive as they were fed by the living Christ.

Though happy at Maricopa and succeeding places we still remembered Dora and received occasional reports from there. Years later we read the following in the Pentecostal Evangel: DORA, N.M. — Just closed a 3 weeks' revival, Sister Wiggins, Pasadena, Texas, Evangelist. Several prayed through to salvation in the old-time way, 16 or 18 received the Holy Ghost, 13 followed the Lord in water baptism, and there were some remarkable healings. Mrs. Sarah Ann Ream, 76 years of age, had suffered intense pain eight years from abscess on the liver and right kidney. Her whole body was racked with pain. The dear Lord touched her and healed her — a wonderful witness for the Lord. — P. J. Haddox, Pastor.

13

PROMISE OF GOD

While still back in New Mexico, one day out in the pasture, I said simply, "Lord, I am your hand maid and if this feeling of pregnancy would bring me a son, I'd give him to You for service."

Hospitals? Who needed them? I had a negative feeling about those sterile white-walled buildings where strangers tended to your needs. The week before my second baby was born I talked over my feelings with Dr. Dykes who had an office in Taft, California. Taft had a hospital and was only a few miles away. He immediately informed me, "If you go to the hospital I won't charge you. If you decide not to go, I'll charge you full price."

Just previous to that discussion I'd met Mrs. Gifford also from Taft. She was a member of the First Assembly of God and a practical nurse. (She was the grandmother of Frank Gifford, the noted ball player.) "I'd like to take care of you and the baby right here in my own home," she declared. Her offer caused me to visit Taft on June the twenty-second. Due to give birth in about a week, I'd be needing to know where the baby was to be born. Dr. Dykes' decision about charging hadn't changed my mind about going to stay with Mrs. Gifford. Since I'd have to pay the hospital charge anyway, I decided I'd rather pay the doctor than the hospital.

Nothing encouraged me to bypass the hospital except my own feelings. The doctor kept insisting, "You have to go where it's clean." Later I learned from Mrs. Gifford that many babies were dying in the Taft hospital at that time. Perhaps my "whim" to have our second offspring at home had been a directive from the Lord.

After I went to stay at Mother Gifford's the doctor came and was amazed at her spotlessness. As soon as I settled in I knew I was in good hands. Not only was she clean but she knew just what I needed. Calling her "Mother Gifford" seemed fitting. She brooded over me as if I were one of her own.

Perhaps it was because of my feeling as though I was wrapped in my own special security blanket and I'd made the right decision about staying with Mother Gifford that my second child arrived with relative ease. Doctor Dykes beamed down at me and announced, "Well, Mrs. Cunningham, you've got yourself a nice big boy!"

I said, "I prayed for a son and God gave me a son. He is God's promise to me." I knew that to be true.

Tom Cunningham's jubilation alone made the effort worthwhile. He drove through the streets of Maricopa hollering, "My son got here at six o'clock! My son got here!"

Because I wanted to have my strength back before I returned home my stay with Mrs. Gifford lasted ten days.

When Dr. Dykes came to dismiss me I asked, "Doctor, how much do I owe you?"

His answer thrilled my soul. "You don't owe me anything because you had such an easy delivery. I was afraid you were going to have a long hard ordeal like the last time."

When I learned he wasn't going to charge me a cent, I thought, "Thank you, Jesus. Thank you again." I didn't tell the doctor, but he'd answered my prayer. I'd asked God not to let the doctor charge us anything and He did not. Our precious Loren was priceless. He got here on faith and still lives by faith.

Mother Gifford was another consideration. She'd stayed up with the baby all night that first night. When I asked her why, she replied: "I wanted to be sure he was breathing all right." How do you repay that kind of dedication? She'd protested when I suggested we pay her. "I don't want a thing! This has been a labor of love!" When Tom and I talked it over, he said, "I think we ought to get her a good Bible." That was a fitting gift for such a dear saint of God.

Soon after I returned home Brother Bates and his family had
come to California for a vacation and to hold a meeting. Since
there were nothing like motels in those days, of course we invited
them to stay with us. Brother Bates family of seven stayed two
weeks, holding a tent meeting, and we all found places to sleep —
with some in the church on pallets. Such a preacher he was! Even
some of the hard cores responded to his words.

But caring for the new baby and our house guests, plus can-
ning fruit that I didn't want to go to waste was hard on me and
caused me to hemorrhage and I had to go to bed.

God helped me get over that trying problem which almost
turned into an endurance test. I didn't get to take in many of the
Bates meetings which I loved to do under normal circumstances.
After the meeting closed, Saturday came quickly, so Tom had to
take the tent down and return it to the owner. No time was left for
us to do the janitor job at the church, shining the floors and dust-
ing the pews like we'd been doing, for Sunday's service. We heard
the rumor that some deacons had complained about us not cleaning the church.

When the gripe got to our ears, we decided, "We can just
leave. They can have their janitor job. We're evangelists. Let's get
out of here."

We'd been so drained, by my having a new baby, and too
much for Tom to do. It was conflict. Our pride suffered from the
complaint because we'd tried so hard, but God gave us a new opportunity right as we were feeling we'd been failures. We had
triumph in another wonderful opportunity of service.

ARVIN

"Will you come over here to Arvin and fill in our pastor's
unexpired time?" one of their deacons asked. God was making it
possible for us to keep on preaching without ever missing a Sunday! Immediately we moved bag and baggage the seventy miles to
Arvin. The Lord began to bless so in every service that Tom
declared, "Soon we're going to have to go hunt sinners. Everybody here is going to be saved!"

After three months of blessed Holy Ghost revival one woman who wanted to be the preacher began to work on me. "You know," she told me, "the Lord showed me in a vision that I am to be the pastor here, not your husband."

Naive, I believed that anybody who claimed to have a vision was authentic so I influenced Tom to act against his own feelings by insisting, "If the Lord told her she's to be the pastor, we shouldn't stand in her way. Let's go somewhere else, Tom."

The night they had the deciding business meeting I remained at the parsonage, worrying, "Had I influenced my husband against the will of God?" Deciding it was time for action, I went to the side door and knocked. "Honey," I told Tom when he responded to my knock, "put your name in and let them vote on it. If we don't like their decision, then we can resign."

"You're too late. They just elected her as pastor." I never will forget the disappointment in his eyes.

We knew we were out of the will of God. Our move to Arvin had been in October. We stayed on until January, for the newly-elected pastor said to us, "You don't have to move from the parsonage right away. I've got my own home here. So keep the meeting going."

We didn't have much to live on. Precious folks named Smothers who had been so loyal to us, offered us their tithes, but we'd declined, telling them, "No, your tithes belong to her now."

Our revival kept going until after Christmas and among the many saved and filled was one Catholic ex-priest — saved and filled and spent the night with us and we heard him speaking in tongues throughout the night. Where were we to go next? Tom and I got down on our knees and prayed the whole night through until I received a vision of a basket handle only and a word from the Lord. "Take hold where you can find anything to take hold of. Take hold of the handle that you see," the Lord spoke to me, "and the basket will materialize." Without saying good bye to anyone, we simply packed up and left the next day, striking off down the road without knowing where we were going.

PIXLEY

About a hundred miles down the road we stopped in the little town of Pixley and inquired, "Do you have a church here?"

One man answered, "Yep, sure do. We've got a Pentecostal church out in the country. They hold their meetings in a little school house. It's two or three miles out in the country."

After our visit to one of their services a woman who lived near-by invited us to have dinner with her. We politely declined, excused ourselves and went to the woods to pray and fast. There the Lord said, "This is the handle." We knew we were to help "make the basket appear" because they had asked us to stay and hold a revival.

Tom told him, "We'll hold the revival if you'll let us move it into town." After he agreed, Tom scouted around until he found an empty little store. We moved into the back section. A hole in the roof could have caused problems during a rainstorm, so my carpenter husband immediately busied himself to fix it.

Phyllis, baby Loren and I huddled around the old wood stove trying to keep warm. Anything we could find, we'd burn.

When seats were installed, the front became our church. Brother Finley, their crippled-up elderly pastor, had been driving out from Tulare each Sunday to hold services. Because his arthritis was so bad that he had difficulty moving about, he told us, "I want you to stay and be my assistants."

"Well, then, where can we live?" we asked. The back of the so-called church was not very suitable for a family with two small children.

Someone told us, "There's a well house down the road. You can rent it for four dollars a month."

After we moved into the well house another problem came up: finances.

A dear Sister Johnson brought us groceries. What we would have done without her weekly grocery gift, I have no idea.

Between holding services for Brother Finley we went to try out at any church where we heard there was an opening. At Wasco we were defeated. From there we went to Avenelle — only to find that Gordon Lindsy was still holding a tent revival there.

At Reedly where we tried out, a deacon declared, "We won't vote for this man. He won't stay here long!"

That was a bitter pill to swallow. Because we'd left Maricopa in such a rush, we'd been labeled as "quitters." For a while that was a conflict we faced everywhere we tried out, but it became a triumph because it taught us a lesson. As Tom said, "Next time we get hold of a place, we've got to stay with it!"

The people at Pixley wanted a church building so Tom found a little vacant Methodist church in the next town. Tom called the Board of Mission of the M.E. church in Los Angeles in order to negotiate with them about buying it. The people had saved enough money to purchase a lot and arrange for the building to be moved on to the premises, with arrangements to buy later.

After the purchase of the lot and the arrangement for the church building, Tom felt as though our work there was over, so the people asked Coy's father-in-law, Brother Medley, to come and take over, after several other preachers had been pastoring the small M.E. church and he was responsible in negotiating with the state to purchase a larger lot and for building a bigger church. Pixley had many to come pastor who were good at their calling.

14

FIREBAUGH

Brother Woods, the Presbyter in Fresno, told us, "There's two places you might feel led to go — Firebaugh or Dos Palos." His first suggestion rang a bell with us, so Tom and I agreed to go there.

Firebaugh turned out to be a small town surrounded by acres and acres of cotton mixed with Johnson grass.

After scouting around we found one Pentecostal family by the name of Carter and told them, "We've come to start a church." It was almost like reliving our Arp experience all over again. The Carters did all they could for us, even taking us to some "tourist cabins," which were really the motels of that day. Luxury Plus? Indeed, no! Our cabin was the equivalent of a one-room apartment with cooking facilities. The only bed stood on hard pine floors. I remember them well, for Loren was at the crawling age and I had to watch closely that his little knees didn't get splinters.

Brother Carter offered, "I have two dollars. I'll give you folks one." His dollar gave us the cabin for the first week. Dividing his last two dollars with us gave Tom and me hope. It was a sign that God had some good people there.

Firebaugh's population consisted mainly of Italian Catholics, so we had ourselves a time just trying pronounce their unfamiliar names with our southern accents. Their names and their saloons were foreign to us. The doors of the local pubs swung back and forth — something we hadn't been used to since the repeal of prohibition.

We'd prayed for a Macedonian call and now felt we'd received it, but then Brother Thomas, the Presbyter, asked if we'd go to Dos Palos. Then we were asked to fill in for the Green Sisters at

Woodlake Tabernacle. Other invitations came — the same as they had at Arp. But we returned to Firebaugh to investigate its possibilities. Such a hard, difficult place to work in! Tom and I kept turning over our fleece before God. Where did He want us to go?

On a visit to northern California we took in a crematorium and a zoo. Maybe we could find our place one of these? We were so discouraged. At Chowchilla we stopped at the big tabernacle. Since Pastor Fisher was sick, we filled in for him that night. Before the service his wife served us cold milk at their home. Such a treat!

Brother Fisher pastored an emotionally free church. I recall one man who jumped on to the seats and across the pews which were empty at the time because others were up and rejoicing.

Brother Fisher asked us to hold a revival in three weeks. Fine — except for the fact that we had two babies who needed fed immediately! Anyway, we probably would not have suited such an emotionally free church.

Pastor Wilson of Los Banos asked, "Would you two like to come and try out for revival?" Try out for revival? What happened to the old times when the saints prayed and accepted the ones God sent? That night we spent one of the children's fifty cent pieces for a rooming house, feeling we'd robbed our own children. On our trip a pastor Nelson felt compassion for our little ones and reached into his pocket, bringing out a couple of fifty cents pieces — one for each.

Driving back on Highway 99, we stopped over for one more night's stay at our wellhouse. Good old rancher, Mr. Johnson, wore an infectious grin as he toted a gallon milk can over to our car while we prepared to leave. Such a welcome gift for a couple with two youngsters!

Ever so grateful, we got into our Chevy and started back down the highway. Bump! Crash! Our tranquillity was jarred along with the contents of the big wooden box we'd tied on to the back of the car. Tom and I got out and surveyed the damage. We'd literally "spilled the beans"! There on the road lay a mixture of all the love offerings we'd been given by the saints at Pixley — fruit from jars, beans, rice, oats and the milk which made a little stream down the highway. I'd been very conservative about using any of these staples, planning to store our stash of food at Sister Marvin's until we'd found a place to settle, but suddenly my careful saving was of no use. Our money and our total food supply was gone! Sister Marvin had been filling the place in the Pixley Assembly as the "Lydia"—there's one in most every church.

At Los Banos we had our "revival tryout" and spent the night on Pastor Wilson's sofa. (Pastor Wilson was father of Evangelist Wilson who we had met at Exeter and other places when their family and ours consisted of only one child.) The following day when he walked out with us from his small, neat parsonage, he shared these devastating words: "Oh, yes, we've decided not to have a revival now. Maybe later."

MAYBE LATER? How were we to keep body and soul together in the meantime? We headed on to Salinas where the preacher confessed, "I'm so glad to see you! I've been wanting to turn the church over to someone else." Surely our chance had come! Tom and I eagerly sought God's will about Salinas. In prayer we both felt we received the same answer—one we both fought inwardly. God wanted us back in Firebaugh! Salinas, we were to learn, was not full fellowship Assembly of God.

At a campground we got out our gas burner and feasted on fresh eggs with bits of bread, butter and jelly that Sister Wilson had given us. As any hobo might do, we found a place near the railroad tracks, where we stopped to ponder and pray. Tom and I did more pondering than praying, hoping against hope that we'd be sent somewhere besides Firebaugh. The next day being a church night, we said, "Surely we'll find some place to meet for services."

Our stop was at Hollister where we dressed for church in a filling station and played "crash the party"—going in with our Bibles in full view. How could the local pastor help but see we wanted to preach? Our scheme partially worked. Tom was asked to speak that night, after which Brother Harper said, "Later on we might get you for a revival." Nothing immediate was happening! Tom's sermon didn't even bring an offering.

As we stood in the church aisle all the folks just passed us by. But as we were heading for the car, the pastor called after us. "Sister Russell will be glad to take you home with her."

By then our pockets were completely empty. Without a cent to our name, we were learning the hard way that money didn't grow on trees. Not even in California! It seemed ministry opportunities outside of pioneering weren't for us either.

At a fellowship meeting at Turlock the next day I had no money for lunch so a sister shared her bologna/cheese sandwiches and cookies with the children and me. I had a sandwich left over so I offered it to Preacher Garland who had no lunch either. That sister's act of sharing became a small "miracle of loaves and fishes." Five people ate from one lady's lunch!

Tom had gone with Presbyter Brother Thomas to look again for a meeting place in Dos Palos. Finding none, we decided to return to Firebaugh. God has a way of breaking our will. (Mark 6.)

At Firebaugh that hot and miserable little cabin Brother Carter had rented with one of his last two dollars began to feel like home sweet home. The community fellowshipped together at the City Hall on Sundays. Farmers, ranchers, musicians and school teachers of all Protestant denominations gathered there to hold Sunday School. None of them knew who we were or where we'd hailed from, but the superintendent thought Tom looked like a preacher, so asked him to preach as we joined the crowd.

A revival began! Folks came out in force. Nights were filled with the joyous songs and the music of the interdenominational choir. "What denomination are you affiliated with?" people asked. Our reply was simple: "We are evangelists out for souls." Then we began to hear, "How we'd love to vote on you to be our pastor and get a salary arranged for you." But Tom blew it! After one sermon on holiness, no one mentioned pastoring or salary ever again. He'd been very specific about little no-harm sins!

The next Sunday night we noticed some of our faithful helpers had skipped out of the service, including such important role players as the violinist, the song leader and the pianist. My sermon had also been offensive when I said, "Jesus was our priest, the only One able to forgive and set free." Those words hit the Catholics. Spies had been in the congregation! Those from the Catholic part of town were offended. They had key positions and privileged rights, including the use of City Hall.

The next night when we came to minister, a huge padlock sealed the front door. Locked out! Not only had the Catholics locked us out, but we'd lost the rest of our crowd of non-Pentecostals.

Yet we were determined to stay at Firebaugh for the Carters and several other Pentecostal families. Our decision meant one thing. We'd have to hold services in private homes.

In people's houses both Tom and I were too modest to pass the hat for ourselves and we had no one to do it for us as we'd had in the union meetings. Eventually we both went to work in the fields.

Tom hired himself out for twenty-five cents an hour to drive tractor for a farmer who needed help with his crops. I cut the Johnson grass from the cotton rows for twenty cents an hour. No civil liberties then—I couldn't protest the discrimination in wages due to sex. While my man and I were both putting in twelve-hour days we left our children with a girl who lived with her parents on the San Joaquin River bank. God in his mercy looked after our offspring for the girl wasn't always watchful. I learned that when I went to pay her and found them off playing alone.

At daybreak we left our cabin to get to the fields by six. The sun came up in such a blaze of glory one morning that it blinded Tom so that he failed to see an on-coming car. The black driver hadn't been hurrying or the impact could have been fatal for all of us. The two cars left the wreck with crumpled fenders, but the owners bore no ill will toward each other. Each poor, each an early riser, each needing all the wages he could earn in a day, we detained each other as little as possible.

As a girl I'd worked in the cotton fields with the Blacks in the South. Then, too, we'd shared a common bond and thought nothing of eating our lunches together. Wherever there's common ground for all colors and races, there will be no more "tiffs" between them!

One day I received a letter from Pastor Powers at Hot Springs, New Mexico, saying, "Jewell, we need you to come hold a two-week revival before the Texaco District Council." A second letter came, I felt this was a call from God I could not ignore. Tom took the children and me to the train at Fresno with one suitcase plus a small box to carry our eats. The children and I left at 4:30 P.M. to ride all night and the next day.

During our hot, hour-long stopover at Flagstaff, Phyllis, Loren and I went to the park so we could relax. As I was thinking and praying and letting the two children down to play on the grass — Loren was only at the crawling stage — I had a sudden urge to go back and talk to the railroad clerk. "When does the train leave for Hot Springs?" I asked. "Do I have to change anymore?"

"Lady, which Hot Springs are you going to? There's a north and a south one."

His question made me think of my letter. "Which one has a post office?"

"The southern one. Your ticket's for the north." The train was expected momentarily. I prayed. When the train headed south the three of us were on board. Good thing! I had no money for food or an overnight stay. By the help of God the ticket was changed in time.

Safely on board, we watched the trees and mountains and tall pines of northern Arizona change into a desert. We chugged into the town of Engle about 4 A.M. on the following morning. Upon embarking I found our luggage had been misplaced! I stood with my two small children in an empty station.

A couple C.C.C. boys and the ticket agent were the only other ones there. President Roosevelt's Civil Conservation Corps (C.C.C.) were made up of work brigades financed by the government to help with the unemployment problem during the depression.

The children slept on the seat with their heads on my lap. "No buses going your way," the clerk told me, "but you might get a ride with the mail truck. It's due in 2½ hours."

When the mail truck arrived, the driver agreed to take Phyllis and Loren and me to Hot Springs if I'd pay him. It cost all the money I had left. Such a rough ride! Our teeth felt like they'd jarred loose! I noticed that the mail driver hadn't charged the

C.C.C. boys a dime. He probably thought they didn't have any money, but the lady from California did!

After three days of swaying in a train and the long waits, and a rough 20-mile truck ride, we arrived—minus our baggage. Brother Powers was so glad that God had sent me, but I wasn't sure how I felt. Loren was sick, cutting teeth. His knees bled when he crawled over the cement floors. The spring was a hundred yards away and Phyllis got burrs in her bare feet when she followed me out to get laundry water. I carried Loren with me as he was feeling badly and I didn't want to hear him cry, "Mama!" in such a pitiful tone. Not too great a vacation. But my job was to get souls saved.

The first to come to Jesus was an old man in his seventies. His salvation alone was worth all we had gone through to get there. He was only one among many who were saved during the ten-day meeting.

Our luggage finally caught up to us. After ten days of meetings I needed to leave to go to the Clovis Council, for I wanted to get ordained. Brother Powers took us back to the little depot and we pulled out toward Belen after midnight. The Powers were so kind to take us to the depot and get back to their own beds so late. At 3:44 A.M. we arrived in Belen where the two children and I waited for the A.M. train which would take us on to arrive in Clovis at 1:30 P.M.

No wonder our son Loren has physical endurance as he travels across the world. On other trips with me he spent untold hours without rest between stops. During that three weeks of misery and endurance our ten-month-old didn't cry or fuss much, just whimper a bit with his teething.

After reaching Clovis I had to leave our luggage at the station and begin to walk the two-mile trek across town, carrying both children when little Phyllis finally gave out. Before reaching Sister Gregory's house, we got caught in a downpour.

Music came from inside of a church and I realized a service was taking place. It wasn't an Assemblies Church, but we needed refuge from the storm. Being a stranger, I slipped inside and sat in a back pew with my two children. At testimony time I shared a little about the long trip and the trouble I'd had after my revival was over. I wasn't asking for a hand out or anything; I only wanted to tell that God had been with us.

As I sat down a little sister grabbed a song book, half opened it, and began to pass it around as she announced, "I'm not authorized to do this, but God just told me to take up an offering for this lady." Tears flooded my eyes as I accepted their gift. I was flat broke! "This shall be told of her," said Jesus of one woman who had washed his feet with tears, pouring out precious ointment on him. She'd gone ahead of her authority too.

Going on to Sister Gregory's, I found she had a sick child who worried her so she was up and down all night with him. And each time she got me up to pray with her. My body was so tired and frazzled, I couldn't even pray. After the depot waits and train rides and a two-mile walk in the rain carrying two little children, I was in need of prayer myself. A day in bed would have helped. Chicken pox marks began creeping out all over her little son's body. It came as no surprise when my own two broke out on the way home.

I took the trip back to Clovis to get ordained because Tom had insisted I should go to Texaco District where he belonged. Since I had been out of the Texaco District a year I couldn't be ordained there. At the council Brother Bates asked me to greet the members. I remember some of my remarks. "We are now trying to get a work started in an area that is predominantly Catholic. Our town has fourteen stores and restaurants, seven saloons and a population of only 700. If any of you want a place to preach in California, come on out." No one accepted my invitation, so I waited till later to be ordained in Southern California. Superintendent Bea Hardin helped me get ordained, as a woman preacher's being ordained was not yet accepted.

We rode the train home to Merced because it was closer for Tom to meet us there. Nearing midnight, we finally arrived at the depot which was quite a distance from town. The conductor came to the doorway to ask me, "Is there anyone to meet you?"

A voice from the shadows spoke, "I am."

"Is that your . . ." the conductor began to ask, but we didn't wait for him to finish his sentence. The children and I were caught up in their daddy's big brawny arms, Tom dressed in his bib overalls; I in my train wardrobe. Together we rode back to our little one-room cabin. That night it surely looked like home.

Firebaugh continued to be a challenge as we kept attempting to start a church. One day a Catholic man came to Tom. "Preacher, I have a half acre of land about a mile outside of town. If you'll build a church there, I'll donate it. I want a church there for my children to learn about God."

We went to the District of Northern California camp meeting at St. Helena where we were given a free tent and free meals in exchange for Tom's work in the milkshake stand. He didn't need such temptation—he was already overweight. But it was good because as usual we had no money. Tom even stayed on for a week after the meeting closed to help build a dining hall.

During our stay at the retreat center Loren was still cutting teeth and was constantly sucking his thumb. I had tried putting on "thumbstalls" made out of wire circles, but they did no good. He was adept at wriggling his little fingers out and free—just as he has maneuvered out of other more important hazards of adult life to find freedom. In forming his worldwide "Youth With A Mission" organization he could not be tied or bound. The analogy of thumbsucking simply shows he has always been able to get rid of obstacles of any kind.

His constant thumbsucking caused me to fret. I even tried putting hot pepper on his thumb, but my baby boy simply winced and licked it off, then continued his thumb-in-mouth habit.

One day his father bought him an ice cream cone. It soon mixed with the pepper on his thumb and Loren's little tummy swelled. His temperature climbed. For two weeks he couldn't keep his food down. We had Brother Argue pray for him at that night's camp meeting service and we tried to have faith. Our baby's condition was becoming crucial. He began passing blood. How we prayed!

Then in time God heard our prayers, but Loren did not respond too well before we went back to Firebaugh. There our baby was still unable to retain his food. Tom said, "I'm going to the drugstore to get some Bismuth Powder; that's what Dad would have given him."

While he was gone I picked Loren up and walked to an open lot where I cried out to God, "Please, Lord, don't let our faith be hindered!" All our years we'd never turned to men. Whatever the Lord said, that's what we'd wanted to do.

God saw my tears and told me to go into the house, get some egg whites, beat them until they were stiff and sweeten them to taste. Whoever heard of such a remedy? If we had, we'd have already used it. The Lord's solution brought forth a miracle. Loren ate the beaten egg whites and the next day food did not go through him undigested. Natural processes took over. He was well in a few days, playing contentedly with small toys, sticks and strings.

Once a woman who dropped by to see us commented, "Your baby seems easily satisfied, or else he has nothing to play with." Both assumptions were true. Loren has always been content to be alone. Today he has to spend many lonely nights as he travels abroad. He and his family are very much at home in sleeping bags with a cold sandwich for lunch — more often than not as they visit the different bases he's established.

As a pre-schooler he went looking for a Christmas present for his Dad. Holding up a dime he asked, "Will this cost a 'shut'?" (Trying to say "shirt"). Today he has been responsible for thousands and thousands of dollars of God's money for youth work, yet he still lives on simple necessities. Millions or a dime, his work has cost all that he has, but God owns all the silver and gold and releases it for his servants needs.

That remedy for thumbsucking was the worst trial we ever had with Loren's health except for the time a motorcycle collided with his bike. His back was hurt worse than we'd realized. God has used that injury to His glory in more recent years. Many times Loren had difficulty keeping his speaking engagement because of it. On one such occasion he was to speak at a missions conference and rode clear across the nation of Switzerland on a board in the back of an old bakery van. Then he stood against the lobby wall of the motel until it was time for him to speak. He couldn't sit down—his back was out. But God healed him as he spoke! His helpers stood the board up for him to speak, but they didn't need to carry him away on it! God healed our son's back as he spoke!

We had our own problems to cope with. Back at Firebaugh the District Superintendent Thoman sent us a tent to hold revival. We still had house meetings. We stretched it out to show Brother Thoman and the people in Firebaugh we were still in business. The Presbyter from Kerman came and set the group in order— hardly twenty, but a nucleus of membership. We never saw them again but kept hearing word from Firebaugh.

We'd received a letter from the superintendent to go to Monterey in northern California to try out as pastors for a small church. A preacher took over the tent meetings at Firebaugh for us, but because of the ill-will caused by rowdy boys who set the straw fire which spread in the tent floor, that preacher soon left. Because of this no church was built there for many years.

(Recently we were privileged to attend services in the big spacious brick church in Firebaugh, a growing stretched-out city of lovely homes and much agricultural economy. That night the young pastor whose name was Cunningham—no relative—asked Tom to speak. For a midweek night service there was a good crowd. We felt triumph. Fifty years earlier we had left a nucleus of worshipers who had become instrumental in making the Assembly of God Church there a reality.)

Many efforts were made, after we left Firebaugh, before there was a Set in Order church and a nice building.

15

MONTEREY

Arriving in Monterey at Sunday School time, we left Phyllis and Loren in the car while we went in to look over the church. The lady leader asked, "Will one of you come to the platform and speak for us?" I was chosen to speak and afterwards Tom whispered, "Jude, I don't know what we'll do if they don't accept us here. We only have two cents left. We're at the end of our road."

The devil may have been tempting Tom. It was or could have been a test. But if that was so, he didn't yield to it to go back to carpentering as a full time job. I knew myself that he was a very determined man and wasn't considering leaving the ministry to go back into carpentry, even if he did take on some small jobs there at Monterey later on in that little privately-owned church to tide us over until election time.

Babies are a threat to pastoral candidates. Woe be to those preachers who have more than two! The same also holds true for candidates for the mission fields. Mission boards seem to think we serve a little bitty God who can't go along with His own planning. Nature is closely akin to God, isn't it? He who feeds the sparrow is capable of feeding His own children also.

At Monterey we were invited to a Portuguese dinner where they called a business meeting to vote on whether they should have us serve as interim pastors while they waited a month for the one they'd already called. Thirty days would at least give us time to collect our wits. Besides we would have food and housing. When they asked if I could play the piano I answered, "Yes" — recalling my ability to play the organ by ear. We learned that pastoral candidates are expected to be pianists too. Nothing seemed quite as important as that.

Tom and I still did not have a settled feeling. Conflict still stirred inside us. The T. C. Cunninghams yearned for some long-term assignment.

"Well never let you go hungry," the Avila's said when we went to see about taking over the church in Monterey, California. The Avila family operated both the grocery store and the church which was privately owned and made up almost entirely of converted Portuguese Catholics.

Brother Avila tried to keep his word by bringing us boxes of wholesome food even though we weren't exactly voted in by the congregation. Tom and I had been asked just to fill in until the yearly business meeting.

Although we'd been promised food enough to take care of us during our stay there, one day I felt like Old Mother Hubbard, for I went to the cupboard and found it bare. I visited Sister Avila at the grocery store, sitting and chatting for a while, but she never asked how we were getting along. Of course, I was too proud to ask for her help. Finally sensing that no help would be forthcoming from the Avila's, I excused myself and started toward home, head down and walking dejectedly. Suddenly my eyes came upon a potato. Someone had surely dropped it out of their grocery sack. Picking it up from the ground, I hurried home and made potato soup for supper. God said in His Word that His seed would never go hungry or have to beg for bread.

Unsure of where we were supposed to be, Tom and I considered going to the little town of Tracy on August the ninth and try out for the pastorate we'd heard was open, so called their board for an appointment. Just finding enough money to get there posed a problem. With no collateral of any kind, we certainly weren't in a position to borrow money. How could we pay it back? Tom had no real paying job and our only possession was an old Model-A Ford which was only a few weeks away from being scrapped for junk. While we were thinking about going to Tracy, a knock came at our door. A child stood holding a large grocery sack in his arms.

"Here are some vegetables and jelly that my mother made. She sent her tithes, too — $2.25."

Praise God! That two dollars would get us gas, milk and bread and still pay our own twenty-five cent tithe, and eight gallons of gas and a quart of oil besides!

Tracy had a well-established Assembly of God and the Lord blessed us with freedom in every service. Yet another preacher came to "spy out the land" for a tryout later too — an unethical practice we had to become accustomed to. Instinct alone should have taught preachers to be fair and stay away "in courtship manners" while another was trying to put his best foot forward.

The election was held and we were not selected. Rejected, defeated, we decided its Monterey and stay put. No more tryouts! Our family went back to our small three-room house behind the grocery store. It was furnished but ill-equipped.

Tom made money by building shelving for a small appliance store. In exchange for his labors, he got me my first washer, a radio and a brand-new innerspring mattress. At last we had a good lumpless bed!

Tom started his own radio program and worked hard at building up the Sunday School. I tried to help in every way I could with his church programs and still keep our little home as neat and cozy as possible. My extra job on Fridays was to go around to the town's businesses and collect radio announcements to pay for the preaching time.

One Thursday the little lad across the street came sobbing at my door, "My mama just won't shush her crying," he wailed.

Taking off my apron, I took him by the hand over to his house. His mother was hysterically sobbing. Finally I deciphered her words, "The baby is sick and my husband is in bed. He's been out all night long."

That rose my dander. The poor woman looked exhausted and frazzled, so I said to her, "Ruth, he needs to help you. Look at yourself."

"Oh, Sister Cunningham, don't upset him. He's so handsome and I love him so much."

"Fiddlesticks!" I snorted. "Let's get HIM up and YOU to bed!"

I marched to the bedroom door and knocked while Ruth sputtered under her breath something about being so in love with him. There was no response to my knock. I pounded louder, then called, "Mister, are you awake? Your baby is very sick and your wife needs to be in bed — so get up and see what you can do to help! Let your wife have the bed!"

Still there was no response, so I threw the door open and on our first meeting found him sitting on the side of the bed. He was a handsome brute. I suppose we'd never met before because he always spent his time out night-lifing instead of being with his wonderful and devoted housekeeper, cook and mother of his own three offspring.

My dander rose further. "Mister, Ruth tells me you've been out all night. You aren't working and providing for your family. The neighbors all know this. They also know you're out of jail on parole for a sentence on non-support. You'll not find another woman who'll be as kind as Ruth." I waited to see how he'd respond to my frankness.

He didn't answer, but I knew I had him listening, so I ventured on. Seldom can one get a man like that to be such a captive audience.

"Mister," I continued, "I know there must have been something good that Ruth saw in you. She fell in love with you. Your mother, too, loves you. . . . And Jesus loves you even as you are. How 'bout it, Mister? You need Jesus and He'll right everything today if you'll just kneel down here and talk to Him."

Suddenly Ruth walked in and I could feel him drawing back. If only she'd have had the wisdom to leave us alone! After all, she'd tried to win him to decency all her married days without much progress. I sensed that further efforts were useless then, I had made both aware of their problem. Whether or not Ruth's husband was ever saved, I don't know, but a couple of weeks later, we saw him stacking wood and cleaning up around the house.

Then Friday I went on my usual rounds to collect for the radio program. On Saturday I felt overly tired but well as I took the children and drove to Seaside to preach at night. Two flat tires plagued me on the way home, so I pulled off the two tires to keep from ruining them and, taking a chance on ruining the wheels instead, I drove home on the rims.

Sunday morning I was to preach the 11 o'clock sermon, but halfway through the message I got a stabbing pain in my chest. Somehow I finished, then dragged myself home to get into bed. Every time I turned I felt as though I could not breathe, so I tried to lie completely quiet and still. Phyllis and her daddy prayed day and night, but I didn't seem to get any better. For a week or more I was so weak that I couldn't even raise my head without extreme effort. Blackouts plagued me. How dear little Phyllis prayed for me when she and I happened to be alone!

Tom had to carry on his job regardless of my health. The saints of the church finally understood that I was really sick. Sister Mathias brought me clean sheets and a bedspread. Other dear ones brought gifts of food. Finally, after several weeks, I was able to get up. The last entry in my diary had been left unfinished that Thursday after I'd become too ill to keep writing. In reflection I recalled my vision, or dream, so:

We had pondered, How could we kindle interest in our vision of selling the little church and relocating where people would come? Never have we seen an individually-owned church prosper. That was the case in Monterey.

One night I had a dream just as Joel had prophesied, "Old men will dream dreams." (Sometimes they do in church, when they're too tired and the speaker doesn't have enough power to keep them awake!) But God does give dreams to the young and old alike. God gave me that dream, for with His promises and dealings, there is neither male nor female.

In my dream I was taking care of a baby in a beautifully shined and decorated chest—not a cradle or bassinet. The lid was down. I came to see the baby and found it in an agitated frame of mind, so I said, "I'm taking it out of here. This box will be its undoing." The baby was white, but of a different race.

When I awoke, I shared the dream God had given me with Tom. Together we prayed and agreed this was its meaning: The baby was our congregation which was made up primarily of a helpless little bunch of Portuguese Catholics. The box was the building—so shiny all the time. Once when we'd held a revival, some of us had become so happy that we were dancing. Complaints came from the staid members of the congregation—"We don't want scuffing the floor and that kind of commotion in here." Tom and I believed "the baby" needed to get out where it could grow up.

We discussed a new church building program with the leaders. "NO!" they responded. "We dedicated this piece of land years ago and wouldn't think of moving from here!"

Well—it became another short pastorate—just six months. Tom resigned and took his sick wife and two children back to the warmer parts.

Forty years have passed since. Weeds have grown up around it. People get charmed by houses and buildings. It's great to remember the place where we first met the Lord, but a place is holy only as long as the Lord is Master there.

At Bakersfield we were given two options, a couple of opportunities which we should have prayed more about for we no doubt accepted the wrong one. Tom could have either built a house for Mrs. Simpson or built a church at Old River Community where we had found a few believers worshiping in homes who needed a building.

Oren and Marylydia came along about then and the two men talked it over. Both being carpenters and both being without money, the house for Mrs. Simpson seemed to be more inviting. Together they accepted the job and the garage they built became our home for three months while Oren and Marylydia lived nearby in their trailer home.

I was bedfast—nerves and heart—and Marylydia ran after her little Oren, six days older than Loren who she also watched after as the two boys rode the grounds of an open acreage on the kitty cars.

God talked to me as I lay on the bed, speaking to me through things around me. I could see a message as Carnation milk bespoke of a beautiful flower representing my Lord. Flour. White was the base of bread and Jesus was the real bread.

One day as I wished for quiet, Mrs. Simpson became irritated with Phyllis, the five-year-old, for trying her luck at painting. Who could blame Mrs. S.?

While the dear lady knocked to come in I covered my head because I didn't want to see or speak to her. But God told me to ask her in with His dear rebuke. Had I not listened and obeyed I'd have failed to receive the answer to a prayer.

As Sister Simpson came inside, cheerfully greeting me, she said, "Sister Cunningham, here is a little white suit you may have, to see if it fits." I didn't have to, for I knew the size was right.

I told her, "Thanks a lot. I've been praying for a white suit for the pulpit appearance."

Rev. Spencer, pastor of the Niles Assembly, had paid many visits, always asking, "When will you preach for us?" Always I answered from my bed, "I'm not able, but will." So the last time he asked I promised, "God being my helper, I'll try for Sunday."

Saturday was a good test of my being able, so I could say, "Yes, for sure." As I sat on the side of the bed trying between groans to put on my shoes and my clothes I declared to Tom, "I can't make it."

At that very moment, Pastor Simpson announced on his radio program, "Sister Cunningham is going to be speaking for us at the eleven o'clock service." That did it; I had to go.

Tom helped me into the car. Stopping in front as near to the door as possible, I got out and walked to the first seats and sat there until I could get more strength to go down to the front. Tom had taken the two children to the platform with him, as he had been asked to sit up front. Service was opened as usual, but after a while Pastor began changing the service by saying, "Now we'll have Sister Cunningham to come up and bring a message."

As Tom came down leading the two children, the devil said to me, "You recall Brother Brown fell with a heart attack (A recent tragedy) in his pulpit in New York? That's how it will be and he (Tom) will be leading the two children to you at the altar space as you're doing now."

"Devil! I'm going to go preach and if I die I do!" Praise God! My strength came and when I was finished I said in my mind, "Now, Mr. Devil, what's it going to be?"

The answer came from God. I danced all over the pulpit. Healed. I was able to do my work and care for my children. It was then we got the call from Brother Wicks at Ventura to come fill in for him.

16

VENTURA

When the call came from Ventura asking, "Will you come to fill in for Brother Wicks while he takes a three-month leave of absence?" — I couldn't wait to say yes. Their beautiful and well-furnished parsonage was a Spanish bungalow just a few blocks away from the surging waves of the ocean — a noise that helped lull us to sleep at night after our wonderfully full days of ministering. We preached at midweek services, twice on Sunday, again on Monday afternoons at the jail and on the streets on Saturday. Again Tom and I were dividing the times, souls were being saved and folks were being filled with the Holy Ghost as others stood by in awe and amazement. "We've never seen the likes of this before!" they declared, but we recognized it as God's infilling. Revival had come! Even in the jail we could count the converts. We went to the docks and passed out tracts to the sailors whose ships were docked there.

God was really moving in revival at the First Assembly of God in Ventura. One short week's revival held by Marylydia and Oren reached the heart of one of Father Divine's followers. He had heard about the real Jesus under the anointing of the Holy Spirit, which Father Divine claimed to be.

Money was raised and board members agreed to buy a Sunday School bus which really increased the numbers in the Sunday School. The church was then located out on Ventura Boulevard and since those day, God has had several servants laboring in the coastal city of Ventura who built the work enormously with a bigger building.

As we rode along on one visit to our neighbor Assembly over at Santa Paula, with our bus full of our C.A.'s, God began to give me a sermon. How it burned in my heart! It was to my surprise after arriving that Brother Paul Wells, the pastor, admitted as he got up to preach, "I have no message. Do you, Brother Cunningham?" Tom said no as he nodded to me. (Although I refused the honor on such a sudden thought, in years to come I learned better. I recall at least three times coming into an Assembly unannounced and accepting the opportunity to minister.) Tom preached for Paul, but it was an altogether different subject than what God had put on my heart, which would have been more for the hour.

Can any of my readers recall when preachers let the Holy Spirit choose the preaching in this way?

Once a big, burly visiting preacher sat blissfully rocking to and fro in my rocker, watching me work. A regular drop-in, he always asked, "How are you two making out? I'm still looking for a place to minister."

One of the times when he declared he was in desperate need of a church, attempting to use a dose of the medicine we'd been forced to swallow many times, I had told him, "Brother, go to the church and pray a door open."

While I swept he smugly told me, "What you need is a vacuum."

"What I need is for a big fat preacher to get up out of my rocker and take hold of this broom!" was the thought in my heart . . . But for His grace!

On June 30 of 1937, I noted in my diary, "Loren is two years old. The other day I heard a commotion in the kitchen and found him pouring out rice, flour, beans and anything else he could find to make a mixture on the floor. While I scolded him and started to clean it up, he ran in the living room and turned the radio up full volume." He was a child in a child's world then.

Today I think of another conglomeration he concocted — one of all nationalities, languages and customs from Scandinavians to Asians and Africans to Europeans with their staid traits and the Americans with their free customs and their adulterated English speech. I picture them in long dresses, denims, patches, bow ties, pant suits and levis—eating everything from spuds and sauerkraut to peanut butter sandwiches. They are students on the campuses of the many YWAM schools of evangelism and from such diversified backgrounds. But they're all there for one reason—JESUS!

That little incident at age two was not the only time Loren pulled out all the stops on the instrument either. I am reminded of the thousands, even millions of people from around the world who heard the groups of YWAMers testifying, singing and praying at the 1972 Munich Olympics. As they marched, witnessed and prayed, they gave out flowers to the crowd following the tragedy of the Jewish athletes' slaughter. Winning police approval and even obtaining the patrolmen's help, they sang praises in the stadium where the dismissed pornographic entertainers had been. Such a mission they accomplished as they lifted His banner for all the world to see. They literally made NOISE for the Lord with all their volume. In their goal for saving souls, they also pulled out all the stops under his direction. Loren had watched his Dad all his growing-up days as he worked with the youth in our churches.

Ventura City and its people were making their way into our hearts. A beautiful young lady who had been a back slider came to know Jesus during a visit to our house. Her name was Opal.

One day Bob, a single man who knew Opal, came and talked to us for hours but nothing we said to him made him want to repent. His problem was Opal. "I've got to have her or I'll die," he despaired, but she had a husband.

A short time after our visit with him we got a call from the hospital where Bob worked. The doctors claimed, "This man has downed enough poison to kill three men." They managed to save him because he was at the hospital when he was stricken. Four doctors had been monitoring his progress.

After Tom and I visited him at the hospital, he repented and declared, "No woman is worth dying for." After that, Bob's chart showed that his body was free of the poison—something that the doctors deemed "miraculous."

There in Ventura many sailors and war veterans passed us on the street corner as we stood preaching to onlookers on Saturday nights. Some of them must have recognized us, as we had boarded a ship to hand out Gospel tracts. One of them raised his hand there on the street corner and loudly asked us, "Please remember me in prayer." We felt our street meetings paid off. We felt a deep concern for these mothers' sons.

After three months of our stay at Ventura as pastors elected to fill in, we received word that Brother Wicks had decided not to stay in the north where he'd been elected. Such a let-down, but that was his prerogative—to stay or come back, since he hadn't tendered his resignation. Tom and I were saddened by his decision, as we'd seen much progress in our ministry there.

While Tom continued to build a trailer for us to pull behind the car, I tried to get the house in spic and span order for the pastor's return. Opal offered to keep us for a week since Tom wasn't finished with the project in time. Our timing seemed to be off, but we learned then that God's timing is always right.

Since we had hit the list of the unemployed preachers once again, we phoned Brother Osterberg who suggested, "Why don't you try out at Inglewood?" That Assembly of God church was one to be desired—boasting a thriving congregation in a beautiful city.

During our last week at Ventura we bought new suits and borrowed a newer car to go for our Inglewood tryout. On July 24, 1937, Tom and I followed the Ocean Boulevard toward our destination. Suddenly I felt squeamish. The curves had gotten to me. I vomited all over my new clothes—perhaps God was teaching us not to try to appear to be what we really were not, or that this trip was to no avail.

As we slipped into the auditorium, we were impressed by the gathered throng. The Sunday School class was enthusiastically singing, "Everybody ought to go to Sunday School and help Brother Roberts in his fight against sin! Everybody ought to go to Sunday School."

Nudging the woman beside me, I whispered, "Who is Brother Roberts?"

"Oh, he's our new pastor!"

Tom and I had no recourse but to take our two children and slip out just as we'd slipped in. We'd had our very own wild goose chase! How could we blame the superintendent? No one had informed him that the place had already been filled. No one ever knew until now why we were there.

Tom called Ventura and told them, "We'll be there for the evening service." After all, it was Sunday and we'd not yet given God's Word. Ventura was still without a minister; Pastor Wicks hadn't yet arrived and we had even left that evening open.

God certainly had His divine hand on us and on where we should be that night. In that evening service, Bob finally prayed through, to further joy. Opal had told him, "I'm going to follow the Lord and not go out with you any more." We'd planned to help Opal get away from Bob by taking her to Los Angeles, but then we had realized it was not the Lord's way, to run from a problem.

"Opal," I told her, "God wants you to talk it over with Bob." She knew she wasn't free to marry; she wasn't even divorced. "And further, you'd better wire your husband and tell him to come for you or send for you and then remind Bob once again you aren't free to marry." As soon as she did that, she felt relief for herself. Victory was hers!

After praying through Bob was declaring jubilantly, "God's given me victory over a difficulty I couldn't conquer myself! Victory!" We couldn't help Opal escape or ignore a brokenhearted man who was wondering what he should do. As soon as Bob was sure he couldn't have Opal, he gave up. No more poison, no more heartache. Pastors often fail to become involved in such tedious situations, but they should, with more prayer and this kind of counseling.

Our family went to the beach for the last time. Tom swam. The children and I hunted for shells on the nearly empty beach which today is a thing of the past along the coast at Ventura.

August of 1937 found us on the hunt again for a field in which to labor. Jobless, we had to have faith that the Lord was going to make us triumphant.

17

PIONEERING AGAIN

Our new home cost only eight dollars a month to rent. No wonder! It consisted of a twelve-foot-square tent we stretched out under some eucalyptus trees. A bed was loaned to us and except for that one piece of furniture we were "boxed in." All our other furniture was made from boxes — boxes for shelves, boxes and boards for a makeshift table, and more crates for seats. Phyllis and Loren slept on the floor on metal cot springs — a sort of trundle bed we could slip under our bed out of the way in the daytime.

How can you dress up a tent? I attempted to make a shelf by nailing a board between the tent props so I could display my little boy and girl salt and pepper shaker set — one of the few trinkets I'd received for my wedding. Loren looked at them one day and said, "Tee, ain't they tute?"

My mother had given me a cardboard motto with the corner broken off. The words meant so much to me that I tacked it up on the side of the tent: "EVEN CHRIST PLEASED NOT HIMSELF" — a reminder I needed to read every time I thought of our well-furnished bungalow at Ventura.

Somerton had more than its share of dust, bugs and flies, but I got to liking the old eucalyptus tree under which we'd pitched our tent. With no fans of any kind to cool us, we so appreciated its shade when the temperature climbed to 120 degrees. Even some of the Mexicans, accustomed as they were to intense heat, had to come in from the fields at times.

Why were we here? But we knew God had led. Driving in our old model-A with a trailer Tom and Loren had made — three-year-old Loren tried to help out with his daddy — we traveled from San Diego across the Jacumba Mountain range and into the Imperial valley. The heat of one hundred degrees hit us. Tom stopped the car. "Jewell, I'm turning around and going back to the coast!"

"Well, then let's pray out here."

There was a big cottonwood tree nearby where we heard the Lord tell us as we prayed, "Go on east." We thought it would be back to Texas, but found a group of people in the little Arizona town on the very edge of Old Mexico who begged us to stay with them and help them get a church built. Revival overswept the few midwesterners who had come from their home places back east to find work and better living in the Yuma Valley. "It is like Paradise," one wrote his children, "If you ever see me and mama you'll come here."

But souls had to be won, and we loved the challenge of pioneering another Pentecostal church. Both of our children were under school age then, but working there with those Mexican-Americans was an experience we all could partially share with missionaries around the world in later years.

"Home is where the heart is." And so our little tent became home. All around us lived other poor families, mostly of Mexican heritage. Neither Tom nor I nor the children could speak Spanish, but some of them could make us understand their broken English. When Loren and Phyllis played with the laborer's children, they came down with pink eye, just as the others did. No antibiotics were available to treat what is now considered a simple malady, so blindness could have developed if they hadn't been properly taken care of. How pitiful our little ones looked with red, watery eyes that finally swelled shut with pus. Getting up in the middle of the night, I'd light a lamp and wash off their eyelids which had become matted shut. That eased the pain so they could go back to sleep. Their lids would be stuck fast again the next morning, so it was necessary to give them another hot bathing and soaking to get them open again. Tom and I and our friends prayed and God healed our little ones' eyes with no lasting effects. Neither of them has ever needed glasses. They still all have good vision.

Trials plagued us. Little kids stole our children's few toys. We were also "adopted" by a stray female dog we called "Snooky." Loren had won her over with his love so the mongrel simply wouldn't leave. We had a dog whether we asked for one or not! We could hardly feed ourselves, much less have scraps for a dog. The butcher gave me bones until he found out we used them for soup for the family. From then on we paid for the bones. Snooky finally had a litter of pups sired by the mayor's male dog. That was the last straw. We had to give them away even though they had such royal blood! Losing them broke Loren and Phyllis' hearts and ours as well. Eventually the mother dog had to go too.

Every-day life was busy. Tom and I slaved at building another adobe church—making the bricks ourselves. Once we crossed the border into Mexico in hopes of finding some ready-made adobes, but suddenly we looked up and found ourselves surrounded by men with guns pointed right at us! We'd stumbled on to a military base! We left in a hurry, without any bricks or information about making them!

Tom and I each preached two or three times a week in the old house the people had purchased for a meeting place. They'd torn out some walls and put some seats in. The young boys helped haul rocks for the new church. Their fathers, who were busy working for wages at the fruitsheds and other places, came on Saturdays to help. When the foundation was being dug, we decided "We're making it too small. Let's go out another ten feet." But the building was only 40 by 60 feet even then—a very small church, but adequate for the little village.

Always in need of money, we tried to raise funds to buy lumber. Tom decided to play chef and sell hamburgers at noon to the men working in the sheds. He took a small gas burner and put it in a trailer, complete with table and the ingredients. Every little bit helped! The laborers really liked buying hot hamburgers.

Tom came across an old building that needed to be torn down which he could buy for $50. He climbed up to the roof and found a lot of good timbers left. The men of the congregation helped him tear it down and clean those timbers up enough to use them for the church beams, ceiling casings and rafters. The left-over pieces they sold for over $120! Shingles were the only materials we needed to purchase to finish the building.

Sister Jones was building a church at Winterhaven, so exchanged labor crews with us while the ladies prepared the workmen's dinners. Both of those churches are still in use after all these years.

Tom, an early riser, always went out to the church at daybreak to pray and then had morning prayer with our children. He preached with a burden and we needed the Lord's encouragement to get out and make adobes. I was beginning to get into the swing of things too.

Lack of funds had us always in prayer. Yet we never went without enough to eat. In Canaan Land, who could starve? We'd get the leftover fruit and vegetables from the fields and groves.

We were moving ahead with our building program. Work on the All American Canal to carry water into the Imperial and Coachella Valleys was getting into full swing. Some carpenters from our group went seeking jobs. They were asked if they could do heavy structural carpentry. "No, only house carpentry." "Sorry," the boss replied. The men quickly said, "Our pastor is experienced in heavy carpentry." The boss said, "Tell him to report with his tools tomorrow and I'll put him to work." They came back and suggested I go to work. Just think of it, $1.10 an hour! (union scale for that time).

Tom said, "Brethren, I have a church to build. I can't do it." So he kept building. The custom in our church at that time was for a deacon to place an open Bible on the altar rail on a Sunday morning and the people would place their tithe and offering on the Bible. All that was placed on the Bible was the Preacher's "salary" for the week.

The following Sunday the Bible was placed on the altar and when the amount was counted, it was $1.10. One hour's pay on the canal. Later, Tom said to me, "If the Lord meant that for a joke, I guess I missed the punch line."

Tom kept working until the church was ready to move into. He then went to work on the canal. In six weeks he was promoted to one of the foremen. We paid up our bills and bought some things we needed. Finally we could afford car payments of $25 a month. Tom went to California and brought back a V-8 Ford. Used, yes, but only two years old.

Tom brought me his $44 take-home pay each weekend and I'd pay the bills, buy the groceries and save all I could. The tithes we collected on Sundays didn't even amount to $10 a week then.

Temptation! Six weeks after he went to work he was made foreman of his crew. later, he met his former job superintendent from Oklahoma City who had come to the canal to work during the winter. He said, "If you'll come with me to Chicago in the spring, I'll pay you a lot more than you are drawing here." Tom refused. He didn't want to be tempted to go full-time again and forsake the ministry, but we were convinced that God had made this way for us so we could stay on in Somerton until the church was built and they could hold regular church services there. Tom could work for a while, putting finishing touches on the church on Saturdays.

I filled in whenever he was working so far away that he had to spend the night elsewhere. Otherwise he'd drive as much as eighty miles back home to preach, and then leave our house the next morning at 5 A.M. That meant I had to get up at 4, if I was to cook him biscuits and eggs!

One time he ran his crew all night long while finishing one of the concrete spillways. After a few hours of rest, he was ready to preach. Another time he ran his crew of church laborers until midnight, then he got up periodically all the rest of the night to finish the cement floors. My man was always an ox when it came to endurance. I tried to always be by his side, but he carried the heavier load.

We finally took a short vacation. Upon returning we found that the Mexican folks had experienced a revival in town and needed to meet somewhere for worship until they could get a church of their own. We let them use our building on Tuesday nights. So spiritually hungry, their crowds spilled out of both the church and the yard. Our 40 by 60 building was no longer big enough. Tom and I enjoyed their services and their enthusiasm, even though we understood so little of what they said. Presently there are two full-gospel churches in Somerton. We felt we'd helped mother the Spanish church by letting them use our building.

Frank Yubeta, a teenager, was the one most responsible for that Spanish revival. He'd found the Lord and helped get the Spanish-speaking church going. His great desire was to go to Bible school. I wanted to help him, but couldn't seem to think of anything to make his dream become possible. He wanted to be a preacher rather than a plumber.

Presently he has a family and his children are grown, but they are following in the footsteps he wanted to take by going to Bible school to prepare themselves for the work of the Lord. Some are serving the community. The entire family blesses the local church where they live.

When the church was finally finished, it wasn't very big and didn't draw much applause. The 1939 dedication of the new church had been set, but Tom was still hunting shingles to nail on. Every one helped clean the yards, finish the walls and ceilings, hanging the doors and windows. How folks sweat to get the building finished! The District Superintendent wouldn't come to dedicate it, excusing himself by saying, "It's on the line between Arizona and California." So What? Both states were in the same district!

This is one reason Tom has never turned down the opportunity to dedicate a home mission church to this day. He's known the sting of disappointment!

At the dedication service Tom spoke of "hallowed ground" as Lincoln had at Gettysburg. Ours had been a hard-fought battle too. For nineteen long months we'd battled to raise up our new house of God. The festivities for the dedication included dinner on the ground with visitors coming from as far as San Diego, Yuma and Imperial Valleys.

Once the church had been built, Tom and I felt we'd accomplished what the Lord had sent us to do, so Tom hitch hiked to Ontario, California, to scout out the land. Pioneering had become our ministry and he'd heard they needed a church. When he returned home he reported their need. All the town had then was a mission house for derelicts and a few others. We were aware of their need, but God didn't call us to go there.

Brother Bradley, a modern-day St. Paul, a devout man of God and a preacher of the Gospel, came to visit. I realized the devil had him deceived when I heard him say, "I feel I'm to go away to the wilds some place and wait there for the ministry I'm to have in the future. I'll be one of the witnesses, one of Revelation's 'two anointed ones.'" (Revelation 11:3)

While I was chatting with him later, I realized he was serious indeed. After I prayed with him the Lord gave me a song to sing in the Spirit. "We'll work till Jesus comes, we'll work till Jesus comes, and THEN be gathered home." I knew and hoped he knew that the words were meant for him. I said, "Ever since the Lord's first visit to this world, mankind has felt they should withdraw from the world and wait for His return. That's a lie of the devil to keep men out of Christian action. 'Occupy,' He says, 'until I come.'"

When Brother Bradley started a set of meetings I knew he'd received my messages. God had put a new zeal in him to save souls. Three found salvation the first night. The next night three were filled and two saved. Fifteen souls had been filled and three saved since Christmas—nearly as many as our entire last year. The reaping time seemed to be at Somerton.

Sunday School attendance was on the rise—68 on Sunday. A church's spirit can be judged mostly by the number of souls brought to the Lord.

Conversions were on the rise! We had to take our converts to the Baptist Church to get them baptized. Seven were immersed. We were glorying in what God was doing there when we got a surprise letter from the Arvin church secretary asking us to come for a tryout. That again! We felt no burden.

Men and women were putting the finishing touches on the woodwork of both the church and the parsonage. The work seemed finished. "Whatsoever thy hand findeth to do, do it with all your might" and "Take what is opened to you" were scriptures that rang in our hearts and soon we got a call from El Centro.

"Brother Davidson has resigned, but folks here already had you in mind." Those words from a brother at the El Centro church astounded us. Tom and I had slipped over there to a fellowship meeting, but neither of us were expecting to run upon such surprising news. A short time later we were voted in.

Back at Somerton, dear Sister Collum seemed to express everyone's sentiments. "But we thought we had you!" We'd just been elected to another term there, but preachers are human and on the lookout for greener pastures, larger crowds, better accommodations and more money to pay their bills. Yet we have found headaches often accompany the better things we hope for. (Like deacons who won't deacon, Sunday School superintendents who won't superintend and members who quarrel and kids who have to be kicked out of class.)

So often discord and confusion accompanied the times of change when pastors played an old game of yesteryear. When the words "Fruitbasket upset!" were yelled, everyone changed chairs. Such a scramble ensued, not unlike the scramble for a church when the word was out, "It's open."

Our days and months at Somerton would not be easily forgotten. The sad farewells were hard, but we had to press on. Tom and I gave Brother Marshall, the newly-elected pastor, all the boost we could by donating all our furniture to him and boasting of his ability to the crowd.

18

MY ISAAC

"Mama, I don't feel so good," Phyllis moaned as we were coming home from church in Somerton one Sunday. In our modest tent home, I touched my little girl's forehead and found it burning with fever. "My neck hurts," she whispered, and her head seemed to draw back. I soon realized that her bowels and kidneys were not functioning. A nurse told me, "She has all the symptoms of Spinal Meningitis. You must get her to a doctor!" Frightening words, but I knew Dr. Jesus, so I went in search of those who knew how to pray.

Just a few nights before, the Lord had spoken to me at the church altar. For no apparent reason He said, "You will have to put your Isaac on the altar." This day, I knew He was meaning Phyllis. I stayed in our tent after she was stricken and sought the Lord's healing power. How difficult to say, "Lord, your will be done"! On the third day I felt the only way to put her on the altar was to leave the praying with Tom and others. Reluctantly I turned my back on her, in this way putting her on the altar. "There she is, Lord," I told Him and left her daddy and Brother and Sister Russell to pray. They were the ones I knew should intercede for her, since I could not. I could only cry with fear, "Have your own way, Lord." God touched her immediately! Phyllis had no fever at all the following day. Miraculous! In a few days she was able to get up — my "Isaac" had been given back — and my heart soared with gratitude to the Lord when I saw her up and playing again. Now I could leave her with her daddy and go calling on absentees with Sister Russell, the prayer warrior. (We need more of these kinds of saints!)

This experience contained a lesson I needed to learn and pass on to other parents. We must have our Isaacs on the altar, for God will sometimes test us in stressful trials. But after God has heard our vows in the midst of theses kinds of tests, it is easier for us to let God have them for His service, as we would find out with our other two children in future years. Putting them on the altar again and again, then watching them leave for parts unknown has never come easy for me, but I've found it's easier than it would have been if I would not have said, "Here she is, God. Here he is, God."

Everywhere we'd pastored previously, the parsonages had been furnished, but not at Somerton. We had to make do with anything we could find. Visitors often came from the coast and other cities, preachers were always stopping by, and I was ashamed of what I had to use to serve my guests. The bucket lids we used for plates had to go. Trusting God, I made out a C.O.D. order to Sears for three coated enamelware buckets, a dishpan, some pots — everything needed to cook in. The works! When the order came in I had no money, so it had to sit in the post office for days. Later the dishes I had wished for arrived too.

What I'm going to tell you now is a very unusual experience. We had a Baptist preacher in to hold a revival. Among his converts were an atheist — a rich tourist from Detroit — who was so possessed with unbelief he could only grasp faith after hands were laid on him at our humble make-do altar, a plain wooden slab. There he found something money couldn't buy. The Lord gave power to rebuke the demon of unbelief. He arose from his knees a new creature. His face shining, he went about smiling and shaking hands.

In contrast, that same night a young, poorly-clad little country girl found her Savior. There at the meeting place in Somerton, Arizona, all kinds of deliverance took place, preached by different men and in different ways, but the same Gospel. All kinds of fish are caught when the great net is put down. On Sunday a children's altar call was given and hearts were touched as so many of them responded in their childlike manner — crying and wiping their eyes.

One day Brother Burke stopped by and asked me, "I was at the post office and they say there's a package down there with your name on it. What is it that they've been holding so long?" In church that night he confronted the crowd, "There's a parcel down at the post office for Sister Cunningham. She won't say what she's ordered, but she evidently doesn't have enough money to get it out. I'm going to take up an offering for it right now." After passing my tambourine, he came back and dumped the contents in my lap. Through tears I saw that it was sufficient. Then I rose to thank them and tell how I'd ordered the kitchen essentials at the Lord's leading. Later on, kind Brother Hulstein bought me a complete set of dishes. No more bucket lids!

Tom and I'd collected $80 for finishing the church, but then I decided to launch out on a fund-raising campaign of my own. Some gave, some could have cared less. I asked the doctor on the corner, "Wouldn't you be pleased to donate something to the church building fund?" His answer was terse, "Why should I? You folks are my competitors. You pray for them to be well; I make my living curing the sick." At least he was honest! I couldn't help but laugh after he said that, so he had to smile back. I thanked him anyway and walked out.

The city had other building plans. It even erected a dance platform right across from our church, but we prayed it out of use — even to this day. They never did open it up. I don't know their reasons, but the platform stands there to this day. It made me think of the ruins of Charazim in the countryside of Israel and all the other reminders of what God has brought to naught.

Sister Banta was a saint of God. Every two or three weeks her prospector husband would make his way back into town driving his rig. One overburdened donkey pulled the "hack" that Banta used to live in while he was out prospecting for gold. It was really a little makeshift trailer-cart with a wagon cover that he used when he was out digging. He never did strike any rich veins, but you knew when you watched his Spirit-filled wife that she didn't need any of those kinds of riches. God's greatest was already hers. Our meetings always livened up after she sang her little song, "I'm under the Spout Where the Glory Comes Out." Those old-time choruses, something like hers, uplifted the soul. Simple in word and tune, they penetrated the outer crust of souls and touched chords on the inside. Such lines as "There is a place of silent rest near to the heart of God" is something we came to understand. Billy Watts, one of our congregation, had one of the most generous and thoughtful hearts of anyone I'd ever known. But poor Billy had a burden — his wife was housed in a mental institution. One day he stole Kate out of that place on the pretense of taking her for a ride. He brought her home and left her in my keeping. Believing God would heal her, he asked us to stand with him in prayer. One day, while Kate and I were alone in prayer, I watched her. I felt led to say, "Kate, if you will lift your hands and say His name, the name of Jesus, you will be delivered . . . set free!" She would not speak His name even with all my coaxing and tearful insisting. Finally I laid hands on her and demanded, "Dumb devil, come out of her voice and mind!"

At last her hands lifted and she spoke weakly, "Jesus," but Bill's poor young wife eventually had to be taken back to the asylum. Her hold was not firm enough to bring her out of her despair. She refused to respond to further counseling or help.

Converts who have no follow-up seldom stay with the Lord. In order to triumph over mental, spiritual and physical problems, we have to persist in growing in the knowledge and grace of God.

When the heat in Somerton had become so intense that summer we decided to take a short jaunt to northern Arizona. Two things stopped us from leaving right away. The church floors had to be finished so we could move into the new building and, of course, our limited finances. Folks sacrificed and gave us $14.50 to make our journey possible. After working all day with the men on the floors, my diligent Tom stayed up troweling the cement and finally went to bed at 8 A.M. After he had a short rest we struck out.

At Sedonia we preached for Cecil. All of us went to the church to pray on weekdays and left the children playing outside. One day Phyllis came running in crying, "Mama, a dog just bit me." I pulled up her dress and found a bruise mark. She had so many clothes on that I didn't see how the dog could have bitten through them. No blood, so we just prayed and sought God about it.

At Flagstaff the next day we visited Oren Paris and Mary-lydia, who were building the Crosstie Church — the first Assembly of God there — out of ties they'd gathered from the railroad tracks. The third night a health officer came knocking frantically on their trailer door. "Is Reverend Cunningham here? The dog that bit his child was MAD!"

When Tom went to the door the man's face showed such relief. "I'd have chased you down if it had taken days! We've already sent the dog's head off for tests. It came back positive. Rabies!"

What shocking news! Yet somehow it didn't phase me. I simply said to the officer, "But we prayed."

My faith didn't impress him. "You must get her to a doctor as soon as you can! It's already been four days and seven is the bad time . . . then fourteen . . . then twenty-one. It goes in cycles. Promise me you'll take her. It could mean a prison term for you if anything happens to the child!"

Such harsh words! Tom and I immediately regretted leaving Somerton for vacation. We packed Phyllis in the car and took her to a county doctor — the only kind we could afford.

The doctor seemed to have our number. Immediately we suspected that the health officer had already dubbed us "fanatical Pentecostals," for he asked as he examined Phyllis' wound, "Do you believe in divine healing?"

Believe in divine healing? What a question. "Of course," Tom answered. I decided to speak up, "Yes, Doctor, if we can't take the sixteenth chapter of Mark, the fifteenth to seventeenth verses seriously, we'd better quit preaching and go home!"

He eyed us for a moment, then said, "I respect your faith. Have you got someone who will pray with you? If you still want treatments after you pray, you can come back." That was as fair a prescription as any doctor ever gave anyone.

We went looking for the nearest Pentecostals, believing they were the ones to trust. Our relatives were as scared as Tom and I.

When we found a family of Assembly of God people up near Red Lake, we told the woman our problem and that we wanted prayer. "You'd better get the doctor as fast as you can!" she cried, and never did pray with us. We turned around and went back to Flagstaff to the county doctor. He was still reluctant, "Go tell the county attorney how you feel about the treatment and then report back to me."

The attorney had as much compassion as the health officer. He told us, "You can have faith. I respect that; I'm a Christian Scientist. But this thing requires more than prayer." Tom and I weren't Christian Scientists, but we'd seemingly lost our faith. Dangling between hope for a miracle and disbelief that Phyllis was in need of treatments, we were at a loss as to what to do. Doubts filled my mind. Could the dog have reached her flesh with his slobber through three layers of clothes and long stockings?

Finally Tom declared, "It seems to be totally my decision. If my darling daughter were to die I'd be solely responsible for her death and be sent to prison. That being the case, I'd better give in and take the doctor's help."

Five-year-old Phyllis wailed, "Mama, Daddy, please—let's trust God!" That didn't help. That had to be the most difficult conflict I've ever lost.

As Dr. Talmadge said in his most inspiring writings of a hundred years ago, "Often science and revelation meet head on." That was one of those times. My God-given revelation was that all would be well and I never lost that feeling. Science warned of danger. It was enough to make me give in—however reluctantly. On top of everything else Tom said, he chastised me. "You won't be the one to go to jail."

We held Phyllis as the doctor pushed a needle into her little tummy and squirted a half-ounce of liquid under her skin so it could slowly find its way into the blood stream to the affected parts. Every day we went through the same thing, but each day it became less of an ordeal. Ice cream cones following the treatments soothed her anguish. She almost looked forward to going for her shot.

One night she woke up; her breathing was erratic; she was gasping for breath. Frightened, I prayed asking God to intercede. The next day I pressured Tom, "Quit the treatments! She could die of heart failure instead of the dog bite."

With some misgivings the doctor dismissed her when we begged him, "Please, please let us take her back to Somerton." He frowned and warned us, "If you don't finish the last fourteen days of treatment, you might as well not have started them. But I'll agree if you promise to take her to a doctor there if you feel it's necessary." How glad I was he added that phrase "if you feel it's necessary," for it let us promise we would. But, Praise God! She never needed to go.

Years later when she took the health exam for a county job a slight heart enlargement showed up. I always thought it had begun back at the time of the rabies treatments. After that she didn't seem to be able to take the rough and tumble play with her brother as well as she'd once done. In Jr. High she got me to have her assigned to a rest period instead of doing the regular athletics.

I'd said to Tom back then, "Honey, if we don't win against this, we'll have to meet the devil in another form around the corner."

Tom had not failed his duty, but I felt let down by the ones we'd gone to for spiritual help. They hadn't even taken time to pray with us. "Bear one another's burdens and so fulfill the law of Christ."

A note and ten dollars came from Somerton begging us to come back. So Tom declared, "Somerton, here we come!"

Oren had really appreciated Tom's help in building his church while we were delayed in Flagstaff. I'd been so worried about Phyllis that little Loren's third birthday passed by without our getting him a gift except for an ice cream cone. He got one each day when his sister got hers.

The Wilbanks', some rancher friends, often dropped off a quart of buttermilk for us. Loren liked buttermilk. One day when he ran out to get some, Mr. Wilbanks said to him, "Sorry, son, we have none left."

"Why didn't you save us some buttermilk, Brother Wi-banks?"

At another time Mrs. Wilbanks had dropped by for another reason. She asked us, "Do you need any furniture? A friend is moving to the coast and has five rooms of furniture to sell." Tom made a trade with her. She offered to loan us the money for the furniture if he'd build her some more shelves. My prayer for furniture was answered. Five rooms of old fashioned but good furniture for only $25! An oil stove with an oven, a kitchen cabinet and breakfast table set, a leather davenport with a fold-out bed, two large leather chairs, a library table, two bedroom sets with mattresses and dressers complete with mirrors. God is not a supplier of cheap plastic. All these pieces of solid oak would be antiques now. But we left them behind when we left the parsonage.

Back in Somerton we used the new building.

We attended a camp meeting at Big Bear located in the Sierras above San Bernardino, our children sang with their dad playing guitar, "Call that Religion? No, no!" Six-year-old Phyllis sang the lead with her four-year-old brother chiming in on the "No, no!" Every time he slowed down, she gave him a nudge with her elbow.

Years later, their vocal training came from Mrs. Marfield of Pasadena, well-known teacher of the art to the movie stars. She also taught our last child, Janice. For years all three have warmed the hearts of audiences across the world. Singing is the most soul-warming art; it stimulates one's whole being. David said, "I'll sing as long as I live."

19

EL CENTRO

We went to El Centro to buy brand new furniture for ourselves. Such fun! We bought a refrigerator, a gas range, a washing machine — the works! All that, plus a salary of twenty-five dollars a week — heaven on earth!

A bungalow in the better part of town was available for thirty dollars a month rent. But after a couple of months we had to step down a peg to a cheaper one, since all the rent had to come out of our salary. Seemed we couldn't win for losing!

Dear Sister B had to put one rowdy out of her class right in the middle of class discussion. When Tomboy Marty (as she was nicknamed) came to the adult session unannounced, I left my class to investigate. The teacher declared, "We can't have one rotten apple that'll spoil the rest." That did it! Tomboy left the church in a huff; the years haven't brought her back.

Those problems and more were to be reasoned with along with lots of kindly-bestowed blessings from the well-established congregation of El Centro, At that time they could boast, "We've only had two pastors in ten years." — A record to be proud of.

At El Centro Tom and I lived up to the other pastors' records and stayed our five years. Many souls came in, especially after the earthquake of 1940. At that time we'd taken on Brother Davidson's street meetings on Kress corner every Saturday night. One night we had just concluded services and were walking to our car when suddenly the whole portico which had been as a shelter from rain or the hot sun only seconds before we left collapsed behind us. Telephone poles bent over like limber twigs.

We jumped into the car to drive away, thinking at first that a tire was flat. Then we began bouncing from side to side, while the motor was even running! Light wires snapped causing mini lightning bolts. Darkness fell like a cloud. Screams of terror and yells for loved ones came from the main street we'd just left.

"Earthquake!" we cried as we jumped out of the car and raced back to see if we could help. Folks ran past us wailing and calling for their kin. Some began scratching frantically in the newly fallen debris of wood and concrete that had buried those unfortunate souls who had run out in the open instead of staying in the partial shelter formed by beams and walls.

As the earth wiggled and moved beneath our feet thoughts flooded our minds. WHERE CAN WE GO FOR SAFETY? . . . TO THE DESERT? INSIDE? OUTSIDE? IN THE HOUSE OR ON THE STREET? WHICH? THE HOUSE COULD COME DOWN ON US WHILE WE SLEEP. WILL IT BE THIS WAY ON THE GREATEST DAY OF ALL DAYS? Dumbfounded we watched. At one place the earth cracked open and swallowed up a whole chicken house.

A black man who worked as a shoe shiner at the barber shop said later he was spared. His friend said, "The Lord was with you." "Well, if He was He sure was running!" was the man's answer.

Two boys followed their dad up onto the high curbed sidewalk — only a split second behind their mother and two other children who had reached the sidewalk first. Before one could take a breath, a wall above them fell and buried the mother and her two offspring alive. Like a madman the father pulled at all that debris, down through cement held together with slabs and poles and timbers of shorter length. Other men tried to pull him away saying, "There's no chance they're alive." They were right. Nine people, ready or not, met their Maker that day.

Even though Tom and I had preached there for more than two years, it was only after that awesome, horrible experience that we really saw folks come to know Him. Earthquakes are necessary sometimes to loosen the bondage, just as it was in Paul and Silas' time.

First Assembly of God, El Centro, was considered a strong church in that period of the Assemblies of God history. We were called there as pastors when Tom was still in his twenties. Quite an assignment for him.

In the early days of our ministry there, Roy, one of the deacons, was also serving as Sunday School superintendent. He was a very good and faithful man and later entered the ministry, but he had a short fuse.

At a Sunday School picnic in a city park one Saturday, Letha, a little girl of about eight years, broke a rule. The superintendent gave her a spanking.

A short time later her "big brother" (about thirteen) heard of the spanking and came riding up on his bike and confronted the superintendent. While still astride the bike, but with one foot on the ground, he proceeded to tell the superintendent off. Roy's temper flared. Grabbing "big brother" off the bike, he turned him across his knee and gave him a much harder spanking. To add to the problem, both Letha and "big brother" were the daughter and son of one of the other deacons in the church.

On Sunday morning the father of the two disciplined children, who lived across the street from the church was absent from services. After the service Tom called the superintendent into the office and sent someone across the street for the other deacon, bringing them face to face to settle the difficulty.

Though Tom was several years younger than either man, he took control of the situation, saying to the superintendent, "Brother R, I want you to apologize to Brother W for what you did yesterday."

The brother started in, "Now Brother W, if I have done anything to offend . . ." Tom broke in, "Now Brother R, you know what you did. Don't beat around the bush, ask for forgiveness." He did and Tom got both of them on their knees for a time of prayer and forgiving. Both men embraced. Quick and decisive action on Tom's part nipped some potential trouble in the bud.

"Big brother's" ego had been deflated the previous day, but he survived and grew into a fine young man.

Up until this point in our lives our "first love" had been pioneering or home missions, but it had changed in time to pastoring, evangelizing and helping plant churches.

The Lord in His wisdom had given us a rest from some of the hardships for a time as He sent us to El Centro. Once when I called Tom "The Pastor" a sister corrected me. "You are co-pastors," she declared. "You preach as much as he does." We did labor together in the extreme heat for five years.

For two years we lived across the street from the park and I had a new privilege. I was able to feed the bums. I lent out one of my quilts, too, I learned.

The children's school was close to the park and we enjoyed the two years we lived there until we built a parsonage. Our work at El Centro became a labor of love.

Revival first came following the death of a baby related to the McKinzie family. As we ministered to them in the death and burial of the little one, we were also breaking fallow ground for the sowing of Gospel seeds. The McKinzies, Wilkersons and Dugans came into the fold one by one. Those names are still familiar at the church at Tenth and Park, El Centro.

December 7, 1941. That Sunday Tom and I went to a little Chinese store to get something special for Sunday dinner. We were standing there when we heard the earth-rocking news: "The Japanese have bombed Pearl Harbor!" In the days following we watched as all our Japanese neighbors were herded into trucks and busses. Their businesses and homes were sold dirt cheap and our hearts ached for them. Our sympathies became less definite when the one sister who had ministered to the Japanese and worked with them in their church found a short wave radio receiver/sender hookup in their church attic.

Anxiety took over that spring. Even the children were always aware that we were in war. Air raid drills at school, the war stamp program and the Junior Red Cross, black out practices when Tom became a block warden, all made us very war-minded. When siren sounds pierced the air our children's Daddy had to patrol the neighborhood to see that all the lights were out. To relieve their minds I made a game of it by taking a flashlight and reading to them under the covers in bed. The war had far-reaching effects. Young men (hardly more than boys) began registering in the military and were called. The church ladies started an early morning prayer meeting. One morning a policeman came, but not to pray. "Why are you here so early?" he demanded. "Folks are complaining."

"War is on," I told him. "Our boys are leaving. Tell the complainers to come help us!" With that, he gave us his well-wishes.

A banner in the front of our church displayed a star for every boy who had gone to war. We had blue stars to put on it, but we also had gold ones in case one of them was killed. No gold stars were necessary so we were assured of the tremendous value of intercessory prayer. Some came back and shared testimonies of their miraculous deliverance from death on the battlefield.

Tom's Father, J. H. Cunningham and my beloved Papa, R. C. Nicholson, were two of the evangelists who dropped by to hold revival, preaching the Gospel straight from the shoulder. Even the "hard crusters" (the men of the congregation that balked at hearing the Word) were touched. Paul Pipkins and his bride, Viola, helped to build up the younger groups and the Sunday School. Brother Kuntz, such a live wire for Jesus, had God's blessing on his ministry in spite of the pressures of his own family problems. From some of his relatives he received unlovely and unjust treatment, but we witnessed a humble-spirited man of God ministering under pressure. Gladys Pearson and her brother James pleased us when they came and held revival meetings. Paul Franklin came — an old-timer who had witnessed the Azusa meeting in L.A. My brother Coy as well as an escapee from the USSR gave us entertaining messages. Coy's was as always dramatic and the other man in his messages told of the awful atrocities. Yet later the U.S. had that nation as an ally.

God even moved on folks' hearts financially. In one missionary service Sister Florence Christie received a tremendous offering. One person gave her a check for a thousand dollars!

God blessed our youth group (then known as Christ's Ambassadors) and orchestra. During the week the children held services in the Sunday School bus parked nearby. I truly believe our two oldest received the knowledge of Christ within that church bus. After that they helped other children pray through to salvation. I was assigned to be principal of our first Vacation Bible School with one hundred enrolled.

One night our church altar was filled with people kneeling and seeking the Holy Spirit. Loren knelt at the very end of the line. After the others began to get up, he came to me and said, "Mama, nobody mattered about me." Others had reached fulfillment there, but none of the older folk had stopped to pray with 7-year-old Loren. How sad when we neglect the youngsters.

Papa and Bernice stopped by on their way east and Tom and I went with them in their car as far as Detroit where we bought our first new car — a 1940 Plymouth. The church had given us one hundred dollars, so we took a three-week trip.

Friends at El Centro grew dearer as time went on. About the city's climate people said, "Nine months out of the year here heaven has no appeal, but the other three are so hot that hell has no fear." Regardless of townsmen's descriptions, El Centro's climate grew on us. One learned to adjust to the weather changes and cope with the floods when the rains came in such torrents that they swept the gutters and washed away anything movable. Even the wind moved the freshly-plowed soil. Yet farmers were happy because their products were in such demand over on the coast where the grapefruit wasn't as sweet and lettuce wouldn't even grow.

On trips to the Palisades Camp Meeting where we went to get the freshness of cool air and to hear others preach (besides ourselves), folks took the air out of our balloon by asking, "How's it where you come from? Hot, I hear."

Our answer: "We hadn't really noticed." Other aspects made up for any discomfort caused by the heat. Ours was one of the best-paying churches in the whole Southern District. We could have answered with that!

The year of 1942, we moved into the two-bedroom parsonage we'd built on the lot next to the church. Tom and I had labored during the three hottest months of the year from 8 A.M. to 10 P.M.

to make that possible. Late dinners became the norm. Some of the dedicated men came to labor with us after their own day at work was through. We finished and polished floors and papered inside and painted outside. Everything was so beautiful that we were all rightly proud—even little Phyllis who would say, "Mama, let's leave the door open so people can see!"

The electrician expressed surprise as he was finishing the wiring that the house didn't belong to us. "You mean it's not yours, preacher?" Lots of services were given to us—all donated labor. Even our dear Ventura friends came to help and were there when the telephone men arrived. The city allowed us to hook into the water line and put in a paved sidewalk free. Tom became "cement happy" and finished the walk from our front porch to the back door of the church and then built steps down into the church basement where he had his study and spent much time in prayer. He and the deacons purchased the church's first air conditioner, which was only a evaporative cooling system, but we put up beds for sleeping outside during the summer in a screened-in one-room building. We hadn't even a fan in the house.

In 1944, we were going back to our first love when we thought we were to go to Tucson and build a church. After resigning, our last days at El Centro resembled a funeral. Our family's hearts were trying to accept leaving our friends and accept what we felt was God's call—another internal conflict from which we would learn that God always triumphs.

20

OUT OF THE DESERT

Tucson began to try my patience more and more. The children started going to the Flowing Wells country school six miles away. They could walk to the bus stop with their daddy, or else he would take them straight to school each morning and try to be there to meet them every afternoon. Quite a feat for a busy pastor!

Even the authorities caused us consternation. Living five miles out of town, we had no way of knowing the ordinance that said a dog must be leashed. But one day when we returned home little Wimpy didn't run to meet us. The kids called frantically, "Wimpy, Wimpy!"—but no response came. Finally, in desperation, I phoned the pound and asked if someone picked up our little dog. Without any trace of feeling, the man on the other end of the phone answered, "Yes, we did. He's out in the incinerator now." I could only reply sarcastically, "You've made my children very happy!"

Tom found part-time work teaching swimming at the YMCA which helped us pay the rent. Our salary was too meager. Rents were frozen, but still higher than prewar times. War time gluttony spread like a cancer then, so we were pleased when we got a two bedroom house we could afford, only if Tom would paint it inside and out.

Heat also posed a problem. So severe! With no air conditioning or fan, I became more miserable each day and found myself praying, "Lord, get us back to California where you sent us."

But souls were being reached. Some from the Saturday night street meetings found the church the following day. In the same way, new ones were also being added to the Sunday School. Others who came from the northeast were able to rent one of the pretentious, elaborate homes on the hill but they had needs physically—with health problems such as TB—and spiritually. It proved there is a direct and indirect will of God. He will not let His Word return void. We were both preaching with anointing at the street and church services. Taking everything into consideration, I still felt that God had a future for us back on the West Coast—not just because of the climate, although the heat surely was a conflict for me.

One great day the telephone rang and I told Tom, "If that is Pastor Elton Hill at Covina telling you he's resigning and asking if you would like to take his place—by all means say YES!"

Tom spoke a minute, then stared at me holding the receiver in his hand. "It is!" I hadn't the slightest idea or reason to believe that Elton would leave Covina. Tom had preached a revival for him two years before, but there'd been no hint that he might resign.

Right there over the phone Tom answered Elton's offer, "If I can be elected unanimously without my coming for a "try-out," I'll consider it."

"Who do you think you are, Tom?" Elton inquired. "You preached here for a week or 10 days two years ago. Some of the new ones have never even heard you."

"Well, I'll have to make it that way," Tom answered. "I'll put out a fleece. If I can get it unanimously and also get J. K. Gressett to come and build here, then I'll be assured that God is leading us." At that point Tom really wanted to stay and build the church for the Tucson congregation as he already made up the money and bought the lots for the new location.

A few days later another call came from Elton. "Well, Tom, you were elected just as you said—unanimously." Without a word of thanks or even "Praise the Lord"—with no enthusiasm of any kind, Tom answered simply, "Then I have this other fleece of getting J. K. Gressett to come and finish the work I've started here." With an "Okay" from Elton, they hung up.

Tom telephoned around and finally located J. K. Gressett in West Texas where he was in between revivals and was using his truck for hire—his "tentmaking" to keep him going. He admitted to Tom that he'd been having nudges from God to go to Arizona. When Tom called, he was on the spot. It proved that both these men were right in their pursuit of God's will. J. K. was the man for the building and pastoring of the group at Tucson. Folks loved him. As Tom said, he was a builder. Later he was elected District Superintendent and served in that position successfully for many years.

It wasn't easy to tell the Tuscon folks we were leaving. "Only four months here!" they complained.

"Well, we're sorry, but it's the right thing to do," Tom replied. He felt relieved, for we'd "plowed the furrows" and soon the "planter" would be coming. Money had been raised, lots bought, and the builder was on the way. We didn't see the new church for some time, but heard of its progress from evangelists and other visitors from Tucson.

No one was too pleased with our decision to move. The Tucson folks were not helping us pack. They were hurt and couldn't understand our decision, but time has proven it was our time to give it up and go back to the west coast. Tom had no help other than 9-year-old Loren. The piano and refrigerator were the heaviest things, but Tom was able to load them up by backing the truck up to the porch. From there our belongings were taken to a trucking company to ship to Covina. After selling some things, Tom stacked others into the trailer and headed west.

Time has proven it was truly our time to go back to California.

Phyllis and I stayed in Covina as our two "men" were to return to Tucson to pick up a second load. No one helped pay our expenses for those two moves, causing quite a conflict for us. But we were certain God meant it for a triumph both for us and for those at Tucson.

After our very hot, miserable ride across the desert, we felt as though we'd crossed into Canaan land when we finally passed over the last high ridge and entered Los Angeles County. What a glorious view! Groves of walnut trees stood basking in the sun of that fruitful valley. Grape vineyards lined the main thoroughfare as we drove to the small city of Covina which was nestled among the orange groves. The sweetest smelling fragrance I'd ever taken in came wafting through our open car window.

After going up Citrus Boulevard, the main and only business street, we turned onto Second Street past the school house. "The church is just a block away on the corner," Tom explained. While turning the corner his eyes began to twinkle. "You'll not like the parsonage," he added.

Alongside the church stood a white wood frame bungalow with steps and a sidewalk which joined the two together. Though the front yard wasn't much, the large backyard was most inviting. A clothesline hung ready for use.

I looked at Tom. "You joker! You mean I won't like this?" As we toured the rooms of that bungalow which was like a small palace to us, I was delighted to discover a well-equipped kitchen.

The saints there began to come to welcome us before we even unloaded. We sent our children the one block to school. They had transferred their school reports from the country school in Arizona called Flowing Wells. The following year we celebrated the Fourth of July with the townspeople by watching the fireworks in the park.

The Sunday School took a spurt, for Tom made it his first priority. God gave an 82% increase in average attendance in six months. Tom was elected as sectional leader of Christ's Ambassadors and also as Presbyter. Not only were we very busy in church, but we were also preparing for another increase in our family.

On November 12, 1944, around 2:00 A.M., I made a quick call for Dr. Hightower to meet me over at Mrs. Ida Golden's house. Immediately after I made that call a torrential rain storm caused the phone to go dead. Our youngest daughter made her debut at five in the morning. At 9½ pounds, she was filled out—a little butterball. Back at the parsonage, when the other two children were informed later that morning, they ran out to announce to those coming to Sunday School, "Our little sister's here! We named her Janice Rae."

Our three young children and the demands of church work kept us hopping. My Sunday School class was a challenge. I'd never felt I had a call to teach, but God confirmed that I was to teach this class in an unusual way. Somehow I'd lost my watch. When I discovered the loss, I said to my children, "Will you pray for me to find my watch?" As I prayed I vowed to God, "If you want me to teach the ladies' Sunday School class, Lord, then let me find my watch. If it's Your will, I promise I'll do my best."

Soon afterwards a notice appeared in the local paper's want ad section, "Found—gold watch. Owner may claim by describing it." A local store's name was printed at the end of the ad. I went there and described and claimed my time piece. After praising God for its return, I knew I had no choice but to follow through with the vow I'd made with my simple fleece—simplicity has been my only attribute to glory in. I began to teach as well as preach.

Teaching didn't diminish my tasks, but multiplied them—especially with caring for the baby. Janice found herself in the arms of love—love not only from her family, but from the members of the congregation as well. Jannie was at home in her basket whenever she wasn't being fondled by adults or young people. Our youngest child was a blessing, not a burden.

Teaching also became a blessing. Time brought forth good reports of my class. Once Sister Dane, a saintly motherly woman, said in her testimony, "Sister Cunningham got me to reading the Bible." I stirred up interest by having a contest searching out certain events and passages in the Scriptures, then giving a prize to the winners.

Such fiery evangelists as young Dean Duncan and Brother Klink, the former Social Secretary for Kaiser Wilhelm of Germany came to hold revivals. Evangelist Klink's audience sat spellbound as he told of the tortures endured during our war with Germany (WWI). Revivals such as we held there with 85-year-old Brother Skull and Sister Grace have gone out of date. Such preaching! Through their anointed preaching souls were added to our number.

Tom always looked for new ways to build up the Sunday School as he got fired up about going to the Sunday School Convention in Springfield. Janice and I drove him into the City and dropped him off at the L.A. Central Station, then started back home. I rolled down the windows for all the fresh air I could get, for few cars were air conditioned in 1945. Jannie, only two months old, got the croup from the sudden temperature change. I fretted for fear it might turn into pneumonia. For the entire two and a half weeks Tom was away, I slept on the sofa in the front room with our baby daughter's crib near by and kept a fire going. She would choke up if I took her to the bedroom.

All the church services were my responsibility while Tom was gone. It was also my job to get someone to fill in at the Asuza storefront mission. I'd been taking Janice along with me to go there to preach, another phase of work I had acquired by his absence. Tom and I had been exchanging pulpits there and at Covina.

One Sunday while Tom was gone Ernie Friend helped me dedicate Janice. "Friend" was an appropriate name for him, for I'd known him all my life. In the midst of the dedication ceremony with our last offspring in his arms, he looked out at the congregation and announced, "I now dedicate this baby Janice Rae Nicholson." He'd known me as Papa's child and had forgotten to give Tom the credit for being her daddy. I said, "Wait, Ernest. It's Cunningham." Folks laughed as he restated the dedication.

Unexpected things come up as the devil seemed to want to test us. Tom called from a hospital in Little Rock, Arkansas, to tell me, "They took me off the bus with an acute appendicitis and put me to bed. But I refused to be operated on! I'm trusting God," he told me. We both felt this was the best way to deal with illness if God so led us, and we gave Him the glory for a miracle. Even though we both agreed that God also directs doctors and nurses, Tom evidently did not feel that was the answer for him with that particular illness.

After hanging up the phone, a pang of frustration and despair encompassed me. "Children," I announced, "that was Daddy and he's very sick."

"Will he die?" Phyllis asked.

"Yes, if we don't pray, he may die," I answered.

Loren disappeared behind the couch—perhaps he felt like hiding to cry, but he came out later to be with us to petition God on our knees. After that I got on the phone to call the saints to a special prayer meeting. Tom would have been touched if he'd seen so many in prayer for him for six long hours on his behalf as they came and united in prayer in the church.

Later that night Mike Martin, the head deacon, came to say, "We'll send you to him, Sister Cunningham, if you want to go." I thanked him with, "No, God can hear us here. It's all I can do."

At midnight I interrupted our prayer meeting and called a pastor in Little Rock—one I knew by reputation only. "Brother Gotcher, my husband is in the hospital there. He had to be taken off the bus with acute appendicitis. Will you please go and anoint him with oil and pray?"

"Yes, sister. I'd be more than glad to."

Later he called and said, "Tom's all right. He's resting. The nurse says she doesn't know why he's resting so well, but his appendix may have ruptured." Yet at our end of the line we knew and rejoiced. Victory was ours in Jesus! We all praised God and the saints all went home to bed.

Ernie Friend continued to help me with all the church services as well as to help organize for the Christ's Ambassador's banquet which Tom had aspired to plan. My husband did not stay out of its planning, but cued us in as to what he wanted done from his hospital bed in Arkansas. Ernie and I chose the best facility we could find—the Congregational Church at Pasadena.

During that week while I anxiously awaited Tom's recovery and his return home, a man came to our door with vegetables to sell. He spoke in friendly terms and then, without any hesitation, he said: "Sister Cunningham, I dreamed about your husband last night."

"What was your dream?" I asked—hoping he'd give some bit of encouragement.

"I dreamed he came home in a coffin."

For a moment I let a sinking feeling overtake me, but then I turned from the door proclaiming, "Well, brother, we're praying!" With that he turned and walked down the sidewalk.

That night while the children and I were praying earnestly again, I asked, "Lord, now give ME a dream."

God granted my request. The next morning at breakfast I said to Phyllis and Loren, "Children, I had a dream last night." Two sets of little ears perked up. I told them, "I dreamed Daddy came home in his pajamas!"

A few days later Tom called from Dallas. "I've been bumped off the plane to give place to the military, but I'll be coming in on the train." When the train arrived, the children and I went in our Plymouth to meet him at the Pomona railroad station. He'd had a berth on the train. In his haste to get off, he'd pulled his pants up over his pajamas! My dream had become a reality.

The saints at Covina were thrilled to have Tom back. We'd never been saturated with more love and concern than we had there; it seemed too good to continue.

Our Utopia lost its stability when a call came from Superintendent Woodworth that made it necessary to think of leaving. "Tom, will you go over to West Los Angeles to get the church there back together and get the church into the Assemblies? There's a split in the congregation."

That was a real challenge—our cup of tea had always been pioneering. "But, Tom," I pointed out, "Covina is a fine place to raise children." For that moment I had my priorities mixed up. Parents should be concerned about their little ones, but the promises of God cover our offspring. Back in the Old Testament when Israel left the bondage of Egypt, God had said He'd take care of His people—"you and your little ones." We knew He'd care for ours, too, so we promised to go and see the job.

That Tuesday night we managed to slip away from our charge. We didn't like the picture we saw in West Los Angeles. Such a contrast to Covina! Tom and I both determined that we should ignore the aspirations of such men like Walter Stubblefield, one of the deacons, who proclaimed, "Brother Cunningham, here is a fine carpenter who could help us build more rooms." Getting out of there as fast as I could, I snorted to my husband, "They can have it!" Tom agreed and told them, You better not consider us. We like where we are."

Back at Covina that next Wednesday after our regular service, the telephone rang. Brother Henry Gotcher, our neighboring pastor told Tom, "Hello, Pastor. You were elected."

"We what?" Tom exclaimed. We were so upset, we could hardly get back to sleep. Our election became a private burden of prayer for both Tom and me. "We'll think better in the morning," I told him.

The next day we drove across L.A. to Sister Brown's home. She was a youth leader who hadn't resigned during the split. The split was caused by some who had been fighting against joining the Assemblies and Tom had the job of discerning who rightfully owned the church. Frank Smith, the church secretary, had the books, and not wanting to offend those of the opposition would not allow anyone to see them.

Tom visited Frank to ask to read the minutes from the business meeting, but he didn't want to let the records out of his hands. Tom finally suggested a compromise to him, "You hold the books. Just let me see them."

Sure enough, the books proved that the majority had voted to join the Assemblies and they legally owned the church building. The lawyer that had been called in to settle the issue was dismissed. The first hurdle was cleared and the conflict was subdued.

Tom and I had to go back to Covina and tell the congregation about our new burden and how we had to accept the challenge, despite all their love and kindness. In my farewell speech I made the mistake of saying, "Over on the west side there's room for growth that Covina will never have. The orange groves surrounding the town just won't let it grow."

Mike Martin, the deacon who'd offered to send me to Tom when he was sick, spoke up, "Sister Cunningham, you're so wrong."

Time has told the winner of the argument. God sent His servants to build a bigger church and the orange groves were cut down for commercial and residential properties. After World War II such expansion took place all over Southern California and Tom and I were a part of some of it.

21

WEST LOS ANGELES

At the end of World War II, we went to the west side of Los Angeles to look for a house we could rent or buy. None were available. One possibility remained—we could live in the evangelist's quarters, a small place above the platform at the church, which could be reached only by a very steep staircase without a rail to hold onto. The area directly at the top of the stairs would be our living room. Behind the partition we planned to form a combined kitchen and bedroom. Making the best of it, we moved in. A short time later a small rental house seven blocks down the boulevard became available for one year, and only if Tom painted it inside and out—a lot of "onlys."

I knew it was seven blocks from the church for I had counted them when I was learning to ride the new bike we had given Phyllis for her twelfth birthday. A fourteen-block ride to the church and back—it became my bike-riding training course.

Living on Olympic Boulevard, a six-lane thoroughfare between downtown Los Angeles and the coast, was not too safe, especially because Janice was only a year-and-a-half old and we had no fence to keep her in. One day I heard car horns honking, and looked out to see the cars stopping for my little toddler. I realized the true meaning of the old song which says: "Angels watching over me." Angels had to be watching over little Jannie that day.

At the end of the year we were all glad to move from that dangerous place back to the upstairs church apartment. Tom created a second bedroom by cutting a small door to the attic. No one could enter except by crawling through. He built a ladder to the new flooring where he'd laid 2 × 12's across the joists to make a twelve foot area. This gave us plenty of space for another bed and our overflow, which was overwhelming us, as we had no closets, garage or storage places of any kind. Storing our overflow in this new area proved to be bad for our woolens. The moths found and ruined Tom's overcoat and my coat with fur trim.

That upstairs apartment became Janice's growing place. She'd tumble down the stairs almost as often as she'd walk down to go out to play behind the church. Normally an early riser, one morning she came back upstairs calling, "Mama, Rose Ann's grandpa is in a pretty bed down there in the church!" One of our elderly saints had died and the body was in a coffin awaiting the funeral. This was our two-year-old's first acquaintance with death.

One day as I crawled out on to the joists beyond our temporary bedroom to find some of the things we had stored away in boxes, Janice unknowingly followed after me. Suddenly, hearing a muffled cry behind me, I looked back and saw my baby girl had missed her footing and knocked a building board off the ceiling. She was dangling into the sanctuary between two joists. Her little arms were all that held her suspended in the air. The center joists happened to be closer together than the rest. Otherwise, she'd have fallen eight or ten feet down on to the pulpit below! Again angels were watching; God spared her from harm.

Another conflict was added to our many trials. Some of the folks decided they wanted freedom with no organization. They up and left the organized church. Bill Enos might have been a spokesman for many of them when he came back apologetically saying to us, "I should never have left. This is my church, where our children were married, where we dedicated our grandchildren and held funeral services for our parents. I'm here to stay." He became President of the Men's Bible Class, and a Godly, endowed leader for all the charity functions of the church. He led our Sunday School picnics at the mountain camps for the FOURTH OF JULY picnics where most of the church folks, the pastor's family included, went to fellowship for the whole week.

Sister Banning, the founder of the church now called Faith Tabernacle, had angelic-like qualities. Although she wasn't there anymore, her acceptance made it better for me, too, as a lady preacher. I appreciated her the entire nine and a half years our family spent there.

Some of the American boys returning from the battlefields of Europe and the Far East came home with embittered hearts. War does that—softens or hardens hearts. Much prayer went up on their behalf and God gave us ability to minister the Gospel with anointing and love for them so that many of them later became deacons and leaders in the church.

The Sunday School increased to record numbers because Tom bought a couple of buses and Alma Tate and Wes Burroughs drove them to pick up the Sunday School children.

A twenty-four hour prayer chain was initiated. It didn't go on as long as the Moravian prayer chain of 100 years that started the flame for missionary endeavors around the world, but ours did continue for weeks. Our first attempt at a missionary convention lasted for days, so that folks had plenty of time to think about what was needed to fulfill the mandate to "carry the Gospel into all the world." Outstanding missionaries like Charles Greenaway, Andrew Hargrave and Paul Bruton, Sr. came from their fields in Africa and Alaska wearing silken robes or fur hats and moccasins and sharing awesome stories of their adventures in the mission field.

An annex was under construction beyond the north wall of the church. A sliding glass door could be opened wide enough for a jeep to be driven from the outside right into the annex, which still had not been sealed or walled in from the auditorium. Tom got the bright idea of borrowing a jeep from the display room in Santa Monica with the thought that we'd buy it. Faith in action! Driving it through the sliding doorway, he took it into the auditorium to the space in front of the pulpit. He'd forewarned the congregation by saying, "You'll see something tomorrow night that you've never seen before!" True! How many have ever seen a jeep in church? That vehicle was purchased and sent to Africa where it was used to help build some thirty churches.

A vision for missions was established through that experience. There our own son Loren received his call along with several others. He'd saved up thirty dollars to have a painter, Earl Scheib, paint his car, but God moved Loren to give it all to the missions offering. Later he came into the study to announce to his father, "Dad, I've been called to be a missionary." Tom did not discourage it, but after Loren left the room he fell flat on his face and cried as if his heart would break. Tom knew what sacrifices missionaries made — living far away from their families, facing disease, loneliness and the strange customs of other cultures. But before he got up he had given his son back to God. Many times we had dedicated Loren and the girls to the Lord, but his decision to become a missionary was something we were not exactly prepared for. Yet our love for souls abroad caused us to say triumphantly, "God's will be done!"

In 1947, while we were still living in the attic, I helped pay for gas so the children and I could share a long, tiring three-day-ride with friends who were going back east. It turned out to be a bad deal. After we'd paid our twenty five dollars we found that there would be two additional riders we hadn't known about. Our friend and her little daughter were to share the back seat with Phyllis and me. Loren, so small he could hardly see out the front window, sat in the front with the two men who took turns driving. The men smoked and stopped occasionally for another drink of beer. I had tried to back out when I discovered the two extra men were going, but was told I could not. Such a miserable, never-to-be-forgotten three days! In western Oklahoma the children and I got out and took a bus the rest of the way.

After our two weeks revival in Arkansas we rode a bus two days to Monroe, Louisiana, to help Tom who was using his vacation time to hold a revival there for Pastor Waldon. Tom had asked me to come help him on the last week and to return home with him rather than travel with Cecil who was heading west and had room for us.

While riding the bus to Monroe we saw the reason for the riots which eventually took place in Mississippi. The bus driver was so rude to the blacks I could not help but have a few words with him, even though I feared that I would be put off the bus.

We spent the last night praying for those seeking the Holy Spirit. By midnight I was so worn out after praying and preaching the sermon; the bed looked so good. Then Tom said, "We have to load up and go to Texas tonight. We had three days without rest. Before we reached home again, I developed an illness which kept me in bed for months. A pain around my heart proved to be a blood clot — I learned its medical name was "thrombosis." For the first months of my illness I lay in bed in my attic room, then Tom borrowed a trailer house which he parked in the back yard of the church so I could stay there. One of the children always slept with me in the trailer's second bed. Whenever I'd have a sinking spell, they would go to the window and call out, "Dad, Mama needs you!"

Wrestling that malady from early fall through the winter and on into spring, I was able to walk only a few feet on my own. On one of those days, I was out at the building site sitting on the lumber pile and watching the carpenters build the Sunday School annex. One of the men told me about his wife having a blood clot in her leg. "The doctor said to put heat on it so it would break up and dissolve," he told me. So the very next morning I noticed a knot as big as a walnut puffed up on the vein in my lower thigh. "Tom, look!" I said. I had my remedy, though, for Mr. Willingham had already told me what the doctor prescribed for problems such as this. "Tom, go get me an electric heating pad," I told him and he did as I asked. The heat did its work; the knot on my thigh broke and left a big spot which spread until it finally cleared up. That was the last of that sort of heart trouble, but my nerves broke after that.

During the move into the annex I overdid my strength again. I was so excited about having a place so clean and easy to reach. No more living in a trailer house! No more climbing stairs! Our newly-built home with three bedrooms was made for would-be Sunday School rooms, with a kitchen which would become the church's dinner preparation place later on.

At the time, it seemed my nerves had completely broken. I felt that if I did not try hard to keep quiet, I'd simply lose my mind. I'd find it was no time for me to go to church, for I could not stand crowds. A sign was put on our door: "NO VISITORS." Sleep seemed to escape me, but walking the floor was not the cure. Someone had suggested, "If you hang your head over the edge of the bed, it'll help the blood flow more freely," but that didn't help either. Four hours was a regular night's sleep for me. I was afraid to use the sleeping pills Tom got. It was also against my faith training. Papa would not take a pill even for pain relief.

While up in a cabin in the mountains with an elderly sister as my nurse, I got alone with God. Under the tall pines I prayed in desperation and one day I heard God's voice again: "Child, there are some things people can help you with." He seemed to be so very close to me and I felt His love and concern. Not wanting to lose my divine healing faith I'd always had, I was made to understand that God was approving my faith in miracles, but also He would not condemn other means of healing if I didn't have miracle faith.

I told Tom when he came to get me to take me home and what the Lord had made me know out under the tall pines. It's letting means and methods come between us and God which is wrong. God first, then whatever is needed as our help, receive it. If no miracle comes, then means — whatever we feel are the right means, for means can be proffered which are not right for our need. God will lead and will answer if we hold out to accept as from God.

"Take me to a doctor," I told Tom.

Whatever the pills or shot had in them, they straightened out my nerves and I was able to be back in church and do my housework.

Sitting in front of the big picture window, I'd pray for those passing by and plead the blood of Christ over them. God gave me such a burden for souls then. My love for missions increased. I watched Mexican, Blacks — some crying, others laughing or fighting. I prayed for them and also prayed, "God, give me a new burden for people, even though I can't stand to be around people right now." Although I felt I had to be alone at that time, I got a vision for a deeper ministry than I'd ever had before — not a vision of fanfare, pulpiteering, or being in front on stage, but simply of becoming a soul burdened for the lost. Because of that time of seeming conflict, I actually received a deepening of my spiritual awareness which later enabled me to reach out in child-like faith to touch a cripple and declare, "In Jesus' name — Be whole!" And I could put my arms around an old drunk as he knelt in one of my evangelistic meetings, and pray for him with real love for a lost soul. After seven months, I could finally say with David the Psalmist, "It was good for me that I was afflicted." David's reasons and mine were the same — as he had, I'd also learned to know and love God more, and to love souls for whom He died with a greater love and concern.

The summer of 1948 came and the children and I again went back to the mid-west where I was called to preach. There Loren received his call to preach. It came on a Monday night. I dismissed our revival to go to the C.A. Rally where I was to be speaker — for youth to say "Amen to God's Call." Loren was the last to get up from the altar. Finding me, his face was smeared with dust and tears as he said, "Mama, God called me to preach!"

Patting his shoulders, I answered, "That's good, son. Obey the Lord."

He had just turned thirteen. I encouraged him then, as his Dad did later on. My son promised me that he would "try out" in my revival one week night, so I bought him a pair of new shoes. When he asked, "Why shoes?" I quoted Isaiah 52:7 to him: "How beautiful on the mountains are the FEET of them that preach the gospel, that bring good tidings." He may have been barefooted.

That fall, back in Los Angeles, God opened the door for us to preach to the Jews. All those around Los Angeles ever seemed to talk about was how Hitler had killed six million Jews in the "bloody holocaust." We got permission to speak, and the merchants said we could entertain outside for one hour each Saturday night when the street was blocked off by the city of Ocean Park, and rows of seats were placed for the Jewish community to come and sit on. We used that time as opportunity to preach to them. That was our outdoor cathedral!

I took the Christ's Ambassadors and their instruments from church. Tom's burden was to study and pray in order to get his message for the Sunday A.M. service. The singing and music was appreciated by the half of the crowd that faced us; the other half stubbornly kept their backs turned to us. A rabbi, always present in his long overcoat, would continuously admonish his people, "Do not change your beliefs!" When I spoke, the audience reacted unconventionally. Some spat at me, others interrupted by rudely asking such questions as, "If God really loves us, why did Hitler kill six million of us?" To those who asked about the slaughter I tried to answer satisfactorily by quoting Psalm 69:21. "In my thirst, they gave me vinegar to drink. Let their table become a snare." I told them, "Ever since your ancestors delivered Jesus up to be crucified by the Romans, your people have experienced many troubles."

One night, a young Jewish gentleman from Israel came to me to ask questions. He began with an introduction. "I've just returned from Israel, and there are lots — what do you call them? — giving out New Testaments."

I said, "You mean missionary evangelists? That's great!"

"Why do you believe Jesus is the Messiah?" was his direct question. I read Isaiah 7:14 to him as the rabbi looked on. When I came to the word "Immanuel" in the verse, I asked, "Rabbi, what does the word 'Immanuel' mean in Hebrew?"

"God with us," he answered.

To that I replied, "You said it!"

In that fall of 1948 it seemed to be the time for the Jews, as God touched many of their hearts during those open block street meetings in Ocean Park. A couple of Jewish missions were opened then within a few blocks of our open air "cathedral." Jews for Jesus began to make themselves known in and around Los Angeles. One of our Assemblies was eventually turned over to the Jewish people who were coming to believe in Jesus as their Messiah, and we often visited their services. How they worshiped! Such spirit they had as they sang and danced so jubilantly to the name of Yeshua! Their roots for worship went back (as the Gentiles must also) to the time of David, Solomon and Ezra.

Ministry was also started to the down-and-outers in the skid-row section of Los Angeles. Frosty Foster came from Oklahoma

City to open a mission and I agreed to preach there once. After a hundred hungry derelicts got inside, the door was shut. The mad scramble was on! Men rushed for the front seats. I thought, Maybe some of our churches ought to go to dishing out beans! The Lord blessed the man who tried to lead those men in singing. God anointed me to preach to the crowd, but one fellow drew a fist as I was dealing one-on-one with the men afterwards. Time to give up mission work—let Frosty have it!—I decided right then and there. Yet we continued to pray for them and send pies for Christmas and Thanksgiving dinners. There is no end to the work God wants each of us to do!

22

MR. MISSIONS IS CALLED

Our tabernacle underwent a remodeling. We polished and shined the hardwood, stripped off the old dark paint on the lower wall as well as scraping, sanding and recovering the theatre seats. An upholsterer finished all 300 seats in a beautiful leather-like material. Faith Tabernacle took on a look of splendor.

Across the front on the wall behind the pulpit a picture of Christ told the world what we had come to proclaim: His Good News. Once when the two big doors were opened, a traveler stopped by and told us, "I had to come and take a closer look at your picture of Jesus." That puts down the notion that pictures of the Lord might be classified as "graven images."

At one New Year's Eve watchnight service we rejoiced as one soul prayed through at the midnight hour in the middle of that one long aisle. Just as the bells began to ring and the horns started to blow all over that part of Los Angeles, our seeker found the Lord's acceptance. Along with the new year, a new Christian was born.

During a Memorial Sunday evening service, I was preaching about Naaman, the leper who refused to wash in the Jordan River to cleanse his leprosy. I noticed Dr. Stanley Woodard come through the door and sit in a far left hand seat. I knew my message was for him, and had hoped that he'd be there. He was late, but I believed that the Lord sent him, so I went over what I had already preached. He'd been working late in one of the big city's hospitals as an anesthesiologist. A confessed agnostic, he did not believe in the hereafter—no heaven, no hell. For six years we'd prayed with his wife, Edwina, for his salvation. When the altar call was made at the close of that service, the doctor left his seat. Taking the long way around to the front, as though he wished all the crowd to see, he passed row after row of folks. The congregation was not standing, but Doctor did not seem to be ashamed at all as he walked the many steps around all the seats and down the far side. He didn't even reach the altar, but fell at the second row of seats. By the time I got there, he was crying like a child. I handed him a handkerchief and he prayed through to his assurance of salvation. That good doctor is still working in his medical career and singing in the church choir. He and Edwina raised their three children for God.

Once I had to be hospitalized to have a lump removed from my breast. Dr. Woodard was not on the case, but when I awoke the next morning he was the first and only one at my bedside. I looked up and asked, "Doctor, why? You work downtown."

He smiled and answered, "Oh, I just came by to make sure that they did it right for you! It wasn't malignant, we're glad to say!" He grinned and I praised God. What a friend!

Our Sunday School was taught by teachers like Mother Cain who taught two generations and then resigned after she was past eighty. As a special tribute we held "Mother Cain's Day" which brought folks from miles around to honor her.

We also started a Christian day school, patterned after the one Pastor Erickson had at Maywood Assembly. Brunette Parker became the principal over the one hundred and twenty-five children who registered. The Sunday School buses found a dual role then —they began bringing the children into school throughout the week as well as on Sundays. The school became a feeder for our Sunday School and church as well. Christian day schools were new then, but the concept soon began to spread nationwide.

Four-year-old Janice had become a regular in children's church which was held at the same hour as the youth class. We scheduled them at the same time so that both groups would meet in our after-service downstairs in the auditorium. Mary Lou, the children's church leader, asked the children for prayer requests one day. Jannie raised her hand.

"Yes, Janice?"

"Please pray for my daddy," she requested. "He's lost the victory."

No doubt our baby girl had heard her daddy bemoaning someone or something that would "cause him to lose his victory," as the old saying went. That soon became a great joke around the church.

Janice's first lessons in the three "R's" came while she attended Baptist Christian day school because ours was not yet in operation. The year after that, she came to Faith School and skipped from second to third grade.

Faith Tabernacle's orchestra and choir had become the life blood of the church. Norbert Smith and others accompanied Tom on the guitar. Phyllis played her accordion when she wasn't at the piano for Martha or Edwina who were the main pianists. Loren played his trumpet and I'd blow my sax. Feet would get a-dancing and hands a-clapping when all those strings, reeds, trombones, tambourines began to get into the swing of exuberant Gospel songs. Jannie, as little as she was, would often pick on her ukulele. Children were welcome to join in, for at Faith Tabernacle we played just about anything that could make music for God. Our choir didn't need robes to get them in harmony! Girls dressed decently then and they didn't need cover-ups either!*

David the Psalmist said, "Praise the Lord with stringed instruments and organs! Praise Him in the dance!" Occasionally our people did this, too, when someone felt like praising God, but no one ever directed people to dance as if it were ritual. The Spirit had to lead them. Our crowds grew because our services had life. People came just to hear the songs and praises and then they stayed for the testimonies, sermons and finally many came to the altar in search of fulfillment in Christ. Souls sought Jesus!

After our two-year stay in the Sunday School annex, we had to move or pay taxes on our living quarters. Besides, the annex had been built for Sunday School expansion and we were filled to

---

*Loyd and Juanita Myers led the orchestra and choir. We regretted the loss for us when they got a church in Iowa.

capacity. Records show that the average attendance then was just around three hundred, but we were constantly working for more.

Tom and I took notice that a big white frame house on the corner of Sawtelle and Richland was sporting a FOR SALE sign on the lawn. One morning I walked outside to where Roy Philips was helping Tom finish a cement sidewalk in front of our living quarters and said, "Tom, let's buy that house."

"With what?" he retorted.

"With faith. Roy here will lend us the $500 to hold it."

"What for?" Roy asked, just getting the fringes of the conversation and hearing his name mentioned.

"For the house, Roy. The one on Sawtelle. We'll get our furniture and car mortgaged for the down payment. But we need your $500 to hold it till then."

"Okay," he said. "Here."

I'd already phoned the realtor who'd said, "We'll shake $500 in the owner's face and see if then she'll come down to $9,000, so I sent Loren on his bike with the money as soon as Roy lent it to us. Not only did we get the $2,000 for the down payment, but we repaid Roy's $500 back too. The deal wasn't long in closing and the Cunninghams owned their first home. To us, it was a mansion. Tenting days were gone forever.

A new conflict came into our lives. Television! Folks were sitting at home watching such shows as "I Love Lucy" and "Gun Smoke" rather than coming to services. Tom and I tried to pass on what we were personally finding out — in order to not have TV run our lives, we had to consecrate that machine to its rightful place and then rededicate our time. It was meant for our use, not to rule over us. We had to learn to turn the knob to OFF!

Our beautiful house on Sawtelle was sold after only three years, due to a mistake in my own judgment. The $3,000 profit a buyer offered looked good to me. Tom was off to a Sunday School convention and the only one I had to consult was Loren who immediately exclaimed, "Sell our house?"

"But we could buy two others!" He finally got my point.

In 1955 Phyllis transferred from Southern California College in order to accompany Loren back to Springfield Central Bible

College. Loren had spent a year at U.C.L.A. while working part time at Ralph's Grocery. (Added fringe benefits to his job included cakes and fruit which he brought home because they needed to be consumed. We'd all miss those goodies!) I could no longer look for Phyllis to come home from S.C.C. on Friday nights in her little Chevy.

Janice, her dad and I watched the pair of them drive off together in the old Dodge so laden down, it looked like a wagon with it's axles dragging. Then we trudged inside the house with heavy hearts and had a cry together. Since that time, watching the three of them drive off to new horizons has been a way of life for us. Our prayers go with each of them always.

While at Faith Tabernacle Tom said to me, "Jewell, you know the Lord has placed a burning desire in my heart. I desperately want to go to Israel and walk where Jesus walked. I want to experience the Bible first-hand."

I'd seen the intensity of my husband's feelings mirrored in his eyes, but he had never let the church know his wish to fly out on the General Council's airplane called "The Ambassador" the following Monday. He'd never admit he hadn't the funds to make the trip.

The Saturday night before the planned flight, I had a dream confirming that Tom was to go. "Honey," I said to him, "I saw you going with your suitcase."

During his Sunday School class the following day Tom was announcing the next lesson when Red, the dry cleaner from downtown, interrupted him and asked, "Rabbi." (A name he jokingly called Tom.) "I thought you were going to Israel." Tom's friend had overheard him discussing the possible trip while on a visit to his shop. But Tom had never expected his words to get back to the church circle.

My husband immediately responded defensively, "I won't be going."

"Why?" Red asked.

"It's just not possible. I have no money."

The face of the Class President, Bill Enos, lit up as though he suddenly had received a great revelation of truth. "Well, if it's money you need we can change that!" And change it they did.

At the morning service, he took up the five hundred dollars needed. Because of that gift my dream took the form of reality as I saw Tom stepping off our porch with his suitcase in hand. He was to go to Springfield so he could travel on to Israel with the group of pastors on The Ambassador.

The date of Saturday July 1, 1950, was destined to be a life-changing experience for Tom. He tells the story in his own words:

"I had roamed through the streets of Old Jerusalem as any wide-eyed American tourist would. The sights were intriguing, bringing to mind many passages from the Bible.

"Returning to my hotel in the late afternoon a friend on the tour and I decided we would use the remaining portion of daylight visiting the traditional tomb of Lazarus in nearby Bethany.

"We found the Arab in charge of the tomb and while he was fumbling with the padlock to open the gate a little arab girl, about ten years of age, came up and stuck out a little up-turned bronze hand uttering an Arabic word, 'baksheesh,' meaning alms or tip. It was a very common sight for tourists in that part of the world. In fact, we had been told again and again by our guides not to give to these beggars for it would encourage them to beg more and more, making life miserable for tourists.

"If I had a heart of stone I could have turned away, for by this time the guide had the iron gate to the tomb opened and my friend was descending the stairs into it and the guide was motioning impatiently for me to follow.

"But I looked at the child. She was carrying her baby sister who was asleep with her little head on big sister's shoulder. Looking into her pleading eyes I saw traces of the dreaded eye disease that causes blindness, even to children, in that area.

"With the guide still motioning me to come on I paused long enough to take an Arab coin, worth about seven cents in American money, and drop it into her hand. She clenched her little hand, flashed a smile showing white teeth that would have done credit to any toothpaste commercial, uttered a word in Arabic that I thought was a thank you and headed off in a trot.

"I went down the stairs into the tomb, much to the relief of our guide, and later we returned to our hotel. I thought no more of the little girl while our tour group chatted and enjoyed our evening meal.

"Finally I retired to my room. Tired because of the full day, but happy for having experienced so many things. Before retiring I knelt by my bed and prayed. I besought the Lord in behalf of my family so many thousands of miles away, seeking His protection for them, etc.

"I was concluding the prayer when suddenly I thought of the little girl. I had completely dismissed her from my mind after going into the tomb. Now, as I looked into those diseased eyes again, their pleading seemed stronger than at the tomb. The little bronze hand was still extended, but this time it was not reaching for a coin worth about seven cents, but seemed to be reaching for the Bread of Life. I began to weep uncontrollably. I buried my face in my pillow, turning my face to the right, then the left, to get away from those pleading eyes.

"That night I made a vow that when I got home I would challenge my church and all others I could influence to get the message of the Gospel into all the world. That has been nearly four decades ago and I can say as Paul said before Agrippa, 'I have not been disobedient to that heavenly vision.'"

When Tom Cunningham came home from his first trip to the Holy Land, his heart was truly burdened for the lost souls across the world. In truth he became a different man. "Missions" was no longer just a word, but a ministry for him. Never one to do anything half-heartedly, he put all his fervor into preaching world evangelism to his own church and accepted from the Executive Presbytery the portfolio of Secretary of World Missions, a beginning for carrying out part of his burden for lost souls.

Covina First Assembly of God. We boasted 300, plus,
our Sunday School was the largest in the city. 1945

Tom's Men's Bible Class at Faith Tabernacle
The group helped necessitate an addition to the Sunday School facilities

Our 1st pastorate, West Fork, Arkansas, 1932-33. Same church, but different car and an "Enlarged Tom," 1969.

Arp Assembly of God, Arp, Texas. This is the 3rd building after the blacksmith shop. Tom preached at their 50th Anniversary in 1983.

A small, privately owned church in Monterey, California. Our pastorate, 1936-37.

Our last pastorate, First Assembly of God, Long Beach, California.

23

LONG BEACH CALL

After selling our first home and leasing a place in west Los Angeles for over a year, we picked out a house to buy on a nice street with friendly neighbors on Armacost Street, a better part of West L.A. Tom, Jannie and I pitched in to re-do the place, hoping that finally we had found a home for life. When Phyllis and Loren would come back from college in Springfield, their rooms would be ready, but Loren was still going to have sleeping quarters in the garage. One day when Tom looked at Loren's picture the realization hit him that his son was gone. How he wept tears of remorse that day. "Oh, Jewell," he sobbed, "how many times I've been too busy to go places with my only son. Now he's gone for good!"

One Saturday not long after that the two of us were out calling on Sunday School absentees. The people always welcomed us so graciously that I said to Tom, "Let's stay here the rest of our lives." We'd been elected indefinitely and the folks made us feel so loved.

My husband's blue-grey eyes relayed to me a message that said I was not going to like what he was about to say. "Jewell, I must tell you that Superintendent Woodworth has asked if I'd let him appoint me to fill the former pastor's term at Long Beach First Assembly. I promised him I'd look into it next Sunday."

"You what?" I cried. What a jolt! "Tom, I know that I've had times of discouragement and have let you know about them—like how, in my evangelistic zeal, I couldn't take the pressure of going in slow motion at times. But I really do like it here. I've even learned to ignore the fact that some of the deacons aren't "with me" because I'm a lady preacher, but there's never been any spoken disagreements. I'm so happy now that we're settled in our home with the new bedspreads and matching curtains I made, and . . ." Tom wasn't listening.

That following Sunday found us at the First Assembly of God in Long Beach where we were "spying out the land." The city and the climate were great, but the church didn't seem as desirable. Their Sunday School Superintendent had forewarned us about a split in the congregation. "Those who stayed in the church have been hurt and wounded in spirit," he told us. "They seem to have no forgiveness left in their hearts. The ninety members who went off to the other side of town not only took the preacher, but also some of the valuable fixtures and furniture. What they left behind was a huge mortgage, so the church had to be refinanced." With all this in mind, Tom and I knelt to pray in the empty church basement and then continued to pray when we were home again on Armicost Street, L.A.

Challenge called! We both felt God was asking us to make the move. Somehow we had to announce to our dear friends at Faith Tabernacle that we'd be leaving. It had been a place where we'd experienced both trials and conflicts, yet neither could outweigh the magnificent triumphs. Leaving was difficult for the children too. All three had grown up in Faith Tabernacle. Janice was still a little girl—not quite in her teens. All four of us—Loren was off with his quartet at the time—had to have our cry.

Love and concern had come in abundance during our nine-and-a-half-year stay. The list of those we cared for and those who cared for us would encompass nearly everyone there, but I knew I'd especially miss Sister Stapp and Sister Stella who'd been my burden bearers in times of affliction. Jannie would especially miss Naomi Smith who'd been her faithful baby sitter in her childhood days while I was bedfast.

The day came for the all-day farewell service with a potluck dinner of Southern cooking out on the patio. While sitting on the long porch of the annex with some of the ladies, a terrorizing shout came to my ears, "Janice fell through the ceiling!" By the time I ran across to the auditorium and through the side door, she was lying in the church aisle in a semi-conscious state, but still breathing! Grabbing my baby up in my arms, I carried her over to the divan near the front entrance. I prayed. How I prayed! Janice came to and the Lord assured me she'd be all right.

"What happened?" I asked. Someone told me the story: "Janice was leading some other youngsters up into the attic. She knew the crawl door was there and had gone through it to walk on the rafters." She often did this, for she knew the place well, recalling the times when she lived in the upstairs apartment. But that day, jumping cross the rafters, she'd knocked off a piece of ceiling and had fallen through, catching hold of a chandelier as she fell. It swung her out past the row of sharp-backed seats into the aisle — a miracle that saved her from having any broken bones! The incident served not only as a going-away memory for us and our friends, but it is still a reminder to Janice today, as a mother of three boys, that children can be very adventuresome!

During the afternoon service the folks all marched down the aisle to shake hands and bid us "Godspeed." The Cunninghams lined up in front, except for Loren who was involved in evangelism with a quartet he'd put together.

A fleece I'd put out to the Lord the first Sunday we'd gone to Long Beach was covered. I'd asked Him then, "If it's Your will for us to be here, give us another nice home to buy." Mr. Graham, a realtor and a member of the church, took us to see a home at 3635 Cerritos in the Bixby Knolls area, the very best part of Long Beach. Without even looking inside the three-bedroom Spanish bungalow, we declared, "We'll take it!" Loren could finally have an inside bedroom — he'd always had to act like an orphan child because he'd been housed in a garage or something of the sort nearly all of his growing-up days. However, having that kind of living quarters surely helped condition him for what was in store for him later in life. The Spanish-type bungalow in Bixby Knolls became home to us for $12,000. In 1985 a real estate broker told us, "It's a bargain for $145,000 and it's for sale!"

We loved hearing the Methodist Church bell peal on Sunday mornings; Janice's school was close enough for her to walk each day. Things were good for us in the natural realm, but little did I know I was in for a real spiritual conflict.

At Faith Tabernacle I'd been honored as the second pastor, but at Long Beach I ran smack into conflict. Even though Tom hadn't told me what had occurred in an early board meeting, as surely as all true ministers of Jesus Christ can discern the Spirit, I could feel oppression. I could not understand, though, just what the bad spirit was that kept binding me. One Sunday night I was preaching (It had been our custom for me to preach in the evening services.) when I had to stop the message and cry, "Turn me loose! Someone is sitting on me!" I could have mentioned the name, but God would not allow it.

God was saving souls at Sunday night services for "His word will not return void." After a month or so Tom finally admitted the problem. "Jewell," he said in a sorrowful tone, "you need to know that the board voted and decided that I should be the only preacher. They have voted against your having any part in the pulpit."

"What?" I cried.

"It's nothing against you personally." But their ultimatum broke both my body and my spirit.

At a board meeting shortly after moving to First Assembly, Tom outlined his three pronged program. A strong emphasis on evangelism. We're with you Brother Cunningham. A strong emphasis on Christian education to train those won that they might engage in Christian service. Again, "We're with you, Brother Cunningham. And a strong emphasis on missions. At this statement one brother objected saying, "Remember our heavy mortgage payments." Tom said, "I will not forget this and I promise you that no family in the church will give more, according to their ability to give, than the Cunningham family.

Though one or two had reservations they all accepted the program. What a time of victory! Remember, the church had gone through a split and many good people were lost to the church. However, the remaining five months of 1955, the church gave more to missions than the whole church had given for the entire year of 1954. In 1956 the missions giving increased over 1955 by 34%. The giving for 1957, our last full year at the church increased over 1956 by 52%. And during that year we paid 50% more than we were required to pay on the principal of the heavy mortgage.

Mr. Orla Kern, treasurer of the church for many years came to me again and again saying, "Brother Cunningham, I don't know where the money is coming from, but we've never been a day late in one of the big payments. God is sending it in."

Tom didn't seem to understand how deeply I was hurt. I wondered if I should somehow try to push open the door that had been shut. How was I going to unburden my soul? I became physically ill and took to my bed. My heart had a new ailment, different from the kind that had put me in bed for so long at Faith Tabernacle. My physical heart began to beat irregularly from over-anxiety. Its rhythm was out of whack and so was I. I couldn't do my work or take care of the house.

Tom had to get Janice off to school and still keep the regular services going, as well as call on the sick and absentees of the church. Phyllis came home after her graduation and occupied her twin bed in Janice's room weekends and evenings. In my pitiful state, it was so good to have her back home. She became our helper in the educational and music departments in church. She attended the University of Southern California and worked part-time as a secretary for Howard Hughes' company. Finishing up her master's and doing secretarial work, she didn't have much time for social life.

Finally, after resting and getting my body and nerves restored, I was able to get up and around again. In time I got over my ailment and Tom eventually told the deacons, "Jewell's been more successful at getting souls saved than I have been." Finally, we both triumphed. Tom won his battle to expand the missions outreach and soon mission giving doubled. In no time the heavy mortgage was easily met. When at last they accepted me as a preacher, I felt like Job. "Should we receive good and not evil from the Lord?" (Job 2:10)

We took Janice and her friends for a picnic at Disneyland on her eleventh birthday. Unable to pay the price of picnicking in-side, we found a spot just outside to spread our lunch. It was the first but not the last time for us to see Disneyland. In years to come we would have the prices for the rides and all the enjoyment with Janice and our other kids — even our grandkids later on.

For the first time Tom had some easy days. The Sunday School and all facets of ministry were expanding, so he even found time to go golfing with some of the men. The students and staff of Southern California College, including Dr. Harrison, the college President, came often to our Sunday services.

Tom's sermons were on doing good, and the faces of his audiences began to reflect sunshine from heaven. The clouds of despair and malice had been driven away.

A new loan had been obtained by the church, mortgaging the facilities to meet the demands of the retiring pastor. Surely that was enough to make a cloud, for it was a staggering bill to meet each month from so few. But nothing is too hard for the Lord, as was proven there in 1956 by the First Assembly of God in Long Beach, California.

While praying in the basement on our first Sunday there, I'd felt a burden for the restoration of the revival that church had known. I'd also felt the need for the healing of many hearts.

Moving from our beloved Faith Tabernacle where the folks would have plucked their eyes out for us (borrowing an exaggerated sentence from the Apostle Paul) would not be easy. That kind of love was not ours at Long Beach in the beginning. It is doubtful that anyone could have been elected unanimously there after the split had caused such internal friction.

Loren returned home after finishing two B.A. degrees at Central Bible Institute (now called "College"). He also started to attend the University of Southern California part-time to work on his masters. Meanwhile he became Assistant Coordinator of the overall Educational and Musical Departments of our church and Phyllis worked as his assistant. He had three choirs — children, juniors and adults.

Jannie helped in youth ministries and in children's church. When she was nominated C.A.'s secretary-treasurer, I was afraid I'd end up having to do the work, so I insisted on her withdrawal. Mothers! Still not even a teen-ager, she was willing and eager to serve but I hindered her election. We all participated in the music of the church. As a family we were very much involved and happy in the service of the Lord together.

Such fun we had — Halloween parties for the kids, beach parties for the youth, grunion huntings and clam bakes, parties in our home, marriages and backyard homemade ice cream gatherings and feeds. The church gave a birthday party for Tom and even had a surprise twenty-fifth wedding anniversary celebration for Tom and me. I'd have dressed up in better finery if I'd have known what they were up to. Loren performed the ceremony, Phyllis sang accompanied by Janice. Carl and Vi Scarbrough presented us with a silver tea service on behalf of the church. Such kind, loving and good folks to work with!

One day an unwelcome visitor arrived. Looking up, I indicated to him that the pastor wasn't in. He pulled a long envelope from his front shirt pocket and never budged from the spot on which he stood. Over and over he insisted through the glass, "I want to see the pastor," so I finally sent him around to the side door.

Once inside, he followed me into the office, saying as he went past the altar and glanced up at our large picture of Christ, "I haven't been in a church since my mother took me as a baby."

"What's hindered you?" I asked.

"Too many years in jail and then in the pen."

"What in the world did you do?" I inquired.

"At first I was in for stealing a bike, then one thing led to another. It didn't bother me a bit to knock someone on the head for his money. I'm out on parole now from San Quentin." By that time we were inside the office. Ignoring my first offer to have a seat by the door, he brazenly walked over and sat down behind my chair at Loren's desk. My mind sent up a prayer — I pled the blood — as he continued on with words that I began to realize could be a threat. "Like I said, I don't mind bashing anyone on the head for money. I'm not going back to that place! I need money!" Quite a threat when he was sitting right behind me!

After my secret earnest prayer, I'd felt I should keep him talking while I decided what to do. The Lord told me to empty my purse for him. Some dollars were still tucked inside, those I had leftover after I'd spent part of my birthday gift. A spark of compassion arose in me. "go pay your rent and get your meals across the street," I told him. "Tell the manager to charge it to the pastor." Somehow I wanted to help him. "Why are you so down on society? It wouldn't be such a jungle as you say it is if you were on the right side of life." Picking up Loren's photo from the desk, I handed it to him. "My son's about your age. He doesn't think life's a jungle. No doubt he's had better opportunities than you, but the Lord is no respecter of persons. Mack, Jesus loves you as you are. If you will give your heart to Him . . ."

Just then the door swung open and Tom came hurrying through to his office. "Honey," I called, hoping he'd take notice of the frantic note in my tone of voice, "this man's in need of prayer. Well . . ." But Tom continued on, hollering back, "You seem to be doing okay. I have to go."

Have you ever felt totally alone and had to depend totally on the Almighty? Gathering my wits I finally got the young fellow down on his knees. The last thing I said to him was, "Promise to come to church tomorrow."

"I promise" were his words to me.

The next day I scanned the faces in the congregation. The intruder was nowhere to be seen. In the afternoon I heard over the radio that the Baptist Church nearby had been broken into the night before and some equipment had been stolen. Someone at the boarding house where he lived had been hurt. I phoned the police to tell them to pick the man up and gave them his address. Justice must prevail. I hoped and prayed that he would remember the words of my prayer. The last I heard of him he was on death's row for even more serious crimes.

"Lord, will there be few saved?" The disciples' question was answered. "Strive to enter in at the straight gate: for many, I say unto you, will seek to enter in, and shall not be able." (Luke 13:24) Many will seek to enter and not be able. Why? Our will decides for us, as did that young man's.

In February, 1958, as Tom sat on the platform in the sanctuary of First Assembly of God, Long Beach (now known as Christian Life Church), the large choir, under the direction of our son Loren, was singing a beautiful song.

Everything seemed to be going well. In early February during our annual business meeting the membership had heard the reports of the year before, accepted the same with appreciation, transacted normal business and adopted a program that Tom presented with an 80% vote. Though the twenty-nine months he and I had pastored the church had brought some problems, now things seemed to be moving ahead. Often, just when things are going so well and the Lord's servants feel so "settled in," the Lord interrupts. This was no exception. Tom recalls what took place on that day in his own words:

"Sitting there with Bible in hand I was anxious for the choir to finish so I could bring a message to my congregation which was burning on my heart. I glanced at the beautiful pulpit for an instant and a still small voice within whispered, 'Two weeks from today you will be reading your resignation from that pulpit.' But why? Wasn't everything going well?

"However, twenty-six years in the ministry had taught me not to question the Lord. So, when the choir had finished I preached my message with all the strength I had. After the service I said nothing to my family about the message given to me.

"In March of that year our Southern California District Council of The Assemblies of God convened in Bethel Temple, 1250 Bellevue Avenue, Los Angeles. Since this was close to our North Long Beach home, I commuted each day. On the third day of this convention I walked into the foyer of that beautiful church just before the beginning of the morning session.

"A friend of mine, Rev. Paul Boyer came out of a telephone booth in the foyer. He greeted me and said, 'That was George Carmichael that I was talking to. He said you are to call him. They are ready to open a mission in Lebanon.' Eight years before, Rev. Carmichael, then Middle East Field Director for the Division of Foreign Missions of the Assemblies of God had spoken to me about accepting a missionary assignment in another area of the Middle East. I replied, 'No, I do not feel that would be the Lord's will for me, but if you ever decide to open in Lebanon, let me know.'

"I said to Paul, 'I'll call him later.' Walking away I said to myself, 'Could that be what the Lord was talking to me about?' I dismissed the thought for the time, thinking I would call Rev. Carmichael in the late afternoon.

"However, it was days later before I called Rev. Carmichael, and then it was to tell him I would not be available for the assignment. That day I was elected Assistant Superintendent of the Assemblies of God of Southern California.

"The day following his call I was driving north on the Long Beach Freeway, heading for the last day of the convention. Breezing along I approached the Atlantic Avenue overcrossing of the Freeway when that Still Small Voice spoke to me again. 'Your new position will involved you in world missions and you will continue in that for the remainder of your ministry.'

"Two weeks from the day I first heard the Voice, I read my resignation, effective April 1, 1958. That week I went to our District Office at the invitation of Rev. L. E. Halvorson, District Superintendent to discuss the assignments he would give me in my new position. During the discussion Brother Halvorson asked me what work I would prefer. I replied, 'Brother Halvorson, if you will assign me the portfolio of missions, home and foreign I will be glad to do that and carry on in other responsibilities you might assign me.'

"Rev. Halvorson was a leader who believed in delegating authority. He gave me a free hand in carrying out the work of missions in our District. Remembering the closing part of my statement, 'and carry on in other responsibilities you might assign me,' he gave me enough other duties to keep me well occupied. Something I was glad for.

"I served my District in full-time capacity for more than twenty-one years. During those years I saw our District consistently lead all other Districts of the Assemblies of God throughout the nation in missionary giving. In fact, no other district ever came near us in total giving to foreign missions.

"During those years we sent out one hundred forty-eight new missionaries to many fields of the world from Southern California. Through those years I made numerous trips to the foreign fields visiting our missionaries and ministering in many countries."

Phyllis came from college first. She had some credits from S.C.C., and it helped shorten the time. She got a job with the Hughes company and also was taking a course at the University of Southern California in Los Angeles (USC) with Loren who was going there after graduating from CBI. These made a Pair. Well, Phyllis gave me her car and got a new one. Also, she paid for me to study real estate and I went and took lessons — enough to get a license from the California Real Estate Commisioner, Fred Grisinger, and got involved in that, and it helped my feelings. I could have made money, but now I had another problem, I had to get victory over the board's opposition and now this new materialism. So, I went to God on my knees. He not only caused me to be accepted as a preacher there, but in time He gave me a broader ministry. I was having good success in real estate, but quit and preached.

Loren was asked to stay on and be the assistant to their new pastor, who had been called while we were still living in Long Beach. Tom had always said, "When a pastor is through somewhere, he should move on and let the new pastor have all the attention." This was how Loren felt now, so instead of staying there, he went to assist Brother Gaston, the pastor of Inglewood Assembly of God. It was a beautiful church with a large congregation, and a growing Sunday school. Loren led the three choirs for the church there. Then the Lord called him and gave him a vision of sending out young people into missions all over the world. From that point on, Loren followed the Lord in this vision, and out of it was born the organization *Youth With A Mission* (YWAM). During this time he also finished up his studies at University of Southern California, getting his Master's degree in Administration of Education. Loren is still involved in YWAM, and his Master's in education is helpful as he now heads up YWAM's Pacific and Asia Christian University (called PACU) in Hawaii, which he built by faith.

Phyllis married a naval lieutenant named Leonard Griswald in a big church wedding at Inglewood Assembly. Then they moved to San Diego where he finished his time in the Navy, and she was secretary to Pastor Hill of the first Assembly of God.

Tom was at camp meeting, so he sent Janice and me out with a $500 check and orders "to go buy us a house in Inglewood." We had just sold our home in Long Beach the night before, so that next morning, Janice and I set out by bus on our mission. When we came into the first real estate office on Westchester Street in Inglewood, the man seemed doubtful of our intentions, until I plunked down the check on his desk! Then he was immediately interested and took us out. We liked the third house we looked at, and bought it. It was on a hill, and a nice street — West 61st Street. Tom didn't even see it inside for three or four months, because the folks living there wouldn't let us see the inside until they were out.

After we were settled in our new place, we had a backyard barbecue with all the staff of the district office. I had placed signs all around stating clearly, "NO SHOP TALK!" But I found a couple in the garage bedroom talking shop. It was Tom, of course. He was so enthused about his work!

For twenty-one years, Tom stayed busy in his work, holding a desk job, and preaching and assisting in both foreign and home missions. His portfolio has been enough for two people. I had to pray myself out another door of ministry, so I became Evangelist at home, as well as across the nation and abroad.

Janice left to attend Evangel College in Springfield, Missouri, where she met and later married Jim Rogers. They have both been busy in Youth With A Mission ever since, currently heading up the Editorial Services Office which is responsible for YWAM publications. Jim and Janice have three children now — a set of twins, Jeffrey and Joel, and another son, Jonathan.

After three years alone, seeing his vision materialize, Loren met Darlene Scratch.

After twenty-one years of service, Tom resigned. The *Division of Foreign Missions* gave him an endorsement as *Deputation Representative of Foreign Missions*, which has been a confirmation of our burden to keep promoting missions. Our evangelistic burden is thus extended to a worldwide scope, and for this we are grateful to the Lord and to the many people who sponsor us.

It was imperative that we take our leave of Long Beach so we moved with Loren—first for his stay as Assitant Pastor in Inglewood, as assistant to Pastor Gaston. Then we all went to Monterey Park so Tom could be close to his office in Pasadena.

Janice was away at Pine Crest during those summers while we lived at Monterey Park. Although Loren was still staying in his room, he and his dad had little time together. I never mentioned about seeing Loren slighted, because his father was too busy to discuss with him the problems of his young ministry. Our son was trying to get going in his little office up above the church property in Pasadena. Both Cunningham men had their own separate burdens for the Lord's work.

Family ties were not as strong as before. My own burdens were of an entirely different nature. I was still getting calls for evangelistic meetings. We'd all been in the process of change when Janice announced a change in her own plans: "We need to be getting ready for a wedding." She'd just come back from a YWAM crusade in the Caribbean when I found myself totally engrossed in this new project—getting ready for our youngest child's wedding.

Life's course altered quickly after that. Loren came home from one of his YWAM speaking engagements in the San Francisco area with news of his own. Coming into my bedroom one night, he asked, "Are you awake, Mother?" As he sat down on the side of my bed he told me, "I met this girl . . ."

I knew that he hadn't dropped in for idle chatter. Without even looking at his face, I knew he was serious. "Tell me about her, son. What's she like?" I inquired.

"Her name is Darlene Scratch. She's got light-colored hair and blue eyes and I guess you'd call her a blonde. She's a pastor's daughter from Redwood City and also a registered nurse."

Before he went any further in describing her, I felt she was going to have my blessing! And so, after a few months, another grand wedding took place. Loren and Darlene have two children, named Karen and David. Phyllis and Leonard also have two children, Sheri and Kevin.

Missionary Talmage Butler and T. C. Cunningham board a plane for a cross-country flight in Africa.

The Jeep that came to church. It went to Africa where it was used by the missionary in opening 39 bush churches in 4 years.

Tom addressing the Women's Ministries Rally at our District camp.
Barbara Forrest, District Women's Ministries Director is the fourth woman from the left.

Loren and Darlene Cunningham
and their children. Their son
was born in Switzerland.

Phyllis singing with sign language.
Besides singing in the choir and
church, she interpreted for deaf
people who attended our services.

Jim and Jan Rogers, and a team they took around the world
establishing YWAM bases. This picture was taken in Korea.

24

OPEN DOORS

Tom also became a Teen Challenge overseer and a director of missions work called Home Missions. These new assignments took him abroad occasionally as well as affording him the opportunity to encourage others to go into the mission field. With his help an average of seven new churches a year were started in the district and he was also able to send out an average of seven new missionaries every year during his twenty-one years as a full-time district executive. How could anyone carry such a load? God gave him strength.

That he had been a giant baby at birth might have also helped. Tom Cunningham who weighed into this world at a whopping eighteen pounds has been a slave to work ever since he was a child.

Those years of dedication to Christ cost a price. I watched his hair turn grayer and his stride slacken. The calm-mannered man became less patient. I had to think that was partially because of the many grueling church difficulties. Family picnics were no more; vacations less. Tom's devotion to missions cost all of us a price. His burden for lost souls was of prime importance to him.

Although ours was a pleasant life, Tom, busy in the excitement of covering the world for missions, did not seem to realize my problem. I had such a burden for lost souls, but he'd pulled the rug out from under me. For 28 years I'd depended on him for a pulpit where I could release the burden the Lord had put on me when I was a little girl of twelve.

The only fights we ever had was over the pulpit — like "who's to preach?" I think we both have had all the time a bad case of preacher's itch. Well, I'm not sure that all who are called don't have it or develop it in their time. Arguments, yes, though neither of us ever win, for we don't have a referee or moderator. Good thing we both have the same Scotch-Irish extraction, so we can laugh or cry or jokingly communicate — all understandable.

Tom has always shown to me ministerial courtesy. One reason may be because his father-in-law made him promise as he made the other two in-laws, never hinder my daughter's preaching.

I fell down on the floor and I stayed there in prayer until God spoke to me, and He said, "You preach Jesus and I will open doors." I didn't take that as a reprimand that I hadn't preached Jesus, but recognized it to mean, "Don't change the message."

Soon after receiving that word, at the District Council meeting, Bill Robertson, the newly-elected Superintendent, asked, "Will all the evangelists please stand and introduce yourselves?" I stood. "What is your name?" he asked, although he knew me well.

"I'm Aimee Semple McPherson — open for calls." A laugh rippled through the audience and then he asked me, "What is your real name?"

"Jewell Cunningham," I reported. At least a half-dozen pastors made their way over at recess to invite me to speak at their churches.

Typical of those invitations was one the Lord prompted me to take, the furthest out in the Imperial Valley, one of the hardest to find in the desert. My first opportunity to meet the pastor and his family was at lunch time. Just as I sat down to eat lunch the pastor's son came and sat opposite me at the table. I arose, reached across the table, saying as I introduced myself, "I'm Mrs. Cunningham, the one who is to be the preacher this week. And you are Jimmy? Well, Jimmy, will you go take off your hat, wash your face and comb your hair? Then come sit with us and eat." To my surprise and his parents' astonishment, he did it.

The next day, Jimmy was there again, without a hat, but not washed or combed. Again, I reprimanded him, "Well, Jimmy, your mother has a good dinner prepared for us. Would you show her respect by going in to wash and comb before you eat?" This time his mother fearfully followed him, maybe thinking,

"She'll cause my son to leave!" Not enough discipline taught? But at the last I felt I'd handled the problem by God's help.

Even though the pastor, his wife and I prayed on our knees at the altar three hours every morning, it seemed that the week-long meeting was going to be closed without making a single convert. Jimmy, the pastor's unsaved son could not help but hear our travail before God. Because we were a bit noisy as we interceded each morning in the chapel just outside his bedroom, he tried to shut out that noise by turning up the volume of the worldly music he played in his room. His parents didn't seem to realize what Jimmy was listening to — maybe rock music.

After the last night's church service, I sat in the front room of the parsonage waiting for the pastors to come back from a call. Suddenly the door burst open and a big, robust part-Filipino burst in. I recognized him from reputation — I'd been told by someone he was the village deputy's son and also the gang leader of the town's rebels. A little amazed, I could have been frightened, but God gave me a peace about this young man's presence.

I'd sensed in our church services he was the culprit holding the others back. His influence was that strong. But on this particular night I realized his countenance had changed. The contempt was gone. He was radiant. Tears streamed down his face as he began to say, "Sister Cunningham, God saved me tonight. Where is Jimmy?" I pointed toward Jimmy's door and the transformed young man went inside.

Months later, while attending a fellowship meeting in the area, I heard for the first time a report about the results of that meeting where we'd planted the seed with prayer and tears — "He that soweth in tears shall reap in joy." Since our meetings the church had established a choir and a youth group. The pastor's son, Jimmy, had joined as a member along with that roughly-hewn character of mixed Filipino and American blood who'd become a new type of leader! Square-shouldered and robust, he'd changed into a rebel for Jesus along with his friend Jimmy and I heard he became the youth leader. We can not forget that triumph.

My heart trouble, which had been brought on because of anxiety and depression from not knowing where I was to fit into Tom's ministry, had become so bad that one day I had some sort of an attack. Frantic, Loren ran across the street to get a heart specialist while Jannie stayed with me, praying fervently and rubbing my chest and arm. For a few seconds (which seemed like minutes) I had NO HEARTBEAT. By the time the doctor got to my side Janice's prayers were answered and my ticker began to beat again. But the continuing irregular beat made me so weak that Tom took me to L.A. to a specialist. Two or three other doctors were consulted, but none seemed to know of any healing for my staggering heartbeats.

A charismatic revival was going on in Los Angeles at that time. One evening a young woman I'd never seen before drove in walked up to our door and declared, "I want to take you to the meeting to get healed." Somehow word of my condition had spread around.

"I'll be glad to go with you," I answered. We went to a tabernacle and sat next to the wall. Many different denominations were represented. I gloried in listening to the various men being introduced — Brethren, Baptist, Methodist, Catholic. A grand sight! Perhaps God in His majesty was knocking down denominational barriers built by man!

Father Seeburg from St. Petersburg, Florida, with his clerical garb, looked the part of the Episcopalian priest he was, but when he spoke, the Holy Spirit flowed through him. He not only preached, but he also danced a bit in the Spirit and spoke in tongues occasionally. Such a glorious sight for one such as I who was bred and born in the briar patch of fanatical Pentecostalism!

Except for occasionally putting my hand over my heart when it fluttered, I enjoyed every second. When the prayer line formed at the end of the service I joined, but felt no obvious miracle. When I returned to my seat by the wall, the lady who'd escorted me there began to speak in tongues. A hush fell over the congregation. Leaders stood waiting for the Spirit's message.

The interpretation came from another woman at the back of

the congregation — another one I'd not seen nor talked to before. Her message was, "If you will go to this place far off where you have been called and preach my Gospel, I will heal you and give you a new heart. Thus saith the Lord." My spirit soared. I knew the message was for me — who else? But how did this lady know about my call?

The next morning I said to Tom, "Honey, I must accept Eva Bloom's invitation and go to Hawaii to hold the first revival in her new church on the island near Pearl Harbor." I told him about the message and we began to make plans even though obviously I hadn't been healed.

God told me to invite Wanda Jaus, a preacher and also a registered nurse, to accompany me. Her presence was no accident. On the plane crossing the Pacific (There were no jets then, so the trip took twelve hours.) she would periodically take my pulse. "Forty-six!" she exclaimed once. "Jewell, how are you alive?"

"Pray," I directed, and she did. She prayed throughout the trip. Every time I weakened physically, my constant companion would send petitions on my behalf to the other companion — the One who has gone with me all the days of my life.

Landing at the Honolulu Airport, we viewed the vast expanse of white sandy beach which edged the sparkling waters of the aqua blue Pacific. Clutter hadn't found its way there yet for the tourists hadn't begun to arrive in droves. The city was much smaller. Since the Hilton and other hotels hadn't been built as barriers to Waikiki Beach, no high-rises stood on the horizon. Natives greeted us with fresh flower leis. I'd heard of the warm and festive reception given to visitors in Hawaii, but this was the first time I'd ever experienced it.

Glancing off the runway we saw a plane ablaze. Flames shot out from it and I prayed no one was caught inside. What a heated arrival! And hard on a weak heart that had just traveled 3,000 miles.

On that island, surrounded by the waters of the blue Pacific, God began to break down my prejudices. Everywhere almond-eyed faces stared up at me. The place was filled with Japanese. In my mind's eye, they were still the enemy. It didn't help to look out the back door of a big sprawling tabernacle-type church where I could see the sunken Arizona where eleven hundred American boys lay buried beneath the waves.

At that time the Lord moved upon my heart to forgive the Japanese, who, we were told, had hidden a radio on the hill behind the church building. From that place they'd given the signal to the swarm of Japanese fighter planes to break Hawaii. Folks told us later that the man who signaled the planes was converted to Jesus Christ and became a witness for the Lord.

I coaxed the Kerrs, who were also there and had obtained privilege to use the school to hold meetings for the Chinese, to tell the congregation about their escape from Communist China where they'd ministered for thirty years, but they said, "It's too nerve-wracking for us to talk about it." The Kerr's ministered to those who could only understand Chinese and I used the room to preach to those who could understand English.

My companion Wanda had gone home to move out to one group of Hawaiian islands. The Jaus's—Wanda Jaus and her husband Gorden—came back that year and started a church on an island she called Flower Island.

By car Pastor Eldon Vincent and his wife took me to see the pineapple groves, an orange juice cannery and the graceful hula hula dancers. After that trip I was glad to fall into bed.

My bed and the pulpit were my only interests except for sitting and eating the meals so deliciously prepared by Eva Bloom and her sisters with whom Wanda and I stayed. Following the daily prayers around the table with Mother Bloom, I was beginning to look forward to being served papayas and fresh pineapple. Sister Bloom said, "We'd like to show you the sights, but all you want to do is preach." She could have added, ". . . and stay in bed!" In order to follow the Lord's command to preach, I HAD to rest. Preaching His Gospel was NOT to be put on the back burner.

While preaching one week for Paul Epler out at Wahewah one week, one night we had a Jericho March—going around the seats, praising God, our singing accompanied by the instruments some of us carried. One man was standing still, unmoved by the joyous praise. I resisted the urge to get hold of his arm and pull him to the marchers. Later Paul told me that he was not mentally alert. I've been cautious since not to urge folks who do not join in more active praise.

After two weeks of holding revival at the church at Pearl Harbor, we traveled to the other side of the island to an old school house auditorium to minister for a Japanese couple who urgently wanted to get the Gospel out.

It was my privilege to preach at the First Assembly of which Elden Vincent was the pastor and builder. Brother Vincent also served as President of the Assembly of God College on the same location. Men and women from the South Pacific Islands including Samoa attended that college. Since I was present at the close of that term, I had the honor of being asked by the president of the college to bring their Baccalaureate message.

With my limited formal training I could hardly give them a message about reaching the stars in education, but I gave them what I had, using the story of Jonah to tell them about following the Lord in obedience.

Brother Yasuhara, the master of ceremonies, had reminded me before I was to speak that I had been given a time limit. By the time I got Jonah in the whale I had to stop short and announce, "Sorry, young folks, we'll have to leave Jonah. I'm out of time. We can't get him out." They began to clap for me to finish, so Brother Yasuhara gave me the nod to continue and I got Jonah out of the whale and on his way to Ninevah. Such a joy to speak to receptive ears!

After thirty days on the island of Oahu and twenty-five sermons in five different churches, later I thought, "I'm better, but still not well. I'm going to call Tom and tell him I want to come home."

Even though he admitted he was missing me, he said, "We've sent a new couple, the Claud Redigers, down to American Samoa and we'd like you to go there to encourage them." I hung up the phone thinking, "Here I come, Samoa!"

My big pot of tea is . . .

Jewell at age 7

. . . the Martha work for my family and

. . . the Mary work around the world.

My smallest church—
Indian Reservation in Arizona

My largest crowd—Dr. Paul Yonggi
Cho's Church in Seoul, Korea

Jewell's Bible Class—
Faith Tabernacle

My interpreter and I—Seoul, Korea
(Kim is a pastor in New York now)

25

SAMOA

"Where are you going?" the stewardess asked and I answered, "Panga, Panga, Tualoafo or somewhere — I don't really know." I could have added, "I don't really care either. This is probably as close to heaven as I'll ever get on my earthly travels."

The stewardess smiled. "It is all the same place — Panga Panga and Tualoafa are all in America Samoa." As we flew down through the clouds a spot of land came up in sight from the ocean, then a hill. "Oh, Oh!" I heard myself sputter, "we're going to hit!" But we didn't hit. Somehow we found some solid ground — hardly enough to land the big plane on. Samoa! Maynard Kecham, the overseer of the Asian Work, had sent word on ahead to the Redigers that I was coming. Claude and Wilma had received his message, so they were on hand to meet me. Their home was surrounded by native houses called falas which were little more than picnic shelters. That same night I learned that the main ingredients in a Samoan diet were fish and tari root cooked by natives on an outside fire, although a Samoan lady named Mali fixed good meals for the missionaries table.

As I got better acquainted I began to walk around and meet people, asking them to church. I soon learned that they were not permitted to go to a church that was not their own. The chiefs didn't allow it. Feeling alone, a smile from one of the natives and a welcome made me feel more at home.

During our nightly meetings I had no way of counting the converts. Some believers were seeking in their own language and could not tell me what was going on. The singing was led by

Brother Yetti with no instrumental accompaniment of any kind. A big Samoan, Brother Yetti was most impressive. from the waist up he was dressed in western attire — complete with a white shirt and a buttoned collar. From the waist down he was wrapped in a white sheetlike piece of cloth which they called a "lava lava." It reached halfway down the calf of his naked legs. His feet were bare except for a pair of sandals. Such singing! They sang and chanted Anglican style. I was asked to come to the platform and preach while the good brother interpreted.

After a few nights I told them, "I want to teach you a chorus using hand motions." With all they had in them, they watched and followed dramatically while I showed them the hand motions to "Jesus Set Me Free." How earnestly they listened to learn the English words as I sang:

"Once like a bird in prison I dwelt,
No freedom from my sorrow I felt,
But Jesus came and listened to me,
Glory to God, He set me free!"

"Now clap!" I told them. Never have I seen such enthusiasm! They liked that dramatic way of singing so well that the Samoan Church carried it on long after I'd gone.

Wilma and I took off and flew to Western Samoa in New Zealand territory. For three days I ministered there. The lady chief gave us a good reception and an invitation to hold services in her huge falla. At that time there was no such thing as a Full Gospel church there.

With the cooperation of the young pastor of the Congregational church in western Samoa, we held services under the big coconut trees outside the little village of Apia. Dinner was served first on a makeshift table covered with coconut leaves. After the table was removed, the crowd sat on the floor while I preached from a makeshift pulpit. What a joy to learn ten years later that the lady chief had accepted Jesus and then married an American-Samoan believer! Thrills our hearts to hear of such progress, made because of our church planting.

As we visited around the island the pastor of the Congregational church asked, "Will you let my children entertain you by singing?"

"Fine," I agreed as four little Samoans lined up. "But I understood you had six children. There's the little one in the bedroom, but where is the other one?"

"We gave him away."

"You what?" Surely my ears were betraying me.

"My brother had no children so we gave him our 7-year-old son. He is not a Christian, but he had no son."

That gave me motive to refer to the Bible and ask, "Did you hear about the prophet Samuel who asked Jesse when he was being presented his sons to choose one to anoint for the king? Samuel found one missing so he asked, 'Are all your children here?' The Lord may ask of you on that day, 'Are all your children here?' Won't it be awful if the one you gave your brother will be missing there?"

That shook him and his wife up. I meant to shake them.

Those islanders received me with honors that only they were able to give—big meals consisting of all kind of fish, lobsters, crabs (raw or nearly raw) served on banana fronds spread on the floor. Natives like to frequent beaches and eat crabs on the spot. Young men caught them and brought some to share. My Okie appetite caused me to pass by the Samoan cabbage and tari root, but I minced and nibbled at the longish fish—but only when my host was watching! For snubbing my nose at their choice of food Claud Rediger reprimanded me. I promised then, "I won't insult anyone's honor, but I'm not going to eat something to make myself sick."

I was going to smile and let them know I loved them. Why else would I have been there at my own expense? Some missionaries have made an end to their ministry by foolishly trying to eat what the natives ate—food they've spent their lives becoming accustomed to—eels in Alaska, monkeys in Africa, dogs and cats in Asia and possums in the Bayou. God's mandate wasn't eating and drinking, but speaking the Gospel and doing good.

Feasts? If you're invited to a feast—eat what's set before you, asking no question. "WAS this meat offered to idols?" That was Paul's question—rightly dividing the word of truth.

In the South Pacific my sermon material needed to be revised. How could I use the symbol of the Gospel train or Jesus as "the bread of life"? For their culture I had to change the symbols to a ship and a tari root. Jesus became the tari root and the highway to heaven had to be a trail.

While still there in 1961, I met Governor Lee as he and his family got off a plane. He had been appointed by the American government to oversee the island. The Samoans had freshly topped the landing space with a black asphalt substance and Governor Lee and his wife and two teen-agers began to bog down in the sticky mess. He tried not to let on, but we all laughed with him. "Governor," I told him, "I'm a missionary from the states. We need to help these people get good water and sanitation and schools. Promise me you'll help them." He promised he would.

The following year Loren went there with his "Youth With a Mission." Because of their visit there, a wave of revival started when a couple of chiefs who had been the giants in the land were saved. Previously they had not allowed their people to come to church or become interested in religions other than their own denominational Church of England.

Loren and his YWAMers went across the island contacting those from the staid Church of England—Samoans who made no profession of faith at all. The next time YWAM visited Samoa they helped build some of the presently existing churches. They "conquered the land for Christ" by getting the chiefs saved. I'd advised my son, "If you'll take your group down there and get the giants saved, God will send victory." Loren did—so God did. Others followed and preaching was heard. The results have been rewarding. Many churches are now scattered across the islands. Many of the islanders are moving to the states and they are carrying the messages further. One young man who now has a big church in Honolulu had carried my shoes on a trail walk over the mountain to hold service.

The missionaries took me past tall coconut trees, the Mormon conclave and then over to a small church which had deteriorated so that it had been condemned and hadn't been in use for two years. The believers borrowed seats from the school and decorated the walls with coconut fronds. The makeshift pulpit was covered with a white cloth so I could preach. Upon entering, we had to watch out for a wide crack where the building had pulled away from the side.

None of this hindered their enthusiasm. Samoans packed the room. Others stood outside, for they were those who'd been ordered by their chief to "stay out." My heart went out to them as I preached "Believe God will give you a new church." From that they somehow got the idea that Sister Cunningham was God. When Loren came the following year, they said, "Your mother was going to send us money for a church."

God answered that prayer another way, for the youth Loren took did help build a church there. The revival gained the momentum of a mighty wave as more and more youth groups found the island and evangelists came.

A little preacher who with his family walked four miles over the mountains to the other side of the island to come to our service asked, "Will you come and hold a service for us? You'll be the first evangelists to ever come."

How could I say no? Yet I had no way of knowing what I was getting into. We could have gone by barge, but the waves were coming in with fury. Even a native woman said, "It would make me sick." We left the missionary's car (the only vehicle I'd seen besides a bus) and started out Indian style following a trail which was difficult to negotiate. It would have been even more so if Mali, a native woman had not walked in front cutting out briars and heavy brush to get them out of my way. Some climb for a woman who'd been sickly with a heart condition! When we reached the top of the hill I could have hugged those big raw-boned men with their machetes who'd spent the day clearing the trail that far.

Thirst had gotten the best of me on that long climb. Spying a stream I started to dash for it. A man grabbed my arm as I knelt to drink. "Sewage," he explained.

Civilization! Friendly people actually existed on the other side of that South Pacific mountain—people who were also ruled by a chief who detained the day's activities by sitting on his haunches and arguing with Pastor Yetti. "It's customary for our visitors to stay all night," he insisted, but Brother Yetti kept saying, "We can't."

We weren't prepared for his insistence of hospitality, nor his arguing time which ran on for hours. Finally we were called to dinner spread out on the customary banana leafs under a falla. I was told to eat first, alone, while the little preacher fanned me with a big palm spray, their custom for a visitor.

A barbecued pig—head and all—had been placed in the middle of the spread. Surrounding it were marine-life dishes. The long legs of a lobster and the eyes of the pig made it difficult to have a hearty appetite.

The pastor stopped fanning for a second, so I asked, "Will you join me?"

His protest was immediate. "No. It is not our custom."

"Just this one time, please. Put your fan down and let's do it my way."

Finally he obliged. Soon the others sat cross-legged on the floor with us and we feasted together. I noticed no one ever needs to ask a Samoan to eat—all they need is a chance.

After the dinner was cleared away all the natives sat on the floor to listen to my sermon. We had a baptismal service in which Brother Yetti did the baptizing, then I changed into my walking garb and we started in our single file line back down the hill. Such an enjoyable walk as we sang while Maurice Luce played the French harp. The mountain resounded with the joy of the Lord as Samoans were singing praises to Him!

Back down the hill we trudged. On the sand we sat and rested. Bushed, I lay down. No one wished to hurry on as a cool breeze wafted over our faces. The stars never looked so close nor so bright as they did in the tropical sky. As I looked heavenward I suddenly realized, despite all the strain of that grueling day, my ticker had not caused me a moment's trouble! I told myself, "Your heart is beating right!" A miracle!

After ten hours of rugged walking, climbing, no rest all afternoon — a water baptizing with Brother Yetts doing the immersing — the four mile trek over the hill and back, holding a service — all those strenuous things hadn't done me in. I cried out to God, "Lord, You have done what you said. You've healed me and given me a new heart just as You promised in the prophecy! Thank you, Lord!"

At the last service with the Samoans, Brother Yetti handed me a big handkerchief tied around a bunch of nickels, dimes and quarters. "It took us two weeks to collect it," he said about the $24 gift.

A small fish cannery and U.S. paid school teachers were all there was to support the economy. I wept as I thanked them and pronounced God's blessings.

Tom had paid my way and after six weeks I was going home. The next day I prepared to fly alone to Hawaii. At the little airport I looked fondly into the faces of all my dear Samoans. Even Brother Yetti's youngest daughter rode out several miles on her bike to tell me good bye. She hugged me as they prayed. The scripture came to me, "By this all men know you are my disciples."

Feeling refreshed in body and spirit and finished with my pioneering, I was ready to go home. I boarded the airplane. The all night flight arrived at Honolulu at 4:00 in the morning. The young immigration officer questioned me, "where is your passport? You said you went over to western Samoa?"

"I don't have any," I replied. "But the deputy who had been given charge while the Governor was stateside had written me a permit to go to the New Zealand territory, but they kept it."

His tone of voice grew more harsh. "So you'll have to pay a fine. As he escorted me to the baggage compartment he ordered, "You stay here until you pay your fine."

"No," I retorted. "I won't tell a lie. I admitted I had no passport, but I did have a permit and I won't pay a fine. I can sit here as long as you can, but I won't tell a lie." So I sat.

The officer finally said, "then go outside and get someone to recognize you and tell me you're an American." I started out, but when I was halfway out of the baggage compartment where I'd been held in house arrest, another officer stopped me and said, "Go back."

My Irish was rising up! "Will you make up your mind?" I demanded. "One of you says 'Go' and the other says 'Stay.'" Disgusted with my growing problem, I went back. "Lord," I prayed silently. "I asked You not to let me have any trouble, but here it is. Help me!"

Again I was presented with papers to sign. I said, "I'll say I went without a passport."

And the officer replied, "I'll write that you owe no fine."

That settled that — or so I thought until I reached home. In a few days I got a note from the State Department asking for the fine. So I wrote a letter. "Dear President Kennedy, I went with the Governor's Deputy's permission over to the western Samoan territory to do missionary work, and only with a written permit. As I confessed, I had no passport, but . . ." Well, he wrote me back, "You do not have to pay a fine."

Victory! I didn't want a good reputation smeared — even if the fine was small. P.T.L.!

My dear friends, the Vincents, had shown the patience of Job, meeting the four A.M. plane and having to wait for me to get released. Great folks! After a short visit they took me to another plane to go home, twelve hours after I had landed.

Tom stood waiting as I came down the steps to the turf at L.A. Never was American dirt more welcome! My spouse surely was tickled with my appearance. I was loaded down with leis and shells and topped with a banana stalk hat adorning my head, trying to look as islandy as possible in my mumu.

From the airport Tom drove me to the camp meeting where I felt like a celebrity in my attire.

Samoa has since been dear to our hearts. We Cunninghams felt as though God had us have a part of pioneering there. In 1978, seventeen years after my visit there, Tom and I returned just as Governor Lee was packing to come home. We went up to his home to see him before he left. The island had so many improvements—schooling, sanitation, roads and churches. Samoa had undergone a face lift and I told the governor so. Tom and I had the most pleasure in what we saw that meant the most to us. Those vibrant Samoans still sang with as much enthusiasm as they had when I was there—hand gestures and all. They'd added a few songs to their repertoire. One talked about falling down and they literally fell on the floor when they sang it. We didn't care if they stood up or fell down for Jesus, just as long as they had Him in their hearts!*

---

*Oh, yes, that was 1961—God gave me a new heart. I haven't had a bad off beat nor pain or organic trouble since—this was why I can keep going—so many have asked me that.

26

ROMA, ROMA!

"Sorry, honey," Tom spoke softly with a pat on my hand. "You can't go along this time. The District won't pay your way."

"What?" I cried. "But, Tom, I've got everything ready — my visa, shots, my luggage. Isn't there some way?"

"No, Jude. I'm really sorry. I know how you've looked forward to this trip." But in 1962 the District just didn't pay for wives. "I'll have to go alone."

Never one to hide my feelings, I protested his solo flight to Africa, but it seemed there wasn't anything he could do. So he packed his suitcase to fly over to the Dark Continent — alone.

After he left I despaired about the situation. "Where can I go? Surely there's some place for me to preach and minister while he's gone. Remembering back, I thought of the time I'd talked to Brother Toppi about going to Italy. He'd really not been enthusiastic about my offer to go there and hold services, but he'd said, "Well, come over some time."

The more I thought about going there, the more enthused I became. I could surprise Tom! Because his plan was to stop and minister to the Italians on the way home the idea of surprising him grew in my mind and I began to plan.

I prayed about going, then I opened my Bible and the text fell to the part of the scripture in Acts 23 11 where God said you must witness in Rome and in Romans 1:15 where Paul said, "I'm ready to preach in Rome also." My heart beat faster with an air of anticipation as I read those words.

I decided I needed to talk to Loren who was still single and out preaching, so I called him in Hawaii to get his advice. "Son, your daddy's off to Africa and I want to go to Rome. We have enough money in the bank and Brother Toppi had given me an invitation. Do you think I should go there?" I didn't think I'd get much encouragement if I told Loren that my "invitation? had been, "Well, come over some time"—so I failed to mention that.

Loren encouraged me, "Mother, if you've prayed about it and you have the funds, I don't see any reason for you not to go." When some friends from Inglewood, Mrs. Mautz and her mother, dropped by I didn't mention my need for extra finances for the anticipated journey, I just mentioned my desire to minister in Italy. They opened their hearts and their pocketbooks and gave me a gift of forty dollars, telling me, "We feel you should go. Here is some help." I took their gifts as another confirmation—I needed more confirmation for this venture than I'd ever sought in my younger days. I called the bank and found we had $700 left in our account. Next I phoned our travel agent and asked, "Bob, how much would I need to fly to London?" Then I'd go by train over the Alps to Rome.

"Five hundred dollars should fly you to London. And you'll still have your train fare to Rome left over."

"Bring me a ticket!" I declared. "I'm a-gonna surprise my Tom. I'll be there when he gets back." I sent him a cablegram which he did not receive till long after I arrived in Italy.

Phyllis and her baby Sheri took me to the airport to catch the eleven A.M. flight to London the next day. The Los Angeles airport was very small at that time. We boarded a prop plane outside the airport. I climbed aboard and felt a tinge of sadness as I waved good bye to my daughter and granddaughter. Yet I felt no fear—only excitement at going to Rome to preach.

A deep peace settled in my soul as we lifted off and began our long flight. No one slept as we flew northeast toward the rising sun. In Iceland where we dropped down for a fillup I watched our military men milling around in their uniforms as I looked out the windows.

In the air again, it seemed we were outrunning the night, for it continued to remain daylight. Even if some of us wanted to sleep, we could not, for many of the passengers were showing the results of too much champagne. They chattered loudly and laughed about nothing in particular. No sleep for my tired eyes — too much noise!

Yet I had the pleasure of chatting with an older lady who was sitting alone. Like myself, she was on a mission for God. She explained, "I just sold my home and I'm on my way to spend the rest of my life witnessing to the Jews in the state of Israel." In that year of 1962, Israel was a newly-established state.

The plane landed at the Heathrow Airport in London about 8 A.M. At a loss as to where I was to go, I followed the crowd and boarded a bus which took us to the railroad depot — a free ride right to the station. Once inside that big place, I spied a couple just sitting there. I introduced myself to Mr. and Mrs. Exeter and soon found they were the kind of folks one would like to have for lifetime friends. They even helped me exchange some of my dollars for shillings and then suggested, "Let us show you the sights here in London. It will be three hours before your train leaves for Rome."

"I'd love to!" I responded to their kind offer. They showed me Picadilly Square, we watched the changing of the red-coated guards. As Big Ben bonged we knew it was nearing time to go back, but first I offered, "Let me buy our lunch." After lunch those fine English souls showed me the street to follow back and bade me a fond farewell. Again I was entirely on my own in a foreign land.

At the depot, while I shared a long seat with another lady waiting for the train, I mumbled to myself about the letters I had written, "I wish I could mail these."

The lady overheard me. "Give them to those chaps there," she said, pointing to some passing teenagers. They were complete strangers to both of us, but I handed them a dollar bill and asked, "Would you please post these letters for me?"

"Yes," they agreed and were off. They returned with my change and were off again before I could give them a tip. The honesty and friendliness I encountered on my first visit to England confirmed my good opinion of the English people.

When it came time for boarding, the passengers grabbed their bags. I followed them past the baggage coach and climbed on board with the others. Such a long, long train!

In no time at all we were getting off to board the ferry across
the English Channel. We all filed into a small enclosure where our
money was to be exchanged for francs. One man's wink at the
other aroused my suspicions. Although I was certain that French-
man had not given me adequate francs in exchange for my ten
dollars, I thought it best not to make a scene. The French were
not making as good an impression on me as the English had.
Because of my keen perception from my father's genes, I knew I'd
been cheated. When I was handed the francs, I did not know how
to count them.

I continued on, following the others. When the customs officer
asked, "Where is your paper?" I had to answer, "I've lost it." A lady
passenger, a total stranger, came to my rescue declaring, "Yes, she
had one. I saw it." With that, customs permitted me to continue.

Following the crowd once again, I boarded another train where
I found an unoccupied compartment. People stood on the side aisle
so I joined them just to get a glimpse of the channel and the countryside that was swiftly disappearing from view. "NOW THIS IS
FRANCE," I told myself. After a gourmet French breakfast in the
dining room we learned there was a strike going on and the dining
car was uncoupled from the train right after breakfast. That meant
I was to go hungry the rest of the way to Rome.

Reaching Paris close to midnight, I was exhausted from lack
of sleep so I told myself, "JEWELL, YOU NEED TO GET A
BED HERE FOR THE REST OF THE NIGHT." Grabbing my
purse and suitcase I got off. To my surprise I found the depot was
in the commercial part of Paris. When I asked, "Where is a hotel?"
a man on the street corner pointed across the street. Such luxury!
In the rather nice hotel I went up to my assigned room and fell
into the big soft bed. No one had to sing me a lullaby! After com-
mitting myself to the Lord's safe-keeping I dismissed all fear of
robbers and molesters. In that foreign land I drifted securely off to
sleep and slept soundly all night.

At daybreak the next morning I awoke suddenly as if some
unseen hand had touched me. I phoned the desk and asked the
clerk, "When does the train leave for Rome?"

"It is six o'clock. You can't make the train. It is too far away and it will leave soon."

Undaunted, I answered, "Please send a porter for my bag and call me a taxi."

In nothing flat it seemed I was speeding in a cab past shady lanes, well-kept lawns and homes. Why were we going so far when I'd only had to walk across the street to the hotel the night before? A time or two I yelled at the driver, "I have to catch the train to Rome," but he only shook his head and murmured, "Roma, Roma!" I finally just sat back in my seat, deciding to take in the view and enjoy the ride across Paris.

Following that speedy ride I was left at another railroad depot. Crowds were mingling and walking fast so I joined them. "What do I do now?" I asked a clerk. He answered in French, but I knew from his motions that I was to keep following the others.

My extra suitcase grew heavy and I wished someone would give me a hand. Just as I made the wish, a young French sailor heard me, reached back, took my suitcase and motioned for me to follow. Angels . . . ? Yes, God has angels in human form! That nice-looking guy then asked in perfect English, "May I help you?"

"By all means, thank you. I want to get the train to Rome and I noticed other trains on the track."

"Follow me," he directed, then led me to my compartment. I followed him with my eyes and realized he was headed for a coach further back. As the train started I made my way through the two other cars and gave the sailor my package of candy.

As we traveled up through the Alps I reveled in the beauty of the mountain scenery, then snuggled in for a good night's rest in my bunk bed. I traveled until very late the next day without food.

The dining car was still derailed, so late on my last evening aboard, I stopped a porter and asked, "Will you please get me a sandwich and a cake?" He came back with a thin slice of bologna between a couple of slices of bread and cake. At my offer of fifty cents, he answered in broken English, "Not enough." Pouring out my change in hand (francs, lira, shillings and some American money) onto the small window table I said to him, "Take what you need." Cupping one hand under the edge of the table, he used the other to scrape all my coins into his hand. "Merci!" he said. After he left I decided the little table by the window was a good place to eat, write or study and watch out for dishonest help. Another night on the bunk bed and to sweet sleep.

Brother Andrew Nelli, a wealthy friend from America who had helped the Italians get a church and a Bible School going, had sent a cablegram ahead telling the Romans they should accept me. This assured me of a welcome.

At four in the morning we pulled into the vast railroad station at Rome. An Italian couple who spoke English had met me on the train. No one came to meet me, so hurriedly I scanned the faces in the crowd until I found my friends and asked them if they would call the church number for me. They seemed pleased to be of help.

Brother Perna, Missionary of the Assemblies of God in Italy who lived at the church I was to visit, arrived at the station soon afterward and drove me directly to an apartment built over the church. Several of the church staff, including the pastor's family also had apartments there. I gratefully realized I would no longer be alone.

So the next day Al Perna, Jr., asked if I wanted to see Rome. I told him, "Yes, by all means!" He took me down the narrow streets. Dodging traffic and looking at that historical town, I thought of Paul and how he'd preached there and lost his head. We visited St. Peter's Basilica and Vatican Square. The Pope wasn't there—we just saw the balcony where he so often comes out to bless the flock. Seeing the twelve apostles' statues on the roof of St. Peter's meant so much to me as I pondered the patience those dedicated artists must have had. I thought of Michelangelo and the others, and the long tiring years of devotion to their art. From a cramped position the artist had painted the murals inside the cathedral just to leave the history in picture form of the greatest of all areas where the Catholic Church was formed. I appreciated the work in a different dimension as I viewed it firsthand and could not help but think of the many saints buried in the basement below. "Life goes on," I commented. "Believers all through the ages have awaited resurrection day."

All day we looked at antiquity until I was glad to get back to rest up for the evening meeting. How I wanted to be at my best! Later at the church I found the house was full. Amazing! On that week night they claimed "Three hundred worshipers are here and the prayer room has been filled from the start."

Sunday morning when I spoke I found an even-fuller house. Seven hundred souls! Besides the crowd, something else intrigued me. Offering-taking time. Buckets of lira! A good sign! Surely I'd be paid well and the cost of my ticket would also be paid. (Those thoughts did occur to me!) But I'd pay my fare and a dollar and a quarter a day for food and room that week.

During the service a note for me was sent up from the back. On the back of a business card I read in plain English, "Come get your car."

WHAT CAR? I thought perhaps Tom could explain it when he came through, but then I remembered that he'd said, "I've ordered a Mercedes to bring back." Since I didn't drive anymore, nor could I pay for it either, I simply let the message pass. But it didn't pass. Another notice came before Tom arrived. I learned later that he hadn't received my cable before he got to Africa, but did get it before he left for Italy.

For a week I'd had good success — seeing souls saved and filled in the prayer room. The ladies there got so busy praying and moving with excitement when the Holy Spirit came upon them that their headdresses came off. They kept praying anyway! One evening I counted seven bare heads. When the preacher came in and saw them, he immediately left with a look of disapproval on his face.

Two young men who'd been praying together got up and hugged each other, then danced and shouted. The presence of the Spirit was evident. (A couple of years later Sister Marin, a missionary, told me, "A couple of young men who were saved and filled in your meeting are now pastoring churches outside of Rome." I couldn't help but wonder if they were those two fellows.)

Brother Perna called me aside and said, "This is the best meeting I've seen here in thirty years." On Sunday I watched as the buckets were passed three times, each time filled to overflowing.

I thought about that glorious week. My first sermon had gone well. I told them how Paul brought the Gospel to the early church and how the church reacted over the years. It's like the stream I'd watched from the train window, I told them. It started clear as crystal, but as our journey progressed the water began to look cloudy with a whitish mud. Surely it came from some digging. Perhaps a mining company was cluttering the stream with pollution. For many miles it appeared to be dirty, but finally the stream cleared again.

The church reacted similarly. The first believers reacted to faith and grace. That "stream" had run clear for two or three centuries until men and their traditions muddied the stream. At last it was running clear again for which we were all praising God. Creating a parable for the newly baptized Pentecostal saints, I said, "It has been as though the Gospel has come again to Rome. Paul preached 'not of works, lest any man could boast, but by the grace of God and faith.' The stream still runs clear in spite of the fact that man's works and rituals have muddied its waters for centuries. It is clear again even as I noticed the stream running parallel with the railroad tracks had become clear once more."

As the week grew on, my bravery increased, so I preached concerning rituals being nailed to the cross. Colossians 2:14. (Ordinances that are against us — in other words, trying to make ourselves righteous by works of the flesh.) I told them that outward adorning was not important but God wanted us to worship Him in the Spirit.

That message was not accepted well because I mentioned the fact that the Bible states in I Corinthians 11 that women's covering is after all, her hair. "Read it, please, from verse 15," I told my interpreter, but he refused, shaking his head and claiming, "It's too controversial."

"Even so, it's the Word," I spouted in defense of my position. Whether or not it was read I don't know since his language was foreign to me. But I removed my scarf in a grand gesture, saying, "The blood is our only needed covering." I knew the ladies on the left of the podium understood my gesture.

It was the right message, but the wrong way of portrayal. The Bible says, "Honor those who have rule over you." In my zeal, I had offended them. So as not to offend in any way (as we are admonished).

The next night I was stopped at the door by the superintendent. "If you don't cover your head, you don't come in," he warned.

Indignantly I answered, "I told the ladies last night that they were bound by tradition, a ritual that the mother church has carried on, one which they needed to get freed from, the same as the Italians who had been converted from Catholicism in the United States. As Paul said, the blood is the only covering necessary. If I preached with a covering on my head, I'd be a hypocrite."

My words made no difference so I spoke up defiantly, "Then let Brother Toppi carry on."

Heartbroken, I saw my meetings close down—something I'd never experienced before in all of my years of evangelism. Offended, hurt, I didn't realize then that in offending them, I could also offend Christ. At the apartment I stood looking out over the city and the light of Rome. "Oh, Lord," I cried, "what have I done?" Tears coursed down my cheeks. "I just wanted to get the sisters loose; but I got myself bound. Here I am—eight thousand miles from home. I have never felt more alone. Even my own seem to have deserted me." In as much goes both ways, I thought.

Early the next morning I went to the church altar in search of peace and comfort. As I knelt in prayer, the janitor was sweeping and didn't even seem to notice me. He'd have noticed me more if I'd have been part of the trash. Being ignored can be the cruelest type of revenge without dealing any actual blows.

Walking to the kitchen, I tried to get a word of friendliness from the little lady cook. Even though she seemed to back my position, all she would say was, "I hate the scarves too."

On my way back upstairs I ran into young Al Perna. Icicles seemed to be surrounding this fine fellow who'd so graciously shown me the sights of Rome. He'd evidently been swayed by my actions the night before.

Later in the dining room I encountered Brother Toppi. "Would you like to visit the homemissions with us?" he asked.

"No, thank you. I'm going to get myself a place to preach." Turning to young Al, I said "Would you call the Naples Assembly of God and see if the pastor down there would like me to preach on Sunday?"

He came back smiling, "Yes, they'd be glad to have you."

Late at night my hosts ate spaghetti and drank wine. I made a vow and declared, "I won't harass you about your wine drinking if you don't get after me about my beads." Some had protested my use of costume jewelry. I told the hostess, "The Bible says, 'If drinking wine offends your brother . . . ,' it does not say 'Not drinking.'" If I should have drunk wine with them I knew my home folks would be offended. I took the morning train to Naples to preach there at 10 A.M.

How I was looking forward to Tom's arrival! He would be like my anchor once he got there on his way back from Africa. My meeting had been closed down; I'd gotten myself in hot water and I longed to have my husband close by. I'd told my Italian friends, "Wait until Tommy sees me! He'll be so excited."

And then Tom arrived. He'd called from the airport and I stayed at the apartment waiting for him. When we met at the top of the long flight of steps, I expected to be swept into his arms. Instead I felt as though a glacier had built up between us. His peck on the cheek was as cool as a kiss from a polar bear. No hug, no embrace. I wanted to ask him, "Have you been to Africa or the North Pole?" but I did not. "WAS HE REALLY BEING SO ALOOF BECAUSE FOLKS WERE WATCHING? NO," I mused, "THERE'S SOMETHING ELSE WRONG." I knew then it was the money I spent. But nothing was said between us while we remained in Rome and he preached over the weekend. Naturally, he did not know, now, he could get the new car. Tom followed me to Naples on Monday.

God had led me and I had obeyed and came. God would get us out of the jam, I knew that. Brother Calibressi, a wealthy Christian man converted from Catholicism, opened to us his penthouse where his son Paula and Maria his daughter were staying, for us to have a few days vacation on the beautiful shores of the Mediterranean. He also offered to loan us the money to get our car. This was not accepted by Tom — he was reluctant to accept a loan from anyone. But later, Brother Calibressi gave him a note saying "Take this to my office in Rome and they'll cash it. Also your ticket is no good, here go get a first class for the train trip back." What a brother! Tom accepted that.

I'd spent the tax money, but Tom was able to work around it, borrowing the money from Brother Perna until we got home and financed the car.

Later I learned that my message was being reinforced by Pope John the 23rd who passed an edict that ladies do not have to cover their heads. My Pentecostal sisters were given freedom to even cut their hair. Traditions are a delicate part of the Gospel to try to reform. Little no-harm sins, too. But Paul didn't refrain from preaching against them, which doesn't make for popularity nor getting the big money.

Let me fiinish this chapter with a humorous event. In 1969 we were travelling with the first YWAM school outreach from Switzerland, in Israel, Greece and Italy. In Rome we spent a few days visiting many of the sacred shrines.

In mid-afternoon we came to the Shrine of the Sacred Stairs. This shrine had three sets of stairs side by side leading up to the second and top floor of the shrine. Visitors went up on the stairs to the right and after seeing some relics and paintings, descended on the stairs to the left.

The center stairs, according to Catholic tradition, were constructed with slabs of marble that came from Pilate's judgment hall. When the group were led into the shrine by our young guide, an American born Italian who was then serving as a missionary to Italy, he told the story of the shrine and it's sacredness to Catholics.

He said, "No one ever walks up those stairs. The faithful will crawl up the stairs reciting certain prayers on their ascent." He then led the young people up the right stairs.

Since I was outside the shrine praying with one of the YWAMers who was sick, I didn't hear the instructions. After a while I came in. At that time the guide was pointing out the relics, paintings and traditions. We were approaching the top of the center stairs when Tom heard a gasp from some of the young people. Not having heard the instructions, I had started up the center stairs! Tom said he prayed, "Lord, please don't let that happen." But He'd already allowed it.

Two women were crawling up the stairs and I'd passed the first one. As I came even with the second lady, she began waving her arms and talking in Italian, rebuking me for walking up the stairs. I grabbed her by the arm and tried to pull her to her feet saying, "get up from there and Jesus will set you free."

I'd never have walked up those stairs if I'd heard the instructions, but I'd argue with anyone for doing what I thought was superstitious. I would respect their beliefs.

Although it was not my intention to break the fast, hard rules, no guide can now say, "No one has ever walked up these stairs."

27

A QUESTION OF WORTHINESS

Controversy has always clouded my ministry. Many places across the world women preachers do not have an easy road. In some areas they aren't accepted at all. During a stay in Paris in 1969, where Tom and Loren had been speaking in a service, Tom spoke to the leader, Superintendent Ware. "Let my wife speak a few words."

His answer? "Folks here don't approve of women speaking in church."

Brushing his decision aside, I arose because I felt the anointing and ordination from on high. I began, "What came the word out from you and to you only? The first persons credentialed by the Lord were women whom He told, 'Go tell . . .'"

The tabernacle where my husband and son had been speaking was holding a service primarily for gypsies. The lady gypsies sat on the floor in the back. After quoting Paul I said, "I want to give my testimony, Brother, to those women back there." I proceeded to tell all that the Lord had done for me.

Having followed Loren and Tom to the front, I had noticed that only men were seated in that part of the tabernacle. I felt unwelcomed sitting in the front row side seats while the other women had to sit in the back on the floor.

"They'll not understand you," the leader objected.

"Well, the Lord does," I declared and continued to tell the story of how Jesus had commissioned the three women. ". . . Go tell my disciples that I have arisen and I ascend to my Father and to your Father, to my God and your God. He put himself down on a level with us human beings . . ."

The Holy Spirit gave out a message in tongues and the interpretation came by the WOMEN. The men had little choice but to listen. Quiet reigned again until I spoke directly to the leader, "See, you can't keep the ladies quiet when the Holy Spirit is in control, can you?"

Such scrimmages were not with flesh and blood but with powers and principalities. Across the world the Lord has helped me fight man's traditions. While in Iran, once the great country of Persia and the strongest enemy of little Israel for centuries, we found the rich were getting richer, the poor getting poorer. Yet it seemed like a peaceful country in those days when the Shah was still in power.

As Tom and I walked down the street from the Blisses' missionary home we came upon bread ovens where bakers made the best bread you could ever sink your teeth into.

In the big palace we were shown the large throne. We both had to try the son's small chair and felt like instant royalty. Watchmen guarded the house of royal treasures. When I started down to the lower floor, the guard stopped me. "Give me your purse first." I did. Then as I was going on down the steps I decided to get my purse and retraced my steps to the desk where I asked, "Why should I trust you when you don't trust me? Look through my purse, then let me have it back." Strangely enough, he did!

On the bottom level Tom and I stood and gaped at the exquisite royal treasures housed in glass and securely guarded by armed watchmen.

That next Sunday morning Tom ministered at a service in the Assyrian church. I wasn't sure the ladies there were even permitted to pray in secret. Imagine how my ears perked up when a woman in the back was asked to dismiss.

From there we went to visit the beautiful Assembly of God church which Brother Plotts had helped build with money from America. A young pastor from the Bible School at Brussels, Belgium, led that group of Pentecostals. Such peace we felt in that sanctuary. Tom was a welcome speaker because he was an executive from Southern California who had helped the Brussels Bible School get started.

As I sat in the congregation the Lord let a scripture ring in my ears: "In the last days, saith God, I will pour out my spirit upon all flesh and your sons and your daughters shall prophesy."

The pastor stopped speaking in his own language and spoke to me in perfect English, "Sister Cunningham, will you come up and speak to the ladies?" He indicated I was to speak from the low podium, so I agreed, stopping at the podium he had indicated. I knew it was that country's custom to keep women on a level beneath the man.

God anointed me with a text that I'd received back in the pew. As I preached the ladies began shedding tears. I told them, "Get busy doing the thing God would have you to do. We are all in this together."

Some triumph has come from my battles for women's freedom. After we came home, we saw pictures of some of the women gypsies in France testifying in an open meeting. I know Iran's day will come too. Prayers are going up for them.

Our missionaries in Iran, Rev. and Mrs. Bliss, had experienced a triple tragedy. A native-driven vehicle smashed into the Bliss car, killing all three of their young children. When we arrived there, tell-tale reminders of their departed offspring remained — dolls and toys were still in place. Their little dog was going crazy searching for his master. Through the anointing of the Holy Ghost we were able to offer them love and comfort with our prayers. Life gone — future hopes smashed forever — is terrible.

How we all cherish thoughts of seeing our offspring grow up to become worthwhile contributors to society. But that was no longer possible for the Blisses. Why? None of us can give an answer. All we know is that God did not deliberately take their children away.

I heard a bereaved father once say in order to comfort himself, "I'd given my child to God and now He has taken him!" The Bible calls the devil the handler of death. Satan should never be accepted as anything but our worst foe. Angels took the Bliss children's spirits home after death ended their otherwise profitable lives. Jesus does not tear down His own kingdom. He came to destroy death, not to use it. He claims our spirit after that last enemy has done his part which came about because of man's fall. I have had to watch my own family's loved ones fight the tortures of death until the angels came to carry them home.

The Blisses entertained us graciously and made sumptuous meals in spite of their heavy hearts. Comforting missionaries and helping to provide their finances has been Tom's continual burden. His own salary? Still one dollar a year! His reward will come later.

Back home Tom took up money to buy the Bliss children's tombstones. The Blisses had been forced to bury their youngsters in a slum area of the city, for the nicer cemetery was reserved for Muslims only. They felt Christians were not worthy to be buried there. This is a conflict we pray will be overcome in years ahead.

In 1971 we took a flight around the world, stopping on the way at a Youth With A Mission base in Afghanistan, leaving behind the freedom of the beautiful country of old Persia and entering the land where we knew the ladies were bound by the custom of veils and covering up on the street. Poverty abounded.

As we flew from Persia (Iran) into the Lions Valley, on to Kabul, the capital we viewed vast stretches of desert with some cultivated land, hillside cabins and caves, sheep grazing and men digging in the earth. Upon landing we found streets lined with beggars from all parts of the world. Many had followed the dope trail clear to its end. Some well-educated young men we met told us they came from influential European and American families. They, too, sat on the streets begging for coins to buy food. The U.S. embassy had done all they could or would for them.

Our taxi driver looked startled as we told him to stop at a run-down hotel. It had been abandoned until one of Loren's Youth With A Mission groups had been given permission to use it for a time. Inside we were warmly welcomed and were given the privilege of speaking with and preaching to some of the wayward lads from the western world. They needed no interpreter.

Sitting on the floor, I shared the story of the grace of God in my own father's life, as he was redeemed from sin and became a preacher of the Gospel for over forty years until he was called home at the age of 84. The YWAM youth then served us good food on a makeshift table.

That work had begun when Janice and her husband Jim Rogers and a small group went driving a van across Southern Europe, Turkey, and Iran, to the border of Afghanistan. They were arrested on the border of that Muslim-dominated area for carrying Christian literature. After holding them in house arrest for 48 hours, the officer finally asked to see their literature. Upon scanning it, he said, "I see no reason why you cannot pass this out. What a miracle!"

Later, when the communists took over, religious freedom was no longer allowed there. The church built by the Presbyterian missionary, Christy Wilson, was the first one built there in a thousand years. The Christian people were also permitted to work so (in accord with an agreement between that country's leaders and President Eisenhower who permitted the first Muslim Temple to be built in the U.S. for their diplomats) a Christian church was built for the diplomats from the U.S.A. The Muslims finally bulldozed down the Christian church where Tom had preached. Our country's free policy of religion still allowed the Muslim Temple to be.

After three years of ministry there the YWAMers had to leave, but some seed had been planted. Several of the best leaders of YWAM were converts in that dilapidated old hotel.

One Swede who had been arrested for giving out Christian literature had been locked up in the top of that hotel. We were devastated when we learned it was the custom to lock up prisoners, leaving them to starve unless friends came to help. The young YWAMers became the Swede's friend, fed him and obtained a lawyer who was finally able to get him free.

Before going on to India we shopped here for rugs. They were too expensive, but we were glad we saw them. We saw the Christian sign. Weavers were still including the Nestorian cross as part of their weaving design.

Tom and I had no choice but to steel ourselves against the beggars. Our hosts were Americans who had gone there to help with social and humanities services. "I know it sounds heartless," they told us, "but you must not give to the beggars at the door." I could have scarcely turned one away if I had seen him and from the up-stairs window it was difficult to turn my back on the man below who was waving the stump of his severed right arm at me. The window wouldn't open or I would have been tempted to toss him a coin, breaking the rule of the house.

We flew over the Khyber Pass to India where Tom was asked if he'd be the main speaker at the Council of the Assemblies of God in India.

South India's General Council was being held at a little village in the Maharasta state. Our accommodations were in a small room off the back of the stage of the tabernacle. I was sick with a cold—almost pneumonia.

One night after the prayer was made for me, I made myself a sari by wrapping about six yards of silk around me and went out to testify to my healing touch. I thought it looked okay. Ladies laughed. Superintendent Jeyarah—I called him Brother Garage —asked me if I would speak the next day.

"Yes," I said, believing God to make me able. And He did. We finished our time there, blessing and being blessed, eating hot peppered curried rice meals at the long tables outside and hating to leave. But we had to go on to Malaysia where the pepper in the rice was hotter. I told Tom I felt the cook there at the Federal Hotel was just teasing us Americans with too much pepper.

Funny thing, I couldn't find my banana. I had put one on Tom's bed lamp and one on mine for the next morning. "Tom, did you eat my banana?"

"No."

"Well, who did?" Then finding parts of the banana and the peel hanging in a small opening under the bathroom sink, I knew it was a rat, not Tom who was the culprit. Strange thing, I thought. A rat five stories up and in a new modern building such as this.

We visited the enthusiastic congregation at the Singapore Assembly. The Fred Sewards, southern California missionaries, had been founders and pastors for several years.

I recalled how she had attracted my attention away from my own praying to listen and watch her deeply agonizing at one of our ladies' retreats in southern California. That was the time when that young red-headed mother of small children was making her consecration for Asia to work for souls and now I was seeing the results effectively portrayed. It was almost all young adults and young folks who were making the church go.

So Margie, your tears and consecration paid off in triumph, I thought to myself.

28

APARTMENT COMPLEX

My friend Loraine called me and said, "We're buying an apartment from Sam Navarra."

"Has he got another one?" I asked. To that inquiry she replied, "Yes, he's got one more."

I had taken 120 hours of real estate courses at Long Beach after I was banned from full service in the church. For some reason I could never get real estate out of my blood, so her suggestion intrigued me. There's an old saying, "While the cat's away the mouse will play." Since Tom was out of town, I decided to venture over and see if we could swing a deal.

While I was at Mr. Gross's realtor's office, Tom phoned me. Somehow he'd tracked me down so I told him, "Honey, I'm already in here negotiating. We're gonna have to sell our home in Monterey Park and the two in Bakersfield, but I think we can swing buyin' this apartment. Tom, it's brand new and beautiful!"

Mr. Gross, the realtor, took us up to Bakersfield to check out our two houses. Both were in fine shape and had FHA loans. "We're going to have to let a realtor up here move these," he told me. "I won't try to sell them over the phone."

We agreed to give him our home in Monterey Park to sell as soon as possible. The sale of that house didn't bring in enough to pay the down payment and the insurance. A financial conflict built up because we needed extra for the taxes. Where could we get enough money in time to keep from losing the apartments?

Our friend Sam, a member of Covina Assembly of God, had given us every break, declaring, "If this apartment is for Rev.

202

Cunningham, I'm not just going to black top the driveway, I'm going to pave it with concrete. I'll also make a built-in desk for him." As the apartment neared the finishing stages, we anticipated moving into our three bedroom deluxe accommodations. Somehow we had to raise more money up front. But how? That became an urgent request. We had to trust God somehow for a miracle.

And then — that miracle came. Tom's sister had willed us money we had not known of and when we received the $10,000 check she'd bequeathed him, we both realized that money suddenly made it possible for the apartments to be ours. Surely she would have been elated to know what that gift did for us in the years to come.

After we moved from Monterey Park, Coy, my brother dropped in to visit. Looking around, he seemed awe-struck. "Jewell, this is a PALACE!"

Interest rates for our "palace" were 7.7% and the payments amounted to $406 a month. Clearing nearly that same figure every thirty days caused us to triumph over a problem that had weighed so heavily on us for years.

Tom had especially prayed that the Lord would open the way so that it would be financially possible for us to visit our foreign mission fields. The Lord answered that heart's desire too! For ten years we enjoyed that extra income. The Lord had a way!

At that time Alhambra was called "The Bedroom of Los Angeles" because everyone was tearing down the little houses to build apartments. I found myself acting as land lady. An older woman living next to us also played that role. Her husband died shortly after we'd moved in. When she'd become so grief stricken that she'd walk the floor at night, I'd try to comfort her. She seemed to resent my religious viewpoint of life and did until the last time I visited her in the convalescent home. I'd followed the priest into her room. When I prayed with her in the spirit, I felt she was saved. We were away for our Sunday appointments, but she left word for me before dying within the next two days, "Tell Mrs. Cunningham I had peace."

One more triumph for Jesus! We had lots to think about while we ran the apartments. The Lord always responded to my prayer,

"Lord, send me some GOOD tenants." We left often for ministry but our assistant kept things going well.

It wasn't too much trouble to keep the apartments up because they were new and I screened the potential tenants. Nobody smoked — I wouldn't tolerate that or any other hanky panky.

Once a doctor came by and tried to rent one saying, "I won't use it all the time. Probably my friend Kelly will drop by some times."

Upon further inquiry I learned that "Kelly" was a lady friend. I somehow surmised he was a married man and she was his mistress.

Later that day another young lady named Kelly happened to come by. Seemingly a good girl, I offered to lease it to her. When the fellow came back who'd been wanting me to rent the apartment to him and "his Kelly," I had the opportunity to tell him it'd already been leased to "Kelly"!

God had answered my prayer about this problem, for our license would have been in jeopardy. The first Kelly was black and the NAACP would have said she had been refused because of her race.

When Tom later decided to change his job and our life style we had sold the apartments and moved from Alhambra into a nice house in Pasadena, then later into a different field of pioneering. Since then folks have often told us, "You ought to have your apartments now. They'd be worth a fortune!" Within a couple of years we would have doubled our profits, but we didn't lose sleep over it.

Statements such as that could cause turmoil to start churning inside us, but we refuse to accept that as a conflict. Our lives have been filled with such stumbling blocks, but we have often found that, as in the case of the apartments, God only used them as stepping stones for us to stay in His triumphant will!

For the twenty-one years that Tom was doing his assignment as Assistant Superintendent for the Southern California District, God had given me a new and wide field of evangelism within and outside the District — three times out of the nation. This could not have been possible. My going outside the nation alone could not have happened, had it not been for the apartment income. The only time I sent back a report of my meetings abroad for our District paper, the man who was secretary then did not include it. He said, "They may think we sent you with District moneys."

Once both Tom and I were away for six weeks and found all was well when we returned. Our assistant manager had done well, the main reason being we had it on the altar. God gives us material things and if we keep those things from getting in between God and our service to Him, we'll be able to enjoy them. "The earth is the Lord's and the fullness thereof." Too often the devil gets the big end of it, because we as God's children fail to claim our inheritance. (Poor is not always heredity.)

Tom heard in September of 1979 that the nation of China was open for tourists and made some plans. He was rejected at first, for the travel agent told him, "You were signed in as a Rev. Tom Cunningham, so they rejected the visa."

"Oh," Tom said, "I could get a lot of folks who would assure the Chinese consulate I'm not a preacher, I just think I am!" So on the next try, with the Rev. left off, Mr. and Mrs. Cunningham were accepted and for eleven full days traveled across China. We'll never forget the excitement of those days. Yet they began to get boring because of the sameness. How our hearts ached to tell them about Jesus! God gave us one soul on the last day of sightseeing on the bus. I led Mr. Tu to accept the Lord. It was so exciting to tell him and others of Jesus for the first time. (Recently we received such a good report from Rev. Philip Hogan, Director of Foreign Missions for The Assemblies of God, that there are now 50 million believers in China.)

29

SOUTH PACIFIC ISLAND

After watching the sparkling blue waters of the Pacific out of the plane windows for seemingly endless hours, Tom and I had become almost mesmerized by the sameness of the view until suddenly a group of islands appeared before us. The plane dropped slowly, its wheels hit ground. After a jolt the huge silver jet rolled to a stop. Loren had told us before the flight, "I've been in all parts of the world, but there's no spot on earth more beautiful than New Zealand." Because of his enthusiasm, his father and I had greatly anticipated this visit.

Flying from Auckland on the North Island to Queenstown in the southern part of the South Island aboard a smaller plane gave us a picturesque post card view of that beautiful country. Looking out the window of the plane at the sights below was like turning the pages of a National Geographic magazine. Sheep grazed on the hillsides of the South Island; shimmering lakes spotted the lush greenery as we neared the lakeside city of Queenstown.

At the Presbyterian Church there, our hearts soared with events that were even more impressive to us than the scenery. Both the Church in Queenstown and the big theater converted into a sanctuary in Christ Church, where we were to visit shortly were filled. A goodly portion of each congregation were YWAMers singing the praises of the Lord and reaching out to the lost in the given areas. Tom's grey eyes met mine and I knew we were sharing the same thought, "The Lord is very much in evidence in some places in New Zealand." But one could sense, in traveling from one end of the country to the other the Lord had

206

second place in some lives. So materialistic! Just like so much we have seen in America.

From Queenstown we were driven to Gore, further south on the island, to stop by a YWAM base. At Gore we rented a car and drove north, crossing by ferry between the South Island to Wellington on the North Island, then to Auckland. Having driven from one end of the country to the other, we had accomplished a feat experienced by few "Yanks."

Tom had an appointment to speak at one of the churches in Aukland, but we totally lost our sense of direction. Finally, in desperation, Tom hailed a cabby to ask directions. "Follow me," he said as he led the way. When we pulled up behind him in front of the church, Tom got out and offered him a generous tip. With a motion of the hand he refused it saying, "You just get in there and convert them."

Tom in his usual joking way couldn't resist saying, as he handed him his card, "If you ever get to Los Angeles, I'll give you directions. I know the streets well!"

From Aukland all across North and South Island we found several YWAM bases and churches. Others told us that the YWAMers were doing a good job ministering and saving souls. Praise God!

Our next stop was Sydney, Australia, where we were met by Tom Hallas who took us to teach at the YWAM Base in Goldburn for a week. The anointed messages were like a mighty force with those young folks' acceptance and consecrations.

We were also scheduled to speak to a couple of the Assemblies in the country. While staying one Saturday night with a pastor there to preach at Brisbane Assembly, we left his home so we could drop in on another YWAM group. One young man stood out in the crowd. Of slight build, he was dressed in shorts and sandals. His shade of skin made me think he must have come from a South Pacific island. "Did you ever meet Mel Tari?" someone asked us. That was our first introduction to the man whose story "LIKE A MIGHTY WIND" swept across the world as it shared how God's Holy Spirit had changed the country of Indonesia.

Not long after we arrived at that meeting some of the young YWAMers started upstairs to roost for the night, but I had other ideas. "Come on down! Let's have some praying and singing first!" I called and they all responded — if for no other reason than they all respectfully called us "Mom and Pop Cunningham."

The young folks sat in a circle and Mel sat in a chair by me. After a few choruses the little Indonesian began to preach on the coming of the Lord, sitting cross-legged and playing with his toes at times. Sandals, shorts and shirt were his attire. The Holy Spirit's presence was so strong then that I realized clothes, skin color or stature are not the measures of a man. Faith is!

I could hardly wait for Mel to finish so that I could ask, "Will you tell us about the one miracle — did a man really rise up from the dead?"

"Yes," he answered simply — as though it were no big thing. "In Indonesia we don't embalm anyone. That man had been dead for three days before I could get there to preach his funeral so his body was already stinking! While the folks were singing hymns, suddenly his body raised straight up in the coffin! He was alive!" Mel's voice had grown in strength. A sense of excitement filled his countenance.

"What did the people do then?" I asked.

"They went bananas!" Mel smiled and then added a statement that astounded everyone. All eyes widened as he shared, "Then the man who I'd prepared the funeral for began to help preach and I don't need to tell you that he had everyone's attention. That service started a wave of revival. Thousands began to turn to God!"

Tom and I went away from that meeting with new hope, as I'm sure the YWAMers did. Joy flooded our hearts as we rehashed Mel's first hand report. That little man was certainly being used in a big way by God!

In Brisbane we attended a second Assemblies of God Church for their fourth service of the day. Fourth! The time? Four P.M.! That Sunday the two of us stood in awe at that late afternoon crowd. A thousand worshipers were crammed inside the building.

Skeptical at such a crowd, I turned to the lady beside me and asked, "Do some people who attended the first three services come back again?"

"Oh, no!" she declared. "That's why we have so many services — to divide the crowd just to make room."

Hundreds of young people dressed in proper church attire stood with their hands raised in praise. Thrilling to my soul! Tom, too, was pleased, but became a little apprehensive when the church pastor asked him not to preach on missions.

"Mr. Missions' " reaction was immediate. "Why not?"

"Because we need a sermon on repentance."

His sermon was on the story of the conversion of a sinful woman of Samaria who had become a missionary by saying, "Come see the Man." (John 4:9) That theme gave them what they had asked for; it accomplished our purposes because of its strong mission undertones. That big church in faraway Australia is much like some here in the states. Americans also have magnificent cathedrals with tall steeples and spires reaching skyward which in a small way tell the story of the cross, but inside the people have no interest in carrying the message of the Gospel outside their own neighborhood.

Our next stop in island hopping was Tonga, by way of Fiji, as the plane didn't go directly to Tonga, one of the few remaining isles ruled by a king. Jim and Janice had been there witnessing the day of the current king's coronation. Upon their return home they couldn't wait to share what had happened. All the YWAMers were giving out Tonga Gospel tracts when a thief snatched one of the girls' purse right out of her hands. Imagine his disgust when he found nothing inside but a bunch of printed papers! Frustrated, he'd thrown the purse over the fence into the palace yard. The king's young son found it and took it to his mother, the Queen. What appeared to be a loss turned out to be a great blessing.

Eventually, the king began to search for answers about his own Christian profession. At the same time, a move of the Holy Spirit had begun through an Assemblies of God missionary, Bernice Proctor, and had spread through the schools. Scores of young people were getting up at daybreak for prayer meetings. Eventually, as hundreds of youth were filled with the Holy Spirit, a spiritual move began which affected the tiny island nation.

Such exciting news for our family! Since all of us had given our lives to spreading the Gospel across the world, we were most grateful to the Lord for giving our youngest daughter and her husband a part in a nationwide revival.

During our visit Tom was asked to be in charge of the Sunday evening service at the home of the Prime Minister. As the speakers for this service, we sat in the front of a big room on soft upholstered chairs while the rest of the worshipers sat on the floor. How strange! Other empty chairs were not being put to use, so we figured it must have been their custom to have everyone else sit beneath the ruler and the dignitaries. One man sitting on the floor with the others was actually a doctor who was there to help those in need!

While on the island of Tonga Tom again used his gift as peacemaker by mending relationships when he found malice had built up between two of the missionaries there. He brought them together in the spirit of reconciliation, clearing up a misunderstanding which had been undermining both their ministries.

Using verses two and three of the second chapter of James, I shared to the Prime Minister, that if we show respect of man, we sin — pointing out that such respect in parliament is all right, but one should not put himself on a higher plane in church, for there we are all to be brethren — Giving him a gift of candy which I hoped would somehow sweeten my words.

Stopping over again at the lovely tropical island of Fiji we spoke at the large church that Superintendent Cakau had built. The Fijians sang loud and enthusiastically for Jesus, nowhere on the face of the globe have we found worshipers with more enthusiasm than those islanders.

Since Jim and Lou Hanse had been laboring as missionaries in the South Pacific, Tom and I were disappointed at not seeing them because they were on furlough at the time. We'd first met Jim when Loren had brought him home to Faith Tabernacle as part of his quartet. That particular Saturday I'd lined up blind dates for each of them to take to the park in Los Angeles. Jim and Louella's marriage was a result of that meeting. Tom had also endorsed this assignment.

In Fiji, about midnight, I walked out on the balcony of the hotel where we were staying. Tom was always a good sound sleeper and easy off to sleep land. But, unable to get to sleep I decided to avail myself of the fresh ocean breeze and the tropical splendor. On the patio below, native dancers and singers swayed and sang to the music of their unusual instruments. They moved about so gracefully that I stood there enthralled. For that short space in time I felt like an intruder who'd been transported temporarily to a world other than my own. New Years Day in 1978 dawned on us in Tahiti and we found no missionary home, so we went on to Easter Island.

Five hours from Tahiti by jet we reached Easter Island which has been written about so often in the pages of history. The hotel looked much more like a second-rate motel. After three days of our four-day stay the clerk dropped a shocker. "We are so sorry, but we cannot keep you any longer. A big plane load of people from Hawaii are coming." Stymied as to where we might stay, Tom and I just looked at one another, for our plane was not due to pick us up until the following day. We had no choice but to look for another place.

We combined our search for lodging with a sight-seeing trip we had hoped to make while we were there. Pictures we'd seen of the huge statues carved out of stone many feet in diameter and many feet tall had intrigued us. Supposedly they'd been placed at the edge of the water to watch over the ocean. Upon inquiring, we learned we had two choices of how to visit them — either rent a jeep or walk. We chose the second option. "We need the exercise," we decided as we started across the vast expanse of grass land. Nearing the village I suggested, "Let me drop by a residence and see if there might be someone friendly enough to rent us a room for tomorrow night. I'll miss seeing the statues if I have to."

The first house on my path was small, but neat. I noticed the door was open and there was no screen. "Come in," a voice from inside invited in very good English.

A woman was working in the kitchen. "I wonder if it would be possible for my husband and I to rent a room for one night," I inquired.

"I'd be very glad to do that, but my husband is the mayor and we are not allowed to rent any part of the house because it belongs to the town." Just then her husband drove up in a jeep and the lady introduced him to me, "My husband, the mayor." I found myself addressing the mayor with this proposal, "I am Mrs. Cunningham, an American. I'll give you ten dollars if you'll take me to see the statues."

"Climb in," he offered, "but I want no money." Along the way we overtook Tom who was still walking. "Please," I said to the mayor, "please pick him up too. He's my husband." A surprised look crossed his face when he saw me sitting in the jeep.

The two of us had to hoof it back to the village. Everything was extremely high. Food, lodging, sight-seeing, etc. The guide was explaining that the people who erected the huge statues disappeared from the island. No one knew where they went, or why. Tom said something that pleased the other tourists, but didn't ingratiate him with the guide. He said, "I don't know where they went, but I know why. They were priced off the island." Our generous benefactor had gone on his way as soon as he got us to our destination. Later we located a room in a guest house that was built for lodging the overflow crowd from the hotel.

Hot, spicy Spanish cooking made me ill. Even though we were each paying twenty-six dollars a day for bed and board, I felt cheated. Easter Island had one small Catholic church — that was all I could see or find out about. I had to tell the Lord, "Send forth laborers!"

The next day, too ill to eat anything else, I was ever so glad when we'd finally made our way through all the red tape and slow service at the airport. Our next stop was Santiago, Chile — five hours away. Sick and tired, after another long flight I wanted to go home!

It was also with a broken spirit and a feeling of failure that I left Tom in Chile to make the rest of that trip alone. When I said, "Tom, I want to go home," he was of course willing, but it was the first time I could recall ever leaving him with tears. I reached Los Angeles and Phyllis took me from the big airport to her home. Tom went throughout the South American nations for three weeks and had good reports to bring home. But my forsaking that part of the long trip and failing to go on with our planned trip throughout South America left me with the feeling of being a loser, a quitter, with Tom which I've never been.

My stomach trouble healed at home, but would have no doubt in Chile too. I couldn't forget Tom's tears as I flew on the Braniff, stopping only once for passengers in Peru.

In reality I felt I would not have had my purse snatched, as it happened, in the Braniff ticket office, had I not been doing like Jonah buying his ticket to Tarshish.

ARRIVING IN TAIWAN

On our long trip around the world, in early fall of 1971, Tom and I arrived at the airport in Taipei, Taiwan. Though a bit tired from the lengthy travel we were looking forward to this visit with anticipation for we were coming in as guests of General Wu Wen-Ee, Military Adviser to General Chiang Kai-shek, president of Nationalist China.

Before landing the Japan Airlines had given us two forms to fill out. This chore had been handled and we were going through customs. The young Chinese Customs Officer looked over our passports and the forms that had been filled out. He said, "Form _____ is missing. Why didn't you fill it out?" Tom assured him we had filled out all forms given us by the airline, but he wouldn't accept that, insinuating that we were trying to hide something. About that time, Tom heard his name called over the P.A. system asking him to come for a message.

Tom told the customs officer that the page was for him, and that if he would let him go get the message, his wife would stay there with our things and he would come back and fill out any forms he would give him. He reluctantly gave him permission.

The young lady paging Tom said, "General Wu is waiting for you outside." She then pinned a large button on his lapel with the message in English and Chinese, "Guests of General Wu Wen-Ee."

Tom returned to his antagonist, the young customs officer. He took one look at the button on Tom's lapel and his eyes seemed to get as large as the button. In a rather agitated voice he said, "All a mistake, all a mistake." He stamped our papers and gave us a stamped visa. Then he called two sky-caps and hurried us out the door.

There was the General, a dear friend, with two orderlies and a chauffer. they took our luggage and placed it in the vehicle and seated us in he car, and away we went. We had received just short of a state welcome. It's not what you know, but who you know.

Sunday, Tom flew 500 miles further south in the island to help our Southern California missionary's decision concerning a building for his work. I had no one to take me to church, if I knew where, so it gave me a chance to witness to the General's house boy, who was indeed a man, and father of a family.

As I called him—his name was Yeh—I turned it around— "Hey, come here . . ." "You want water?" "No, let's talk. Can we talk down in the parlor?" He agreed and there with no more ado, I asked, "Do you know Jesus?" "Who is Jesus," was his answer. "Oh, He's God's Son." "Which god?" he asked. "No, He's the only God, the Creator God. And He had a Son who died in our place for our sins, that we might live forever."

"And Mr. Yeh, if you'll accept Him as your Saviour, believe in Him, you and your family won't have to go out to nothingness [as I was thinking as a Budhist who has not made their Karma] but you and they will live forever!" "Oh!!"

I can still see that dear little Chinese man as he clasped both his hands together and exclaimed, "That's *good!*"

Leaving him with a Bible and admonitions to follow on, we had to depart as Tom had returned, and we flew on to Tokyo, Japan to minister.

_____
_____
_____
_____
_____
_____
_____
_____
_____
_____
_____
_____
_____
_____
_____
_____
_____
_____
_____
_____

Rolling Ridge Realty

Your neighborhood Real Estate Information specialist

JEANNE &
HAL BURNS

Bus: (714) 597-1891
Res: (714) 597-1474
Fax: (714) 597-4968

30

FULFILLED YEARS

In Guam, where we ministered, we have to recall with gratitude the example of the young sailor lad coming back after World War II ended and building a work there. His name was John Burk.

The Marshall Islands were evangelized by Sam Sasser. In 1970, Tom and I visited his church on our way to Korea, and Tom was to help set it in order, but first we had to get one ordained to be elected as superintendent. The night before he was to be elected, the king himself had been ordained. He was the suitable one for the lead office as he seemed to have been fore-ordained by the Lord, for he was the one chosen to be their superintendent after he was their reigning king.

During a short revival there, Brother Philips from Santa Ana, California, brought forth such dynamic messages that little children as well as adults came into the fullness of the blessing. The wide-eyed youngsters sat on the floor around the altar. How could one ever forget their little arms lifted in praise along with the adults?

The scene also must have been impressed upon Reverend Philip's mind, for he bristled later when some of his board insisted the children leave the sanctuary of his home church during the Sunday morning services. He demanded, "Let me have my children here for me to minister to." Not only was he affected by memories of the youngsters worshipping so effectively in the Marshall Islands, but he remembered the Master's word, "Suffer the little children to come unto me," as well as Peter's mandate, "Feed my lambs."

In Japan we visited where Paul Klahr and others who were faithfully carrying on regular church services mainly to Americans in uniform. Although Tom and I tried to encourage their efforts in our messages, we could see few Japanese were open to the Christian message. Marie and Agnes Jergeusen and their parents and many more missionaries have spent their lives just getting a few converts. Yet their seeds must have caused a harvest — today the reports are much more encouraging.

Tom and I witnessed the Japanese situation firsthand. The cities were so congested. Folks nearly shoved each other out of the way as they jammed the subways and the aisles of the department stores. But such ambitious people! The countryside teemed with men at work. What tore at our hearts most was the graft and the greed which was so evident. A beautiful land, a beautiful people — Japan lacked one major thing. Jesus' love was missing!

In 1968, we had visited and ministered on the Caribbean Islands, down from the eastern side of the United States. Things were so different from the Western Islands which seemingly Americans had only found to evangelize after World War II. In Haiti, Jamaica and Santo Domingo, many churches had been established by the evangelical missionaries. Not cathedrals in any sense of the word, but the Christian churches there are truly serving God among heathen natives who were enveloped by superstition and idolatry. Have you ever looked upon a half-starved child? Nowhere had we ever seen more poverty-stricken people. Scrawny, hollow-eyed children are a familiar sight, in Haiti.

For once in my life where I was sent to preach I took my purse to the pulpit with me. Tom had been sent to preach in a better section of the city. I had no secure feeling that I was safe and in the lower part of the city of Petionville we prayed fervently for our beloved missionaries — the Turnbulls and the Hittenbergers — for we knew how burdensome their task was, ministering with such poor people.

In 1984, we were invited by Superintendent Bohla to the country of Guyana in the northern part of South America. It was not such a pleasurable time, yet we met many dear people attending the Assembly of God churches which had been built in the last couple of decades.

Some years past, Morris Plotts had raised money in the U.S. and sent it for the big Assembly of God church to be built in the capital city of Georgetown. Now there are 175 churches. Such love of God was manifested in those godly oppressed but victorious saints!

Guyana is now under Communist rule, frightening when one realizes it is right off our shores! Yet, despite the oppression against them, both financial and otherwise, church folks there are still faithful and going on with the work of God.

A bread line? None existed in Guyana, for bread is a no-no. The reason? Missionaries told us, "The leadership wants to stop all the imports and have folks grow their own wheat." How were they to do that? One could see it wouldn't be a good wheat-producing country. While we were there one girl was fined and jailed for buying a loaf of bread from the black market. Our own breakfast at the old Dutch-built hotel where we were staying was cut short when the waiter said, "You were given bread yesterday!" Oh, yes! We recalled having one piece! But we had Jesus, the Bread of life. How much He was needed there!

We had no peace of mind there. Our door was kept locked, for some natives had hounded us to buy our American dollars. Some even begged, "Help me to get to America." I'd have liked to have brought some of them home with us.

Brother Bohla gave us a dinner and shared a prayer concern. To continue working in Guyana, his son would be required to attend one of their colleges and be indoctrinated with the Marxist doctrine.

Tom and I each had a couple of churches to minister in. The government did not admonish us, but our host and hostess warned us, "You'd better steer clear of any politics." To this Tom replied, "Hopefully God will keep us so we can continue to preach Jesus."

As we were about to depart the country, Brother and Sister Bohla stayed nearby to watch as we were put through three different customs and other rigid investigation. We'd been able to get in because of a letter that dear pastor had received from the Communist Secretary of State — "Dear Comrade Bohla, Yes, you may have Mr. and Mrs. Cunningham come for five days."

Since we could show our arrival had been approved, and after telling how much money we were taking with us, we were finally allowed to board the plane to take us to home and freedom. Along with us we carried the memories of that visit and a determination to keep in prayer those dear Guyanan saints — mostly people from the east India race.

That trip and the one which took us eleven days across Red China in their earliest days of tourism gave us such concern as to be prayer partners with those living in Communist-dominated countries of the world.

In 1985 the earth shook in Mexico City and a great quake followed. Devastation and fear resulted. Tom and I responded to Wayne and Doris Turnbulls' need to have someone come and minister to those who remained. Many were seeking God for answers.

We each were assigned a tent where we were to preach each night, come rain or come shine. The tents were put up in prime spots across the devastated city.

Tom ministered under a big tent across the city. Youth were flocking in to fill the seats. Because this was the first time in their lives a tragedy which was beyond their comprehension and control had taken place, they were seeking God.

How I ached for those broken-hearted, frightened people! But I got so ill I had to ask for someone to fill my place. On the final night I knew I would miss out on my last chance, so I got out of bed, dressed and was taken to my tent.

While I rested in the car and watched while folks gathered, God touched me. I was called to the platform after the singing and did a little dance myself, praising God for my healing.

The Lord anointed my words. At the end I invited them to the front and said, "Stand here and tell God, 'Here I am — send me!' Say an eternal YES to Him." My heart soared as they came by the numbers. I counted ten across and figured there were nine other such groups. God told David not to count, but He did not tell me that. The Holy Spirit began to bless.

I didn't try to minister to each of them, but said over the mike, "Pray, give yourself to Jesus." One by one they began to speak in another language. I asked Wayne, "Are they speaking Spanish?" He assured me they were not. They were speaking in tongues! What a meeting!

Tom's been asking church leaders since our experience in Mexico, "Is there anyone you know who can speak Spanish fluently who can go to Mexico to minister?" There have been six thus far and they have been building churches to replace the tents.

Sometimes it takes an earthquake to set things right, as it did in Paul and Silas' jail experience and as we first learned in El Centro. God's people sometimes head for the Social Security system to maintain them. As for us, Tom and I can not relax and sit back and enjoy our rocking chairs when there are so many souls to save and jobs to fill, so Tom still gets calls from the Holy Spirit, and various pastors across the nation.

One of our more recent missions meetings was at Aruba in the Netherlands Antilles. After feeling soothed by watching the sparkling blue waters which lapped lazily over the sandy beaches, we were surprised when the customs officers were reluctant to let us enter. When Tom inquired why, he was told, "You have no address for an invitation to visit." These words were true. Pastor Alberga, a Dutchman from Holland, had not been on hand to greet us. Since we had neither his address or phone number and we were denied use of the customs' telephone to get help from an operator, we had no choice but to let the officials keep our passports and visas while we went next door and ordered reservations in the $100-a-night motel.

We'd had better for less money and were very glad to get out the next day as soon as Pastor Alberga came.

The pastor's dedication showed in the church he had built. It was so arranged to include a dormitory, an apartment, a chapel for a Bible school — all of which was erected in spite of opposition from the island leadership who wanted only their own religion practiced. We learned that this was also the reason for the delay at customs.

Enjoying their hospitality as Tom taught in the Bible school for a week, we had an interesting tour of the island. The cab driver informed us, "Nearly all of our income comes from tourists." The eastern coastline was hilly and uneven and there were no beaches. A natural bridge which could have been used for a walkway, was perhaps strong enough for vehicles to cross over the spur of water. The ocean waves crested, then flowed under it, dashing against a natural wall.

On the western side we found a tourist's paradise. Very expensive hotels lined the beach where Tom and I gathered special shells while others were boating, surfing or sun bathing.

On Sunday morning at 7:00, Tom kept his appointment with Brother Alberga to help baptize thirty-seven converts in the ocean. Then they all came back to hear his sermon and it was my turn to preach that night. Sitting in the back with other English-speaking women that night, I moaned, "I'm so sick. My hands are cold and clammy. I must go to my room."

"Oh, no," one said. "We came just to hear you."

"But I am so sick!" I protested again just as the pastor called me up front. Immediately I felt well to preach. After my thirty-minute sermon, under strong anointing, I gave the invitation, "Who will say an eternal YES to God's call? Come and stand along the altar rail, please."

All thirty-seven freshly baptized converts came and stood along the front — too many to lay hands on, as I was too ill, too tired. Yet as I watched, God sent His Holy Spirit as one by one they began to speak in other tongues.

I sat down near a lady who had hobbled in on a three-pronged crutch. Since I couldn't comprehend her message to me in words, she used body language to indicate that she'd fallen out the door and broken her hip. Laying my hand on her knee, I spoke a fervent prayer, remembering Jesus words at Lazarus' tomb when He looked up and reminded His Heavenly Father, "I know you always hear me."

Suddenly this lady tossed her crutch aside and began running and jumping around, squealing, "Look! Look what I can do!"

Our nest empty, Tom and I held many meetings about carrying out both his and my burdens for the Lord. Because of my husband's zealous efforts in world evangelism one hundred and forty-eight workers have been sent out into the mission field and Tom Cunningham has become known world around as "Mr. Missions."

We have been compelled to experience a missionary's life, but God has been with us as we have put one hundred and forty-three thousand miles on our old Pontiac — crisscrossing the states from New England to the gulf and ocean to ocean. The Lord has helped Tom to raise many thousands of dollars per year for the past 8½ years in his task of assisting men and women in the foreign field. Going out with the approval of the General Council, he was given the title of "Deputation Representative of Foreign Missions."

"Where should we live?" Tom asked me after he'd resigned from office. "We can't live here on the west coast and reach all the necessary places."

His words tore into my heart strings. I so enjoyed our Pasadena home in the better part of the City of Roses where a helicopter flew overhead daily as a security watch, plus so many other city benefits. I didn't want to leave and Tom was aware of that fact.

But in all honesty I had to be realistic and say that he was right. When we finally agreed that another move was necessary, I prayed, "Lord, make me willing." Tears surfaced every time I thought of leaving and fought my own selfishness.

We called a realtor and while Tom was off preaching in Asia, the house was sold. I packed, rented a U-Haul and hired some YWAMers to drive the furniture to a place we'd bought in Texas. It had been intended as an investment, but we had to tell the tenants to leave since Tyler, Texas, was to be our new home.

Tom returned from Bangkok to find an empty house. I'd gone to spend time with Phyllis after the house was sold. When Tom caught up with me, he asked, "Why did you sell the house in such a hurry?"

"No use cutting a dog's tail off an inch at a time to keep it from hurting!"

We spent the night with Phyllis and her family, then started on the long trek to Texas. It was as though life had gone full circle. Tyler was the place we'd left behind some fifty years before.

Again Tom recalls: "Facing another District Council that was to convene in Riverside, California, in April of 1979, with still more than a year remaining in the term to which I had been elected, I was seriously seeking God as to the direction Jewell and I should take.

"I was preaching in a missionary convention in the city of Clearwater, Florida, in late March of 1979. Daily I was seeking God for His direction. It came on Friday afternoon, March 30. But it wasn't the Voice I had heard on two occasions twenty-one years before. Rather it was a deep-seated conviction and assurance that the time had come for me to move out into a new phase of missionary work. When that assurance came, I glanced at my watch and saw it was 3 P.M.

"I called Jewell at our home and her first remark was in the form of a question, 'Has the Lord shown you anything?' I told her I was sure I had the mind of the Lord — that I would be coming home in four days, that I would resign my position with our district effective June 1, 1979. I realized this meant that I would go on retirement pay and work for the Division of Foreign Missions for $1.00 per year plus our travel expenses.

"There was a considerable pause on the other end of the line, then she said, 'Well, I have followed you for forty-seven years (At this writing it has been fifty-six years) and I will continue to follow you. But I sure hope you know what you are doing this time!' She made that statement because I had told her our pay would drop 75% on June 1, 1979. Can you blame her?

"Looking back from this vantage point, it will be nine years on June 1. I can say as Joshua of old, 'Not one thing has failed of all the good things which the Lord your God spoke concerning you. All have come to pass for you, and not one word of them has failed.' (Joshua 23:14b)"

Through the years Tom has been promoted from pastoring to executive work, missionary endeavors, convention speaking and world-wide promotion of missions. With all these homes and salaries, nothing has ever given us the combined joy and happiness of ministry together as did our times of pioneering.

Tom's assignment with the Division of Foreign Missions of the Assemblies of God is for a two year period, reviewed each two years for extension.

In the spring of 1987 he wrote his immediate superior in the Division of Forein Missions, Rev. Paul Branna, saying, "When I was praying about my change of ministry in 1979, and reached the conclusion it was God's time for me to launch out, I asked the Lord for ten years in which to serve Him in the new ministry. June 1, 1987 will mark eight years so I'm asking for another extension. Please present this to the Board. But tell them I'm not promising to quit on June 1, 1989. In fact, I think I will pull 'a Hezekiah' on the Lord and ask for another fifteen years in which to serve Him (see II Kings 20:1-6)."

Rev. Brannan wrote back, "Don't worry, Tom, before your letter came the Board had already considered you. In the light of your continued service, we invoked the 'grandfather clause' in your case. You are approved to work as long as you wish."

Tom's remark to me, "Who mentioned retiring? I didn't."

Retire? Mr. Missions and his bride of over a half a century? No way! Sometimes I think Tom has a greater burning desire and zeal to serve the Lord now than he did when we first launched out together in a pioneering ministry. Physically, my husband has become a little heavier, and a little less patient. His silver "crown" has replaced the darker one of yesteryear. I blame his slower pace, his signs of weariness on the fact that he is nearing his eighty year mark.

At our advanced age we still find ministry. God has sent His laborers forth and we find as Paul did in Romans 1:5, "Now he is sending us out around the world to tell all the people everywhere the great things God has done for us, so that they, too, will believe and obey him."

Left to right, Len and Phyllis Griswold, Jewell, Tom, and Mr. and Mrs. Gomez. The Latin American Theological Seminary conferred a Doctor of Divinity degree on Tom.

Twins Jeffrey and Joel, and Jonathan, sons of Jim and Jan Rogers.

The oldest grandchildren, Kevin and Sheri Griswold.
The blondes are David and Karen Cunningham.

Our Texas Home. A double-wide mobile home nestled among the trees.

Most unforgetable of our trips. We arrive in China.

Our 50th Wedding Anniversary. Front row: Jeffrey and Joel Rogers, Tom and Jewell Cunningham. Standing, from left: Jim and Jan Rogers, and Jonathan, Sheri, Len, Phyllis and Kevin Griswold, Loren, David, Darlene, and Karen Cunningham.

Appendix 1

THE GREATEST MISSIONARY OFFERING
by T. C. Cunningham

Years ago I was working in a missionary convention in one of our larger churches. In the last meeting as the pastor introduced me he said, "Brother Cunningham, before you preach please tell the congregation about the best missionary offering you ever witnessed."

Now, there are several offerings that would vie for that honor. But because of the influence it had on my life I chose to tell of the smallest offering I ever witnessed. The year was 1952, and the place was Santa Ana, El Salvador.

I was working through an interpreter, Missionary Paul Finkenbinder, in receiving the offering. The church was a large building for churches in Central America at that time. A cinder-block building with open sides to catch the breeze. At the back of the building a lady struggled to get up on home-made crutches, and hobbled down the long aisle. At the edge of the platform she balanced herself on the crutches and handed up a small envelope.

Opening the envelope, I emptied out the equivalent of 10 cents in American money. Paul said to me, "That's a day's wages for that crippled woman." I handed the money to him saying, "That's sacred money; I don't want to handle it. But I do want the envelope."

I folded the empty envelope, put it in my wallet and carried it for years until it became frayed. In the years following, I have sometimes become weary in my missionary work. At such times I took out the envelope and looked at it. I relived the moment. I could see that crippled woman struggling to the front to give a

224

day's wages from her meagre salary. The memory of it gave me courage and renewed my determination to give the gospel to the whole world.

Even now that I'm in my late seventies, and weariness often tempts me to make the excuse "I've done my share," I can see that offering re-encacted and I renew my determination to keep working to send out the Gospel.

YES, TEN CENTS AMERICAN, was one of the greatest missionary offerings I ever witnessed! Great because of its impact on my life.

Appendix 2

MISSIONS GIVING ON THE MISSIONS FIELD
by T. C. Cunningham

While visiting Agentina in 1978, missionary Ralph Hiatt, Buenos Aires, agreed to go with me to the furtherest south city in the world, Ushuaia, Argentina, just a few hundred miles north of Antartica.

A missionary had opened an independent church in Ushuaia, and in going there he was without support, as his missionary board was not in a position to back him financially. Needless to say, he had a great difficulty getting started. However, he was determined to start a self-supporting church on the missions field. In time he had a stronger church than his brother had further north in Argentina.

We had a house full for the Wednesday evening service. I preached on the feeding of the five thousand, pointing out that a little boy's freely given lunch was the food used to feed the multitude. Giving it a missionary application—"Give what you have and the Lord will multiply it to meet the need."

A good offering was received. Remember, the service was in Spanish, and I preached through an interpreter. Later I learned that the offering was taken for me. I had the deacons empty the offering plates, piling the peso bills rather high on the table, then we all laid hands on the money dedicating it to the foreign missions endeavor of the church, then instructing the church treasurer to disperse it to missions.

Following the service a mother came to me. She was holding her sleeping little boy, about two years of age, and spoke to me in Spanish. I called the missionary to interpret for me. She handed

226

me two notes of large Peso value, and explained, "This is from my little boy's saving bank. It is for missions. I want him to be like the little boy who gave his lunch." The missionary told me this was about a full weeks pay for the woman. Again, this was given to the treasurer for disbursement to missions.